MW00462942

Zoning China

Information Policy Series

Edited by Sandra Braman

The Information Policy Series publishes research on and analysis of significant problems in the field of information policy, including decisions and practices that enable or constrain information, communication, and culture irrespective of the legal silos in which they have traditionally been located as well as state-law-society interactions. Defining information policy as all laws, regulations, and decision-making principles that affect any form of information creation, processing, flows, and use, the series includes attention to the formal decisions, decision-making processes, and entities of government; the formal and informal decisions, decision-making processes, and entities of private and public sector agents capable of constitutive effects on the nature of society; and the cultural habits and predispositions of governmentality that support and sustain government and governance. The parametric functions of information policy at the boundaries of social, informational, and technological systems are of global importance because they provide the context for all communications, interactions, and social processes.

Zoning China

Online Video, Popular Culture, and the State

Luzhou Li

The MIT Press
Cambridge, Massachusetts
London, England

© 2019 Massachusetts Institute of Technology

All rights reserved. No part of this book may be reproduced in any form by any electronic or mechanical means (including photocopying, recording, or information storage and retrieval) without permission in writing from the publisher.

This book was set in ITC Stone Serif Std and ITC Stone Sans Std by Toppan Best-set Premedia Limited. Printed and bound in the United States of America.

Library of Congress Cataloging-in-Publication Data

Names: Li, Luzhou, author.
Title: Zoning China : online video, popular culture, and the state / Luzhou Li.
Description: Cambridge : The MIT Press, 2019. | Series: Information policy series | Includes bibliographical references and index.
Identifiers: LCCN 2019005735 | ISBN 9780262043175 (hardcover)
Subjects: LCSH: Mass media--Social aspects--China. | Mass media policy--China. | Television broadcasting policy--China. | Internet videos--China. | Streaming video--China.
Classification: LCC HN740.Z9 M345 2019 | DDC 302.230951--dc23 LC record available at https://lccn.loc.gov/2019005735

10 9 8 7 6 5 4 3 2 1

For my mom, Xiaoling Pan

Contents

Series Editor's Introduction

Sandra Braman

There are things we forget. That, despite the "Communist" label, Mao saw the value of capital for both productive and regulatory purposes. That cultural policy was one among the domains in which he put capitalist techniques to use. That after the brief but vibrant Hundred Flowers period, when Mao's policy to "let a hundred flowers bloom and a hundred schools of thought contend" did encourage a flourishing of public expressions of diverse views in the mid-1950s, those whose ideas were a bit *too* diverse wound up experiencing reeducation camps, or worse. Some things we don't stop to remember. That during thirty years of managing an ultimately successful underground political and military organization, a leader and a party that had to operate under a wide range of conditions that presented a variety of types of threats and challenges, could and did develop an approach to policy making that differed significantly from decision-making processes as they developed over the course of long empires with well-developed bureaucracies. The "guerrilla policy" style developed by Mao and the Chinese Communist Party during their decades of governing under revolutionary conditions was a "free-wheeling" policy style, one in which all techniques and partners are welcome, irrespective of purported ideological frameworks or previous commitments, and changing things up altogether is always an option.

In her fascinating and multifaceted analysis of the quite different histories of Chinese policies for television and for online video, *Zoning China*, Luzhou Li reminds us of these things, and more, because the guerrilla policy style is still in use and the past still matters. Li makes vividly clear that those interested in the much-cited twenty-first century concept of "adaptive governance" could learn a great deal from studying the guerrilla policy style. Certainly the ways modern-day China makes and implements policy are also worth studying for their increasingly global impact.

During the critical period in which online video developed as a set of practices and as an industry—the imprinting years of the Chinese internet— China's approach to media and cultural policy making was a mix. For television, the traditional approach to regulation, with its strict content controls, continued to operate; however, online video content, apart from the pornographic or the politically extreme, was relatively unregulated. Luzhou Li characterizes this seemingly inconsistent approach to regulation as "cultural zoning." Some topics could only be addressed or openly discussed in online video; Li's informants told her of individuals who would walk out of television production sets and into online video production units in order to "finish" online what they had begun to talk about on television. There were other differences in China's regulation of content between the two media, an important one being the distinctly different extent to which piracy of intellectual property was tolerated.

Zoning China has much to tell us about the often banal nitty-gritty of censorship operations—"banal" in the sense Hannah Arendt used to describe the nature of evil. For television, it involved working with a long-standing bureaucratic apparatus that articulated rules in great detail, constantly recited those rules, and required attendance at regular training sessions on what content would be considered unacceptable by censors. For online video, on the other hand, guerrilla policy techniques were used in a dispersed, fragmented manner, developed across multiple regulatory agencies, evolving quickly but at different rates and in different ways in a market that was becoming both increasingly profitable and increasingly competitive. At the same time, in an environment surely experienced as turbulent, the technologies and services involved were also constantly changing, with new players and new types of stakeholders constantly appearing. The result was, at minimum, toleration and, at maximum, stimulation of the production and distribution of a wide range of content.

Luzhou Li understands censorship as a knowledge industry: "Knowledge, or the capability to know, is of foremost importance in exercising strategic censorship" (chapter 4). Her account combines mainstream economic analysis with political analysis, pushing our understanding of what it means to be in an "information economy" forward. In another book in the Information Policy Series, *Designing an Internet*, David Clark argues that no network design feature for the internet will go anywhere if there is no industry to provide what is needed—there must be not only technological innovation, but also a market and willing producers for the feature to be adopted. Luzhou Li's insight into censorship as a knowledge industry points in the same direction, toward the markets and the producers involved, as elements needing further analysis.

Li also tells us a great deal about intellectual property rights. Much of the most interesting content of China's online video has been user-produced, involving processes such as "fansubbing" and "spoofing" that use pirated content from foreign producers as production materials. We learn that the use of pirated content in derivative works spurred the market for original works as well, also often pirated. The popular belief that China is simply, well, inattentive to intellectual property rights becomes, with Li's authoritative and empirically grounded treatment, a much more complicated story. During the early years of the online video industry, the guerrilla policy approach of the Chinese government made it first acceptable to distribute both original and derivative pirated works, and then, in a convoluted and never quite official way, for foreign individuals and companies to invest in the Chinese media industries. *Zoning China* goes on to examine when, why, and how this situation was transformed into one where intellectual property rights were treated with greater respect and foreign investment much less welcome, although the situation remains fluid. We learn that the history of online video in China is also the early history of the internet in popular culture as generally experienced in that country. Or, as Li recounts: "In China, the internet's rapidly changing context has altered our sense of time and challenged our memory of contemporary cultural life" (chapter 5).

Zoning China provides both conceptual tools for policy analysis and insights into what "policy" actually is, expanding the domain of policy making to include policy that is "not there," and "doing nothing." It describes policy frames that discard officially unwelcome content that is taking up bandwidth as "industrial waste." In Li's analysis of cultural piracy in China, the range of ways pirated material is used to create new content runs from pure creation to pure migration.

For the two very different worlds of television and online video in China, Luzhou Li systematically and rigorously thinks through their histories from the perspectives of mainstream economics, political economy, political factors, national and international policy making, organizational and interpersonal dynamics, cultural trends, and the very real lives of individuals trying to find their own ways through a media world constantly changing in every dimension.

With its attention to the most fundamental of concepts and to the historical roots of contemporary problems and policy-making practices, Luzhou Li's *Zoning China: Online Video, Popular Culture, and the State* is in valuable conversation with Russell Newman's *The Paradoxes of Network Neutralities* and with Rita Zájacz's *Reluctant Power: Networks, Corporations, and the Struggle for Global Governance in the Early 20th Century*, both also in this MIT Press Information Policy Series. All three works examine the negotiations, struggles, and conceptual and regulatory developments involved in determining just what a "corporation" is, although they do so from different theoretical perspectives, starting from different questions, and with different groundings, which sometimes overlap but sometimes do not. All three push the research agenda for those in information policy toward another stage and offer strong theoretical and empirical openings for doing so.

Professor C. C. Lee, a Chinese media scholar with whom I studied in graduate school at the University of Minnesota, used to start his class on communication theory by telling us that the first question always to be asked is: "Are things changing, or are they staying the same?" Things are indeed changing. Luzhou Li's *Zoning China* is a superb analysis of what that means for television and online video in that country. Providing a comprehensible and accessible account of contemporary Chinese policy making across domains, *Zoning China* also gives us a real feel for the earlier years of China's user-generated popular online internet culture and that culture's growth as an industry. It should be required reading for those seeking to understand the "Belt and Road" policy as the Chinese state moves to enhance its global presence in internet technologies, network and service provision, and governance. Certainly, the guerrilla policy style, which Luzhou Li so thoroughly examines, is now among the concepts that must be used to understand any given set of policy tools, the formation of an information policy toolkit, and perhaps also the decision-making style of a particular leader.

Acknowledgments

This book crystalizes an unforgettable intellectual journey in my life over half a decade. There were good times when I made smooth progress and had a sense of great fulfillment and pleasure; there were also moments of frustration and loneliness that too often ensued. Many people have been with me on this journey, in good times and bad times alike. With *Zoning China*'s publication, I finally have the opportunity to express my gratitude, respect, and love to those who have contributed to this book and to my development as a scholar.

The book—which is a complete rewriting of my PhD dissertation—began at the Institute of Communications Research (ICR) at the University of Illinois at Urbana–Champaign. John Nerone was and is my adviser, mentor, and the person I turn to for all sorts of advice and wisdom. He taught me how to read and write with kindness and generosity and guided me through the long process of writing, reading over the entire manuscript many times. I could not have begun and completed this book without his mentorship over the years, and I owe him my deepest gratitude. I am also indebted to Kent Ono, another great teacher and mentor. He played a crucial role in my early years in graduate school, and his unfailing belief in me since then has helped me through the most challenging moments of my life as a young scholar. He is always there, cheering for me. At Illinois, I also had the good fortune of working with Dan Schiller, Amanda Ciafone, and Poshek Fu, from whom I have learned so much. Among others at Illinois, I would like to thank Anghy Valdivia, Cameron McCarthy, James Hay, Ivy Glennon, Sarah Projansky, and my fellows. I still miss the numerous conversations and hotpot gatherings I had with Wenrui Chen and our other friends where we discussed Chinese media, culture, and society during those long Illinois winters.

Beyond Illinois, this book would not have taken its current shape without the support and help of colleagues and friends in mainland China, Hong Kong, the United States, Singapore, and Australia. Some of them helped to clarify key concepts in the book, some provided invaluable feedback on parts of the manuscript, some introduced me to useful sources and works, and some provided timely support at moments of need. I thank all of you: Mark Andrejevic, Adrian Athique, Joseph Man Chan, Kai-wing Chow, Chua Beng Huat, Stuart Cunningham, Li Deng, Prasenjit Duara, Terry Flew, Anthony Fung, Gerard Goggin, Jonathan Gray, Yu Hong, Brett Hutchins, Wesley Jacks, Dal Yong Jin, Michael Keane, Chi-Kong Lai, Francis Lee, Hongmei Li, Ke Li, Chunfeng Lin, Ramon Lobato, Ye Lu, Tom O'Regan, Vibodh Parthasarathi, Aswin Punathambekar, Jack Qiu, Kevin Sanson, Qingqing Sha, Colin Sparks, Sue Sparks, Harsh Taneja, Graeme Turner, Wilfred Wang, Saskia Witteborn, Angela Xiao Wu, Guobin Yang, Juan Zhang, Lin Zhang, and Chunyang Zhu. In particular, I would like to thank Guobin Yang for his support of this book from its earliest days, Michael Keane for sharing his many insights on the topic, Tom O'Regan for his vision and confidence in my work, and my dear friend Angela Xiao Wu for over a decade of friendship and company. An earlier version of chapter 5 of this book appears in the journal Television & New Media, and I thank the editor Vicki Mayer for her enthusiasm for and promotion of the article.

In China, I am indebted to all those who accepted my requests for interviews and so generously shared their experiences with me, as well as those who provided crucial industry contacts. As a member of the generation that grew up accustomed to media piracy and as an early Chinese internet user, my encounters with my informants were not only interviews but also a recollection of a shared past through which I came to revisit the China of my youth, and that sympathy informed this book. Given the current sensitivities surrounding public discourse in China, I have chosen not to list my informants' names.

My editor, Sandra Braman, deserves my heartfelt thanks for seeing the merits of the project that I did not see, for offering candid and insightful criticisms of my earlier drafts, for generously sharing her experience in reading and writing, and for broadening my intellectual horizons. I cannot thank her enough for her time and input in this project and for her mentorship in general. At the MIT Press, I would like to thank my acquisitions editor Gita Devi Manaktala; her patience, kindness, and faith in this project has meant a lot to me. I am also indebted to my production editor Elizabeth Agresta for keeping the book on schedule, to my copy editor Jeffrey Lockridge for his superb editing work, to Nhora Lucia Serrano for her assistance with manuscript preparation, and to the anonymous reviewers for their detailed and constructive criticisms.

I have also been fortunate enough to have the love and support of my family in Wenzhou, China. My brother, Dongyang Li, is my best friend. Although we do not get to see each other often enough, our phone chats have been my morale booster over the years, whether he is in Los Angeles, Nuremberg, or Shanghai. My parents, Mianshui Li and Xiaoling Pan, have given me their utmost understanding and support in my pursuit of an academic career, personal fulfillment, and a way of being that is so very different from that of most of my hometown and, later, college peers in China. I know the culture that my parents come from, and I know how hard it has been for them to unconditionally support my academic pursuits over the years. My mother is one of the kindest and strongest people I have ever met. During the most difficult time in my life, it was her company and care that kept me going, and she did so while she herself was suffering from chronic allergies and insomnia. I cannot hope to repay that debt. This book is for my mom.

1 Introduction

In December 2014, officials from the State Administration of Press, Publication, Radio, Film and Television (SAPPRFT)—formerly the State Administration of Radio, Film, and Television (SARFT)[1]—which regulates Chinese cultural life, announced at several online video industry conferences that content forbidden to be broadcast on traditional media would also be forbidden on new media. If we consider these announcements in the context of increasing oversight of public discourse since President Xi Jinping came to power in 2013, the unequivocal message was that online and offline censorship standards would be unified.[2] Although the official announcements were explicit about the coming restrictions, they also implied the previous existence of a double standard applied to old and new media, which SARFT officials had never actually acknowledged but were nevertheless finally attempting to end.

If we look back at its development in China, we can clearly see that in the two decades before 2014, online video was subject to different and more lenient regulation than television was. Specifically, whereas television was largely the province of the state, market relations dominated the development of online video, from its financial structure to its content development. This produced an online space for people to question state media and the state's preferred ideological narratives about the nation, history, and society.

Liberal-leaning online video culture was certainly not the only cultural formation that developed alongside state media culture in China. If we look back to the 1980s and 1990s, the two decades immediately following China's "reform and opening up,"[3] there was always an unofficial, alternative mechanism of cultural provision falling outside the purview of the state, which China scholar Orville Schell calls the "second channel," namely, piracy in all its permutations.[4] Although some of its works were compatible with state ideology, the second channel also included many that departed from or even conflicted with the party line. The cultural formations that existed as an alternative to state media culture at different stages of the reform, collectively show that a dual cultural sphere has historically operated, generally with state permission, in China. If we look beyond media and culture, the dual track formation is much like the zoning practiced in the economic realm, through which the Chinese state has strategically configured its national territory into multiple zones of development according to market principles.[5] Specifically, we can see this in the creation of special economic zones (SEZs) in coastal cities. As with SEZs, which operate under different constraints in the economic realm, in the cultural realm, the Chinese state has strategically applied market relations more to certain media sectors or forms than to others, which has led to a dual cultural sphere.

The story told here is about zoning practices in the cultural realm or, as I term it, "cultural zoning." In examining how a dual cultural sphere took shape in the context of the internet, I look at the dynamic of television versus online video. Though not always delineated by them, the zoning of culture often comes down to different media forms. The notion of differentially regulating different media forms, whether de jure or de facto, is certainly not unique to China. In the United States, for example, print, broadcasting, and telecommunications have been regulated differently for different purposes.[6] In India, there has historically been a structural division between state communication (broadcasting, documentary) and popular media (print, cinema).[7] However, although they appear to be similar, regulatory differentiation in each of these instances may have arisen out of different considerations and followed different paths. In my view, China's differential treatment of television and online video is a market-oriented development strategy that is ultimately associated with the party-state's perpetual pursuit of political legitimacy through "gradual, measured" development.[8] This differential treatment of different sectors according to their strategic value, both objectively defined and subjectively perceived, is also found in other national sectors, and, like economic zoning, it is commonly practiced as well in East and Southeast Asian countries such as South Korea and Singapore.[9]

Zoning China focuses on the period from the late 1990s—when the Chinese internet including online video began to take shape—to 2014, when online video had developed into a full-fledged medium. Marking both the twentieth anniversary of the Chinese internet and a significant change in internet governance as the new leadership under Xi Jinping began to assert a much stronger dominance over public discourse, the year 2014 thus constitutes an important juncture in internet development in China over the last two decades. Cultural zoning arguably continues after 2014 because, in spite of the significant reduction in latitude online video once enjoyed, it remains more marketized than television. However, cultural zoning no longer operates on a scale comparable to that in the previous two decades.

The purpose of this book is twofold. First, it examines the differential treatment of television and online video in relation to the market—that is, the establishment of cultural zoning. Although the relaxed oversight of some sectors in Chinese media may seem like the loosening of the party-state's grip on the cultural industries, the strategy of zoning actually foregrounds the strong role of the state. Since the 1970s, scholars have critiqued the liberal fiction of the natural market, noting the constitutive roles of the state (as an infrastructure provider and a coordinator among other roles) in the development of global capitalism.[10] The continuing relevance of the state is particularly notable in countries like China. For instance, in zoning culture, the Chinese state limits the marketization of some sectors (e.g., television) while allowing others (e.g., online video) to have more market operations. I am not suggesting that these two interconnected zones (television and online video), whose unstable boundaries continually shift, are entirely discrete, but I believe that the zones are sufficiently discrete to posit a rough divide between them. I argue that, by zoning culture, the Chinese state has strategically configured the cultural realm into multiple zones in relation to the market, which allows it to enjoy the fruits of economic development while simultaneously retaining socialist legacies through its own state media. Like the SEZs, which are considered by anthropologist Aihwa Ong to be exceptional spaces within national territories,[11] online video appears to be a zone of exception to the socialist norms in state media and culture.

Second, *Zoning China* describes how, within a dual regulatory context, China's online video industry developed in parallel to its television and gave rise to an online space for counterhegemonic possibilities. Developing from a number of business models including a YouTube-like sharing one in the early to mid-2000s,[12] major Chinese online video companies, including iQiyi, Tencent Video, and Youku, have since become original, creative forces of production and distribution, connecting domestic private production companies, transnational corporations (especially the Hollywood majors), and a vast network of creative labor from amateur video makers to professional content creators. Although the telecom infrastructure, foreign investment, intellectual property, and lax censorship are all important to its development, I argue that online video in China cannot adequately be understood without situating it within the unofficial, second history of popular culture in contemporary China, particularly the history of piracy. I map online video's close but not entirely visible links to audiovisual piracy, ranging from videocassette copying in the early 1980s to peer-to-peer (P2P) file sharing on the internet, and to a piracy-informed vernacular online culture embedded in practices such as video spoofing in the early to mid-2000s.[13] It is partly because of its singular history rooted in piracy that I consider Chinese online video to be a largely independent medium despite its many overlaps with television.

Lack of Will or Lack of Capability?

The idea of "cultural zoning" most immediately suggests an active, deliberate choice of the state, although that choice could also be strictly pragmatic. Is the latitude granted to online video in China a result of the state's lack of will—or its lack of capability? Is lax regulation a strategic choice or the result of unmanageable bureaucratic problems? The lack of capability thesis is powerful, especially given the complex organization of the Chinese state, which often constrains its ability in policy making and implementation.[14] Although very little research has been done to explore the effects of bureaucratic politics on internet governance in China, scholars have delved into a number of tangentially relevant areas, notably the telecom industry and intellectual property rights (IPRs) enforcement.[15] *Zoning China* acknowledges the difficulty of regulatory fragmentation as a factor when accounting for the latitude given to online video, which was most evident in the years before 2005. As I will show in chapter 4, much of the early regulatory history of online video content involved a protracted turf war between several related ministries, all claiming authority over online video.

Nevertheless, lack of capability is not and could not be the only explanation for the latitude granted to online video producers, especially in light of later regulatory developments. The SARFT was designated as the primary authority over regulation of online video content in 2007. Lack of capability may have continued as a factor (this time, mainly in relation to the sheer amount of online video content waiting to be regulated). But an analysis of policy alternatives and post-2014 developments shows that, though fully capable of developing creative methods and investing more resources to impose stricter control than earlier on, the SARFT chose not to—thus exhibiting a lack of will, which this book emphasizes. After all, as communication professor Sandra Braman notes, "it is only through the exercise of will to utilize existing capacity that anything happens."[16] *Zoning China* accepts that the Chinese state has proven to be both incapable and unwilling when it comes to managing online video in the ways it had managed television in the two decades before 2014. Recognizing that there can be no single causal explanation in a system as complex as China's internet governance, this book uses the concept of zoning to frame its description of the system's byzantine workings and nuances.

The latitude granted by the government to online video was induced by economic considerations. As my SARFT informant Lin explained: "[If we] control everything tightly, there is no way for development."[17] Thus, to encourage development, the government tolerated emerging online practices and content that diverged from those associated with the more strictly controlled television sector, as long as such practices did not fundamentally threaten the government's political legitimacy. In fact, by mitigating social discontent, these relatively unfettered online practices and discourses may have served to stabilize rather than challenge the government. A growing number of scholars have investigated why authoritarian states have allowed free or partly free media.[18] Political scientist Peter Lorentzen, for example, concludes that the Chinese state has strategically granted and adjusted the latitude given to investigative journalism, which allows it to check on local corruption and improve governance, while preventing the spread of discontent and reducing the risk of overthrow.[19] In a study more relevant to matters discussed in this book, Gary King, Jennifer Pan, and Margaret Roberts show that, while taking care to prevent collective action, online censorship in China has allowed for a wide range of criticism of the Chinese state, its officials, and its policies. This easing up, the authors suggest, is an effective governing strategy to monitor public opinion, satisfy the masses, and ultimately strengthen social stability,[20] allowing the Chinese state, it would seem, to achieve the greatest benefits at the least cost. And the state can always revoke or reduce the latitude it has granted should that pose a threat. In this way, political scientist Andrew Mertha says, "the state can have its cake and eat it too."[21] This flexible approach to governing public opinion is reminiscent of how the mid-1950s Hundred Flowers movement (so named for its aim to let "a hundred flowers bloom and a hundred schools of thought contend") encouraged intellectuals to criticize the party and thus set those critics up to be targeted and silenced in the anti-rightists campaign that followed.

Emphasizing this flexibility in cultural governance, my work adds another dimension to what scholars have observed in many other policy domains in China. In recent decades, contrary to critics who regarded it as weak and fragile, the Chinese state has weathered moments of crisis ranging from global economic meltdown to domestic unrest, reconsolidated itself, and seemed to be adept at managing challenges. Political science professor Andrew Nathan calls this flexibility "authoritarian resilience."[22] Along the same lines, other scholars have looked at various institutional adaptations and innovations in China's political, economic, and social domains. In politics, for example, resilience is maintained in part through strategies of containment like the creation of various bottom-up "input institutions" such as local elections and of structures that solicit citizen complaints or that permit administrative litigation.[23] In economics, it is the admission of private entrepreneurs into the party.[24] And in the social domain, it is the creative use of solidarity groups such as temple associations and lineages in rural China, and the encouragement of mass protests at local levels.[25]

This flexible governance in China, Sebastian Heilmann and Elizabeth Perry argue, is shaped by a guerrilla policy style that was developed from the Chinese Communist Party's three decades of revolutionary experience in adapting to a wide range of environmental conditions and challenges. It has continued to shape China's present-day governance alongside the competing styles of administrative, bureaucratic, technocratic, consultative, and legalistic traditions. But because, as Heilmann and Perry note, it is fundamentally against institutionalization, this free-wheeling guerrilla policy style allows China to remain responsive to changes. It exists in contrast to norms of political accountability and procedural stability in liberal democracies and to Soviet-style bureaucratic control.[26] The style is particularly notable in policy fields such as economics and technology.[27] And from their research, Daniel Breznitz and Michael Murphree have also noted that China's policy making and implementation in science, technology, and innovation have been "less institutionalized and more ad hoc in [their] operations."[28]

Some of the many features of the guerrilla policy style are easily discerned in the governance of online video. First, and most obviously, because it is opportunistic and open to experimentation, the style sees policy development as a process of "continual improvisation and adjustment that 'shapes itself in the making.'"[29] Or, as my SARFT informant Lin put it, speaking of her agency's management of online video content: "Wherever/whichever stage the industry develops into, we follow to regulate it."[30] Second, the guerrilla policy style favors fluid policy making, which "avoids binding constraints (e.g., personal pre-commitments or legal-contractual obligations) so as to retain political initiative and room for policy revision,"[31] an outcome commonly seen in the context of new media. And, third, the guerrilla policy style is sometimes characterized by "secrecy," or what Breznitz and Murphree refer to as policy "un-decisions," that is, policy scenarios in which "no formal policy decisions" take place.[32] This is most evident in the policy style's regulation of the special financial structure of Chinese internet companies, as I will discuss in chapter 4.

The guerrilla policy style poses challenges to researchers. The ultimate challenge involves gauging the state's intent. Traditional methods of policy analysis such as analyzing written policy and interviewing policy makers are of limited and dubious value here. As King, Pan, and Roberts are quick to emphasize, even when interviews with officials are possible, researchers are "in the position of having to read tea leaves to ascertain what their informants really believe."[33] Although I did not entirely reject these traditional methods, I supplemented them with numerous stories and anecdotes related by industry professionals describing their encounters with the state. These unofficial sources tell us far more than official interviews about the processes of policy making and implementation, especially their informal side. The accumulation of diverse kinds of data may help us develop a clearer picture of the real objectives and ongoing calculations of the Chinese state.

I validated data obtained from such sources by looking at media outcomes
and at the meanings these outcomes generated in society.

A Note on Internet Censorship

As we discuss censorship in China, it is important to think beyond the false
binary of complete freedom versus draconian repression. Understanding
China's censorship as dynamic, corresponding to a spectrum of ideologies,
a situational and strategic exercise of power in response to specific crises,
defined by old and new media forms, allows us to more fully understand
China's media realities as well. Examining the measures the Chinese state
has taken to suppress information is important, but emphasis solely on
suppression to the exclusion of other avenues of inquiry prevents us from
understanding wider social and cultural impacts of internet use in China.
A different approach is therefore necessary for a more nuanced and sophisticated perspective.

My research approach directly opposes that of dominant scholarship,
which generally analyzes internet control in China through what media
scholar Bingchun Meng terms "a pre-formed lens of democratization."[34]
The democratization paradigm places exclusive emphasis on restrictive
regulations, policies, and technologies (e.g., filtering, blocking, tunnel-
ing), as well as highly publicized arrests and crackdowns, and on the self-
censorship resulting from these measures.[35] Such measures certainly exist,
but not all of them reflect actual operations in China. For example, self-
censorship conducted by Chinese internet companies is assumed to stem
from an awareness of constantly being watched among industry professionals, which effectively disciplines industry practices.[36] Although this is
true in some instances, empirical evidence from my fieldwork shows that,
despite constant surveillance, the absence of external censorship often led
industry professionals to prioritize economic pursuits over political obligations until their boldness triggered state intervention.

Although this book focuses on state censorship, it acknowledges that
online censorship in China and perhaps also in many other countries is
multilayered and more complex than simply "state-centered, technical
configurations."[37] In addition to state censorship, understood here as the
relatively explicit intervention of state censors into the free exchange of
ideas, other structural, impersonal forces such as those of the market and

various social institutions may also work to regulate public discourse in a manner not unlike that of state censorship.[38] This may increasingly be the case in China as privately owned internet companies gain more leverage.

Zoning China engages with a growing literature on internet censorship in China that sees censorship as a process not merely of repression, but also of knowledge production, entailing forms of subjectification that may make people think in a particular way, or even in no way at all.[39] Adopting this perspective, in chapter 4, I will describe the positive exercise of power among industry professionals in response to social and moral values. Another good example of research from such a perspective is communication and sociology professor Guobin Yang's study of how the Chinese state's discursive campaign of "surfing the internet in a civilized way" mobilizes self-discipline among internet users, thereby working to regulate online conduct and speech.[40] Political scientist Rongbin Han finds similar social regulative practices in the "voluntary fifty-cent army" on the Chinese internet. Unlike the state-sponsored "fifty-cent army," whose online commentators reportedly receive a fifty-cent fee from the party for each comment they post online, the commentators of the "voluntary fifty-cent army" actively choose to defend the government without pay.[41] In addition to its implications for online censorship in China, the existence of both groups, Han argues, demonstrates the heterogeneity among Chinese internet users, who are not all and not always empowered social actors.[42] This challenges the common simplistic tendency to understand China's political and social dynamics as no more than a conflict between a state repressing cultural freedom and a civil society pushing back for it, or "an unremitting interplay of repression and resistance."[43] In reality, the state-society relationship is far more complicated than a binary model can explain, and acknowledging this allows us to evaluate cultural politics in contemporary China in all their complexity.

Video as a Medium: A Cultural View

Whereas Netflix describes itself as "the world's leading internet television network,"[44] its Chinese counterparts unanimously call themselves "online video companies"—or, in Chinese regulatory discourse, "online audiovisual service providers." The difference in terminology invokes an ontological question of how to think about cultural and technological developments such as Netflix and Tencent Video. Some scholars, especially those from film and television studies, tend to see these developments as a new mechanism of distribution and therefore a disruptive moment in television, like the many other disruptions television has experienced in its history. Whether people watch its content on tablets or mobile phones, they would probably say online video is still television, or television in transition, recognizing television as a shifting set of technologies and practices.[45] Others though largely taking the same position are more sympathetic to the ontological ambivalence of the recent formation.[46]

Acknowledging this important scholarship, I propose to consider the current digital turn to be "online video," recognizing that video has a history of its own, one closely associated with but also effectively marked off from that of television. In doing so, I am not suggesting that, with online video, the internet is taking over television in China, for "media themselves are not literally in competition with one another,"[47] nor am I arguing for a clear-cut, fixed status of online video given its intricate relationship with television (if television has ever been a stable, uncontested medium). But I maintain that video's rich global history, both offline and online, guarantees it an expressive capacity of its own and that there are productive ways to view it as an independent and legitimate medium.[48]

Although the history of video is certainly about its technological essence, from videotapes to digital files, and from disc players to mobile devices, understanding media based merely on their technologies' capacities and constraints leads us into the trap of technological determinism. In her much-cited work, media historian Lisa Gitelman defines media as "socially realized structures of communication, where structures include both technological forms and their associated protocols," meaning how, where, with whom, and under what circumstances we use them.[49] Thinking along similar lines, historian Michael Newman contends that video as a medium is constituted not only by its technological innovations, but also, and more important, by quotidian, commonsense ideas about these technologies and their uses. The history of video is thus more than a progression of materiality. It is also a history of ideas about technology and culture.[50]

For example, in the era of videotapes, video was imagined as a recording and playback medium and was therefore marked as distinct from conventional television transmission and reception (i.e., live broadcasting). It was considered mainly in light of its potential to allow viewers to "time-shift"—to record and play back television shows at their convenience. Among the many uses of video technology in history, the time-shifting experience has probably contributed most to the conception of video as a medium promising to liberate viewers from television's perceived economic and ideological control over its audience and society.[51] Although video's material formats went through numerous variations, viewing protocols associated with analog video have been recycled and have continued to define video's identity in the digital era. The diverse range of technologies and viewing experiences in the digital context complicate, if not challenge, television's potential for "liveness," its structure of scheduled flow, and its ability to aggregate a dispersed public.[52] Indeed, it is through its sequenced flow of programs that television creates a temporal viewing experience.[53] But television's very planned process of flow as default is deconstructed online as internet companies offer "a set of equivalently accessible alternatives" at any given moment.[54]

The video disruption of television's linear temporality is sustained in China. Perhaps because of this, television and home video have historically been subject to control by different ministries or agencies and the official procedures for importing home videos (including VCDs and DVDs) have been faster and more lenient,[55] with video largely remaining the province of piracy. The nonlinear viewing experience associated with video has also been readily recognized by Chinese users. As one of them put it, "To me, a video site is like a combination of a newspaper and a library."[56] He particularly enjoyed the freedom to select media content from a vast profusion of videos. This agency ascribed to Chinese video users should be seen in terms not only of its changing viewing habits, but also of its political implications. Communication professor Larry Grossberg considers watching television a relatively passive social experience of "waiting inside the home for the outside world to be 'transmitted' into one's private life."[57] In the Chinese context, this passive viewing allows the state to effectively reach families and individuals. The distinct viewing protocols associated with (online) video disrupt the relationship, carefully constructed through a planned flow, between the Chinese state and viewers/subjects, undercutting the status of television as a political and moral medium.

In addition to its viewing protocols, video's social place and identity have been shaped by all the hopes and fears projected onto it. It is at once a medium of corruption and a medium of democratization.[58] In much of its short history, video joined its contemporaneous technological counter-parts in destabilizing our common perceptions about the established role of media in society, a process intertwined with long-standing popular aspirations to have free expression and unconstrained access to media content.[59] The use of video and ideas associated with it in China, for instance, were premised on widespread discontent with state-curated provision of cultural content and were inextricably involved with and affected by piracy. Indeed, piracy has been among the most pervasive ways in which video technologies have been used in developing societies.[60] Capitalizing on video's technological progression from videocassettes to P2P downloads and online streaming, piracy fulfilled long-standing social desires for popular entertainment beyond the scope of state-curated content.

Video is also a technology of production. Associated with camcorders and amateur recording at its most politically engaged moment, video succeeded "as a medium of authentic representation of the real world, and of civic engagement and democratic participation."[61] The same trope of participation has continued to mold our understanding of amateur video practices emerging in a more advanced digital environment. In China, the amateur spoof video making in the early to mid-2000s was valued by viewers as a form of oppositional discourse against the mainstream culture of the nation-state, as I will show in chapter 5. In short, video has historically fallen into a vaguely felt sphere that sets itself off from China's state media.

This sense of video's place within a wider frame of reference and meaning continues shaping the "socially circulating identity" of online video even today,[62] as an anecdote from my informant Peng, an industry professional, makes clear. For some time, the same television series always had two versions across platforms: an abridged version broadcast on television, and an unabridged version streamed online. The abridgment took place at television stations in order to make room for advertisements within an allocated time slot. Although this was mainly a commercial manipulation, it was widely seen as political censorship. As such, the unabridged version circulating online was appreciated by viewers as uncensored discourse.[63] This anecdote suggests that, over time, even fairly similar content online was constructed as an alternative to television in the popular imagination, producing a sense of difference between the two media. Indeed, video as a medium of legitimacy in contemporary China is constituted not only by political economic forces, relationships between industries, and video's technological essences, but also, and more important, by the ideas and discourses that go along with it.

Piracy: A Cultural Infrastructure

Although China has long been regarded as a notorious market for global piracy, some doubt the accuracy of such an assessment. Organizations such as the International Federation of the Phonographic Industry (IFPI) have year after year compiled statistics on the extent of piracy around the world, but because it operates in the shadows, piracy by its very nature calls such statistics into question, and lack of publicly accessible details about how these statistics are obtained only compounds doubts about them.[64] But, even though no one knows its precise extent in China, piracy was on almost everyone's lips when the industry professionals and users I spoke with recalled their personal histories of cultural consumption.

Debates on media piracy are normally framed in the opposing terms of "creative privilege versus organized criminality."[65] But a growing number of researchers, refusing to see piracy simply as a criminal act or as opposition to the establishment, have instead posited its ambivalent role in the long-run trajectory of capitalist development. For one thing, some have argued, piracy certainly addresses inequalities of access between those who are excluded from the circuit of global media flows and those who are not.[66] And, for another, as many others have argued, within national contexts, piracy has also enriched the limited range of state-sanctioned official culture and spread a worldview different from the officially promulgated one.[67] *Zoning China* takes no issue with these arguments and emphasizes the ideological competition of piracy with state media in many places. But when coming to an understanding of the relationship of piracy to China's online video industry, I agree with anthropologist Brian Larkin that piracy is non-ideological in that it does not represent "a self-conscious political opposition to capitalism,"[68] although it does provide creative solutions outside the intellectual property rights regime.[69] Indeed, even as it hurts Hollywood's global economic interests, piracy also reinforces Hollywood's dominance by widely circulating its products, thus creating a greater demand for them.[70] From the national perspective, piracy might well be merely a manifestation of early developments common to immature markets, which support social demands ahead of infrastructure improvement and associated regulations.[71]

Chinese financial writer Xiaobo Wu's account of China's three decades of economic reform shows that the shadowy import trade in the form of smuggling was an important impetus for the development of a private economy on China's southeastern coast. Around 1980, dozens of ships loaded with smuggled goods from Hong Kong and Taiwan moored offshore in the South China Sea each day, and hundreds of boats from mainland China headed down south to meet them. Under the acquiescent eyes of local governments, these boats smuggled in clothing, household appliances, small hardware, among other products, which sustained the functioning of the earliest commodity markets after the Cultural Revolution. Those bold smugglers, traders, and retailers would become the first generation of businessmen in the reform era.[72]

The development of China's material economy corresponds in some ways with the development of its online video industry. Early online video companies either directly distributed pirated content or were heavily sustained by piracy and by user content, whose circulatory history was rooted in piracy. From that base, the companies evolved into buyers of global copyrights and, later on, into producers of original content. The case in China thus parallels the one in Nigeria, where entrepreneurs previously involved in piracy switched to production and distribution of legal (legitimate) videos.[73]

More important, the unofficial ethos of piracy and piracy-influenced online culture in China has shaped and continues to shape the ideological orientation of online video production in its more mature stage. In fact, many people working in online video, an industry marked by a low threshold for entry, developed their professional expertise and original sense of what counted as good work through consumption of pirated Western popular culture. In addition to similar entrepreneurial development, China's online video industry shares the development of content production with Nigeria's, which could not have come into existence as legitimate without the infrastructure developed by its illegitimate counterpart, pirated videos.[74] Within this notion of infrastructure, I include more than just the material. As Brian Larkin argues, because infrastructure can also be "soft," including social knowledge, it can therefore refer to both "technical and cultural systems."[75]

The generative quality of piracy confirms the interdependence between formal and informal media suggested by some scholars, which encourages us to rethink familiar narratives of media industry development.[76] Lately, scholars have also begun to view Chinese online video through the lens of the formal versus informal dynamic, pointing out how early commercial online video companies survived by exploiting informal media economies.[77] Sound as their research findings are, I am cautious in using the terms "formal" and "informal," not only because informal sectors such as piracy are highly organized, demonstrating a degree of formality,[78] but also because the so-called formal media within the purview of regulators are sometimes marked by surprising informality. Television drama production in China, for example, has been marred by questionable financial records and is in some projects rumored to be a money-laundering vehicle for government officials. That said, when I find it necessary to use the term "formal," I do so loosely to suggest media sustained by an organizational logic (e.g., regulation, institutionalization) that structures their activities;[79] and I use "informal" also loosely to refer to media activities that operate outside such structures.

Methods

Zoning China combines a variety of methods including participant observation of trade fairs, interviews with industry professionals, documentary research, and critical discourse analyses of media texts. Access is always an issue for critical studies of media industries. When the industries have limited archives, researchers need to establish industry contacts and to rely on these for further connections.[80] I made my initial industry contacts through a few key introductions by acquaintances and at trade fairs in both television and online video. I "immersed" myself, to borrow media scholar Amanda Lotz's word,[81] in the space of trade fairs, where socializing with industry professionals, observing industry practices such as media buying, and listening not only to formal addresses by industry leaders but also to informal conversations at exhibition booths allowed me to gain a sense of the industries' cultures, fears, and struggles.

Much of this book draws on extensive conversations with industry professionals and early video amateurs and with associated online communities that have been negotiating their survival in a rapidly changing cultural market. I talked with a diverse group of people from both the television and online video industries, including regulators, investors, producers, screenwriters, distributors, copyright purchasers and lawyers, ad sales planners, engineers, and government relations builders. Because I regarded my informants as occupying constructed positions in China's recent sociocultural history, in my conversations with them, I sought not only to learn about policies and industry practices, but also to capture my informants' life histories and especially their personal histories of media use, reminiscences of social and cultural developments since the 1990s, and their views on issues such as marketization, popular culture, and the internet.

This book takes a cultural approach: it treats the lived experiences of people involved in media production as the subject for theorizing China's contemporary media industries.[82] Seeing how their life histories informed these people's practical work pushes us to move beyond looking just at the role of political economic forces in making an industry to understanding its broader sociocultural basis. It is worth mentioning here that, in many instances, my informants were quite willing and indeed enjoyed talking about their cultural consumption histories and their experience as historical subjects of China's changes in recent decades. This often led to hours-long talks that switched back and forth between past and present, personal and institutional, which turned out to be an effective way of dealing with issues of access and openness in my encounters with the informants.[83] I talked not only with people working in the industry, but also with many online video users from different class backgrounds, and I performed a two-week participant observation of mobile video use among migrant workers in Shanghai. Although I eventually decided to drop the section on mobile video use from the book, those encounters still inform the project generally, if not specifically or explicitly.

I complemented my fieldwork with documentary research on industry and policy primarily from 1999 to 2014. Among my sources were government policy documents, the trade press, mass-circulation newspapers, industry statistics and market data, materials collected at trade festivals/ fairs, industry commentaries both directly online and forwarded to me by my informants through social media, and numerous personal reminiscences and commentaries circulating online. The materials I examined described industry news, concrete policies, and regulatory techniques developed by relevant bodies for television and online video; those for online video covered all aspects of its development, including telecom infrastructures, foreign investment, copyright, and content production. My documentary research concerned itself primarily with the political economic context of the industries, but also aimed to reconstruct early Chinese internet culture and use, from which China's online video industry developed.

Vicki Mayer, Miranda Banks, and John Caldwell remind us to keep "a healthy dose of skepticism and reflexivity" in both the research process and its presentation because "all texts, whether found in an archive or one's own field notes, are constructions, versions on the real that may serve different roles in a production studies project."[84] This reminder, I believe, also applies to interview materials, which I assessed critically, moving back and forth between and among different sources to keep them "in critical tension or dialogue with the others."[85]

Chapter Overviews

Chapter 2, "Culture before the Millennium," sets the stage for the rest of the book with a history of popular culture and cultural governance in contemporary China, covering the period from the 1930s, when the Chinese Communist Party (CCP) formulated its cultural policy principles, to the 1990s, when the cultural realm underwent a market-driven rupture. It reviews the development of the dual cultural sphere in history and establishes the policy context for discussions on television and online video in subsequent chapters.

Chapter 3, "Stay Left: Post-2000 Television Drama Production in China," examines market-oriented developments in state-owned television after 2000, focusing on television drama production. It shows that, despite the influx of private capital into television drama production since the early 2000s, the state has managed to maintain a multifaceted regulatory regime over television production from the early stage of topic selection to post-production censorship, which has rendered television a largely political and moral medium—in contrast to online video.

With chapter 4, "Early Online Video: A Political Economic Perspective," *Zoning China* turns to online video as an emerging cultural institution in contrast to television, detailing the political economic forces that shaped the formation of the online video industry in the early to mid-2000s. The chapter first describes the state-led construction of telecom infrastructures, then addresses the particular latitude granted to China's early online video in the financial structure of internet companies and the lax regulation of online video content. It analyzes these arrangements in relation to China's push to develop the internet for economic gain. By focusing on the political economic context, it shows how online video was able to form as an alternative cultural institution to television in China.

Chapter 5, "Piracy, Internet Culture, and the Early Online Video Industry," moves beyond political economy to explore the sociocultural basis of China's online video industry. It considers two vernacular online practices that preceded the rise of video-sharing websites in the mid-2000s—video spoofing and fansubbing—that were to various degrees entangled with the legacy of preinternet piracy.[86] The chapter examines how outcomes of these piracy-informed user practices challenged China's mainstream culture, and how this alternative internet culture influenced the massive rise of commercial online video services in the mid-2000s. It argues that piracy served as a cultural infrastructure for the development of China's online video and accounted for the distinctive discursive features of its early video culture.

Chapter 6, "Bidding on the Rights to Stream: The Industry, Copyright, and New Cultural Flows," examines the transformation of China's piracy-inflected online video industry by focusing on its copyright strategies. It describes how video companies, under pressure from both advertisers and intellectual property rights owners, first began to actively acquire digital rights, especially from the Hollywood majors, and then disarticulated themselves from amateur online communities such as fansubbing groups. The chapter also examines China's looser regulatory regime over copyright-based online video content compared with its regulation of cultural imports via traditional channels such as movie theaters and television stations.

Chapter 7, "Online Video as an Emerging Network of Cultural Production," focuses on the second aspect of China's online video industry's professional turn after 2008, that is, its move upstream into commercial content production. It emphasizes the role of advertisers in generating video companies' in-house initiatives such as web series, which largely evolved from video spoofs. The chapter also examines how amateur parody video makers from different class backgrounds transformed themselves into professional or semiprofessional producers who commercially collaborated with video portals and how, as entrepreneurs, these producers brought about the transformation of China's video industry. It ends with a discussion of the lax regulation (compared to that of television) of these new forms of cultural production.

The epilogue (chapter 8), "The Operation of a Dual Cultural Sphere ... And?" describes the development of cultural zoning in the context of China's increasing management of the Chinese internet after 2014 and the further consolidation of China's online video industry. Bringing together the various themes addressed throughout the book, it offers a final analysis of the idea of cultural zoning.

2 Culture before the Millennium

Popular culture is one of the major institutions through which the Chinese Communist Party (CCP) establishes and maintains its hegemony in Chinese society. "The arts must serve politics" was the cultural policy principle formulated by the CCP in the Yan'an period from 1937 to 1947, a decade that marked the CCP's political and military victory over domestic rivals and foreign invaders. This principle served as the core of China's cultural governance once the Communist Party came to power in 1949 and remained so thereafter. Historian Hsiao-t'i Li tells us that the extent to which popular culture has been politicized from the 1930s onward is unique, not just in comparison with modern Western liberal states, but also with China's own experience in the past.[1] As Li puts it, "the shadow of party and state looms larger and larger"[2] over Chinese popular culture in the twentieth century. Accurate and widely held as these observations may be, they do not speak to the relatively autonomous unofficial sphere in popular culture enabled by private entrepreneurs and other individuals, which runs parallel to and sometimes conflicts with the culture's official sphere.

This chapter offers a short, selective history of popular culture and cultural governance in China from the 1930s, when the CCP's cultural vision became clear, to the 1980s and 1990s, when "the reform and opening up" project that began in 1978 brought drastic changes to the cultural realm. The chapter emphasizes the latter two decades, when developments were most immediately related to the television versus online video dynamic I will explore in later chapters. I use "cultural governance" here to mean the ways in which the Communists mobilized (or demobilized) different forces, especially the market, in regulating popular culture at different historical periods. During each of the surveyed periods, I will describe the operation of a dual cultural sphere, one that continued undisrupted even during the most repressive moments of the Cultural Revolution. I focus on the duality of contemporary Chinese popular culture, not to invoke a dichotomy between its official and unofficial spheres, but rather to use it as an analytical framework for talking about the richness and complexity of that culture, believing, with Chinese history professors Perry Link, Richard Madsen, and Paul Pickowicz, that both spheres were "fully real, and indeed complexly interrelated."[3] In discussing a wide range of examples from the television and audiovisual aspects of China's popular culture, I will show how the boundaries between the two spheres were constantly in flux as the larger political economy changed.

1930s and 1940s: "The Arts Must Serve Politics" and Others

Hsiao-t'i Li has offered a fascinating account of popular culture and its relationship to radical ideologies from the late Qing dynasty (which ended in 1912) to the middle of the Republican era in China (the early 1930s). As he notes, the politicization of popular culture became inevitable when imperial rule in China came to an end in 1912 and intellectuals of diverse political stripes emerged, from reformers to revolutionaries, from May Fourth liberals to leftist writers of the 1930s. All were searching for a direction for the country, and, despite their different ideologies, approaches, and orientations, most turned to the common people—viewed as ignorant in imperial China—and their culture: what they read, listened to, and watched for leisure and entertainment. Since the end of the Qing dynasty, intellectuals have endeavored to win over the people through popular culture—through newspapers, operas, ballads, and tunes, for example. Over those decades, organizational attempts to mobilize the masses became increasingly important, and the strategies to reach the masses by exploiting their culture became increasingly sophisticated. In the early 1930s, leftist writers and artists such as Qu Qiubai analyzed and debated issues such as the class backgrounds of the laboring masses and the petite bourgeoisie in both the cities and the villages, the need to learn from the people, to reform the old cultural forms, and the languages to be used in doing so. A decade later, in what Li considers the CCP's first systematic treatment of cultural mobilization, the party would take up and further develop many of these issues.[4]

In the mid-1930s, the Chinese Communist Party's Red Army, in order
to escape the Nationalist forces of the Kuomintang (KMT), began a military retreat famously known as the "Long March," relocating to revolutionary base areas in the northwestern provinces. Yan'an, a small town in the
northern Shaanxi Province, became the party's headquarters from just after
the Long March in 1936 until the late 1940s. The Yan'an period included
"the war of resistance against Japan," which forced the Chinese Communist Party and the Kuomintang to cease domestic battles and form a second
United Front to confront this national crisis. The decade in Yan'an was
considered crucial to many aspects of preparing the CCP to take power.
The cultural vision and the subsequent organization that mobilized writers and artists in the cause of a party-led project of national salvation was
articulated and developed during this period.[5] The formation of the CCP's
cultural policy should thus be understood within the larger context of the
Chinese Revolution, which was at once anti-imperialist, nationalistic, and
characterized by domestic class warfare.[6]

People usually refer to Mao's 1942 talk at the Yan'an Conference on
Literature and Art when the subject of the party's early cultural policies
arises. But Mao's 1940 speech "New Democratic Politics and New Democratic Culture" is no less important to consider. That it later came to be
known as "On New Democracy" may explain why its significance to the
formation of the CCP's cultural policy is often overlooked.[7] The idea of
New Democracy came at a time when the anti-Japanese United Front of the
Chinese Communist Party and the Kuomintang was being undermined by
the Nationalists' military pressure on Communist-controlled base areas. In
this context, Mao tried to construct a different united front.[8] Challenging
the urban revolutionary line, Mao proposed that the Chinese Revolution
should be led by the proletariat with the aim of "establishing a new democratic society and a state under the joint dictatorship of all the revolutionary
classes [the proletariat, the peasantry, the intelligentsia, and other sectors of
the petite bourgeoisie]" in its first stage and carrying the revolution forward
and building a socialist society in its second stage.[9] It is noteworthy that,
in Mao's theory, the bourgeoisie would still be welcomed into the ranks of
the revolution since its members were thought to have possessed a revolutionary quality at certain periods in semifeudal and semicolonial societies,
although Mao pointed out that China's bourgeoisie was "extremely flabby
economically and politically" and had "a proneness to conciliation with

the enemies of the revolution."[10] This foreshadowed the CCP's pragmatic and flexible approach to private capital in the cultural realm at different historical periods.

To make a broad revolutionary alliance under Communist leadership possible, Mao, like his predecessors, emphasized the role of culture. In a deviation from the classical Marxist base-superstructure model, Mao saw culture as having a definite and active role in achieving revolutionary goals. In his famous 1942 talk on literature and art, Mao asserted that, as a core cultural principle, "The arts must serve politics." The talk was meant to reinforce the political principles of the New Democracy and to wean a majority of writers and artists from their preoccupation with aesthetic theories and artistic practices,[11] or "art for art's sake." "In the world today," he explained, "all culture or literature and art belongs to a definite class and party, and has a definite political line. Art for art's sake, art that stands above class and party, and fellow-traveling or politically independent art do not exist in reality."[12]

In this regard, there are some striking parallels between Mao and Marxist philosopher Antonio Gramsci. Though situated in different social and historical contexts, both understood revolution and political life as a war of position in which the Left must outmaneuver hegemony on cultural and political fronts, rather than engage in immediate revolutionary attacks.[13] Mao's vision of revolution is also Gramscian in that, like Gramsci, Mao emphasized the role of peasants in a revolution,[14] envisioning a worker-peasant alliance as its core. Because of this, Mao argued that a New Democratic culture should be a mass culture: "New-democratic culture belongs to the broad masses and is therefore democratic. It should serve the toiling masses of workers and peasants who make up more than 90 per cent of the nation's population and should gradually become their very own."[15]

But, as China scholar David Holm argues, Mao's remarks here are ambiguous about the intended class nature of the New Democratic culture, and the mass orientation of the CCP's cultural policy they imply is open to debate. On the one hand, Mao asserted that the New Democratic culture "belongs to the broad masses," which suggests a culture organically developed from the masses. On the other hand, however, he contended that this culture "should gradually become [the masses'] very own," which implies that it did not yet belong to them and was not identical with their preexisting culture.[16] The condescension suggested by this last remark was even more apparent when Mao went on to say, "There is a difference of degree, as well as a close link, between the knowledge imparted to the revolutionary cadres [people engaged in revolutionary cultural work] and the knowledge imparted to the revolutionary masses, between the raising of cultural standards and popularization."[17] The critical aspect of this passage, as Holm notes, is that knowledge was to be "imparted," indicating that it would come from the top down to both revolutionary cadres and the masses. Thus Mao's conception of a mass, democratic culture did not imply a particularly democratic and open-ended culture. Mass culture in this context was not a culture *of* or *from* the masses, but a culture *for* the masses. What was imparted to the masses, which required popularization, was presumably a different, less sophisticated version of what was given to the cadres.

Here we see one of the major differences between Mao and Gramsci. As historian Nigel Todd explains, Gramsci emphasized the importance of institutions where the working class could develop its own organic intellectuals connected with an embryonic alternative state power such as the Communist Party, trade unions, and factory councils, whereas Mao tended to see the problem of intellectual and cultural activities primarily as one of recruiting and transforming existing Marxist and non-Marxist intelligentsia into Maoist intellectuals who could enlighten the masses. To Mao, the masses were essentially materials to be molded and liberated from the outside by the party's newly enlightened intellectuals.[18]

To create such a mass culture, Mao resorted to another recurring theme in his 1940 speech: "national culture," saying that "the universal truth of Marxism must be combined with specific national characteristics and acquire a definite national form if it is to be useful. ... National in form and new-democratic in content—such is our new culture today."[19] His call for a national form of culture was warmly received by cultural populists and nationalists of the day, who were in favor of a large-scale and creative use of Chinese old forms as the basis for China's future national culture. Thus Boda Chen, close to Mao and later a prominent member of the leadership during the Cultural Revolution, argued: "This ... requires that one selects the forms [the common people] have grown accustomed to over a long period, pack [new content] into the old form and give it appropriate refashioning: only then can they take delight in receiving it and digest it thoroughly."[20]

Prior to the Yan'an period, in the early 1930s, the party's cultural theo-
rists had already analyzed a wide array of national popular cultural forms of
the day, in both urban and rural settings, among them wall posters, serialized cartoons, historical novels and sagas, traditional popular fiction, sacred
scrolls (*baojuan*), storytelling in the teahouse, folk songs, local tunes, ballads (*xiaochang*), and regional operas (*daxi*), and they advocated replacing
the corrupt, feudalistic content conveyed by these forms with enlightened
content.[21] These endeavors were carried forward during the Yan'an period,
when the nascent party developed its own media and culture—and when,
as Yuezhi Zhao notes, it also sought collaboration with (presumably progressive) privately owned newspapers, which were permitted to continue
operations after 1949 until they were nationalized a few years later,[22] as
were private film studios in the early 1950s, my own unpublished research
found. These collaborations, in my view, anticipated the party's (re)admis-
sion of private capital in media in the 2000s.

What the party nevertheless dismissed then and thereafter, Hsiao-t'i Li
tells us, was the "deleterious dimension of popular culture, those [commer-
cial] soft cultural productions ... presented at Shanghai theaters, teahouses,
or amusement halls."[23] Although the CCP never completely rejected this
pleasure-seeking entertainment-oriented popular culture, it maintained
a generally apathetic attitude toward it. Thus the party largely turned a
blind eye to the Mandarin Ducks and Butterflies fiction that comparative
literature professor Perry Link has investigated. Indeed, this light and enter-
taining side of popular culture, though decadent in the eyes of leftist revolutionaries, was a staple of people's cultural lives, and Li suggests that our
understanding of popular culture in modern China would be sorely incomplete if we were to ignore it. What Li refers to as the "heavily politicized
cultural works promoted by the CCP" and the paralleling "leisure-oriented
Mandarin Ducks and Butterflies type" I see as one of the very first instances
of China's dual cultural sphere in the twentieth century, a duality that has
continued to this day.[24]

Culture after 1949

Unlike their Soviet counterparts, who had no concrete plan for a propaganda system when they came to power, Chinese Communists fully understood the power of culture and had practiced their conception of culture

long before they came to power.[25] In the early 1940s, a series of organizational developments already in place led to the concentration of control of China's leading cultural bodies in the hands of cultural populists allied with Mao. Those arrangements clearly indicated the Chinese Communist Party's ambition to centralize and coordinate cultural activities from the top down.[26] After 1949, the party established a far more comprehensive, centralized propaganda system controlled by key party and state agencies. Thus the state's Ministry of Culture played a crucial role in making cultural policies and coordinating cultural activities before television became a mass medium in the 1980s, although absolute power over culture was usually wielded by the party's Central Propaganda Department.[27]

Much research has documented the CCP's organized attempts to mobilize popular culture to serve the political needs of the socialist state at different historical periods, from the promotion of industrial production in the late 1950s to class struggles during the Cultural Revolution. The socialist transformation of culture entailed state patronage of cultural production and required an erasure of the market as a way of organizing cultural activities. Despite some resistance from cultural workers, there seems to be a consensus among scholars about the party-state's success in achieving cultural hegemony.[28] Opposing this dominant consensus, a small yet growing group of scholars paints a more complex picture of popular culture in Mao's China. In particular, these scholars note the significant role played by the market in regulating cultural provision. Even historian Chang-tai Hung, who offers a comprehensive account of the Maoist transformation of culture, acknowledges that the prominence of state politics in cultural activities during this period did not mean absolute state control over the cultural realm.[29]

A relevant example comes from historian Qiliang He's archival research of Pingtan storytelling, a performing art in the Yangtze Delta, in which stories are narrated as monologues or dialogues using local dialects and whose popularity was second only to movies of the day.[30] As He shows, because the state lacked the financial resources to provide full patronage for the art, only a small number of Pingtan performers were incorporated into state-run performing enterprises. And Pingtan's individualistic organization, chameleonlike performance style, and essential improvisation all made it an art not easily censored, which must also have discouraged the state from pursuing full control of it. In this instance, a vast majority of performers operated outside the state system, maintaining their self-employed status and depending on the market or commercial story houses for their living throughout the 1950s. It was only beginning in 1958 that local governments in the Yangtse Delta took concerted action to crack down on storytellers' self-employment and force them to join newly founded troupes under collective ownership. But, even after that, freelance performances continued because those new troupes were unable to absorb all the Pingtan performers. Thus, far from extinct in the 1950s and 1960s, the cultural market continued to play a significant role in cultural provision.

In He's view, it was only during the Cultural Revolution that the Communist Party managed to exercise full control of the production and consumption of popular culture. Yet Link finds that, even during the Cultural Revolution, unofficial and underground entertainment fiction circulated widely both in hand-copied forms and recorded on audiotapes alongside officially published literature. These original creations, copies of pre-1949 works, and translations or retellings of foreign works told of "beauties, seductresses, spies, detectives, traitors, corpses, and wizards of the martial arts, as well as of China's top leaders, informally described."[31] Link sees a strong continuity between Cultural Revolution–era hand-copied fiction and the earlier Mandarin Ducks and Butterflies genre fiction.

More recently, Guobin Yang examines cultural activities among young people who were "sent down" to rural China for reeducation during the Cultural Revolution, including copying forbidden books and listening to foreign and "hostile" radio programs. Compared with purely entertainment fiction, the forbidden books read and copied by the sent-down youths seemed more politically charged. They included political dissent, works about Soviet revisionism, and internal publications limited to high-ranking party cadres. Yang sees the circulation of these works and more entertainment-oriented ones as part of an amorphous underground cultural movement. Although not all of these works expressed dissent, all deviated from the political norm of the time. Yang considers this unofficial culture as transgressive, but in the sense of disengagement and distancing from power rather than of confrontation with it.[32]

Taken together, the instances of cultural deviation here, whether openly tolerated by the state or existing surreptitiously, clearly indicate that a much fuller picture of popular culture in Maoist China remains to be uncovered. It is important to acknowledge this side of the story because, as Link observes, there is a strong continuity, in themes and technique, between the clandestine Cultural Revolution–era entertainment fiction and the unofficial (but aboveground) tabloids, fiction, and other works appearing in the reform period, whose popularity was much easier to establish.[33] Likewise, He considers the continued existence of a cultural market as one dimension of continuity between the Maoist and post-Maoist periods.[34] And Hsiao-t'i Li finds the relatively "independent and uninterrupted" development of entertainment-oriented popular culture to be a direction that modern Chinese popular culture has taken.[35] In line with Li's thinking, the extraofficial culture that reemerged as the reform began may very well have persisted to digital culture in later decades, whether there is a demonstrable connection between the two or not.

State Media in the 1980s and 1990s

Although never completely isolated, China resumed regular contact with the outside world in the late 1970s, when the reform took off, entailing from the start many significant changes in the cultural realm, especially in state media. The government introduced the "budget contracting" (*yusuan baogan*) system, in which a predetermined amount of money was allocated to formerly state-owned units, and they then either retained any surpluses gained from their own operations or made up any funding gaps. In time, nearly all state media and cultural organizations would adopt the new system. The central motive behind budget contracting was to force state-owned units to generate their own income by "pushing [them] into the market,"[36] where they were expected to survive and grow. Over the early to mid-1980s, many state media and cultural units that had been completely subsidized by the state were gradually forced to rely on themselves to make ends meet;[37] advertising, sponsorship, and other forms of business operations became an important source of income.[38] At the same time, the development of China's market economy created a growing demand for advertising outlets among domestic and foreign enterprises. The defining feature of China's efforts to reform and govern state media in the 1980s and 1990s was to phase out government subsidies and carefully introduce market relations into these media to increase their capacity and audience appeal while making sure not to diminish their political value. Since it is impossible to track all the changes taking place in state media and culture during this period, I will focus on the state medium most pertinent to the topic of this book: television.

The expansion of market relations in television was, first and foremost, embodied in the structural and institutional changes enabled by growing advertising revenues coupled with new technologies, from broadcast (terrestrial) to satellite television. On the eve of the reform, the television broadcasting service in China was centralized at the national and provincial levels, with Chinese Central Television (CCTV) being the only national broadcaster and each province having a television station of its own. Municipal and county governments served primarily as transmitters, relaying central and provincial programming.[39] Beijing's decision in 1983 to allow lower-level governments to build their own television stations resulted in a proliferation of stations at the municipal and county levels and established a four-tier broadcasting structure.[40] Whereas Yuezhi Zhao attributes this policy change to the inability of the central government to provide the necessary financial support for national television coverage,[41] communication professor Yu Huang contends that the main impetus for decentralization came from below: dissatisfied with centralized regulation of broadcasting development and with their lack of share in the growing broadcasting business, local authorities, particularly in the newly rich coastal areas, demanded that Beijing allow them to set up and run their own stations using their own money.[42] Moving beyond structural factors, media professor Michael Keane considers the four-tier policy to be a result of the new science of audience research, which began to treat the television audience as a localized, heterogeneous entity rather than a universal subject.[43]

A shift toward local development aligned with the larger trend of subsidy cuts and marketization. Around the same time, broadcasters at all levels were encouraged to explore alternative sources of financing—above all, advertising; they increased the number of their entertainment-oriented programs in order to attract viewers and ultimately advertisers. Meanwhile, foreign programs were selectively brought in through a barter agreement, whereby Chinese television stations traded with foreign media companies, exchanging advertising time for free television programs.[44]

Although new developments in media culture began in the late 1970s, it was not until the 1990s that China's cultural landscape underwent a market-driven rupture. Deng Xiaoping's tour to the Shenzhen special

economic zone (SEZ) in 1992 and the Chinese Communist Party's Four-
teenth National Congress (the party's highest formal body) in the same
year reaffirmed and expedited the course of reform both symbolically and
officially in the wake of the 1989 Tiananmen Square incident.[45] With subsidies shrinking, state television accelerated its commercialization in order
to realize financial self-reliance. Chinese Central Television, for example,
officially adopted the budget contracting system in 1991, followed by stations at the provincial and lower levels.[46] Television quickly became the
top venue in attracting both domestic and foreign advertisers. In 1992, the
sales of television advertising accounted for 30 percent of the total advertising turnover in China.[47] With growing advertising revenues, both central
and local broadcasters were able to introduce more channels, often market-
oriented specialty ones, and thus more programs.[48]

The introduction of advertising enriched both Chinese Central Television and local stations throughout the 1980s and 1990s. At the same time,
it also induced and sustained the development of cable and satellite television. Cable technology was originally introduced as a means of overcoming
poor reception of broadcast signals caused by tall buildings and rugged terrain. By 1987, there were only about 100 cable television stations, most of
them run by large industrial and mining enterprises, with only a few owned
by county and municipal governments. With the proliferation of television stations and channels, viewers using single-channel, fixed antennas
began to encounter difficulties in receiving distinct broadcast signals from
multiple sources; cable technology was rediscovered in this context to allow
them to receive broadcast signals on multiple channels, with improved
reception quality. Its potential to become a new way of organizing television production and transmission, and thus also a new tool of propaganda
and a possible new market, was immediately seized upon by different levels
of party cadres. After 1987, cable television underwent accelerated development, eventually expanding from dispersed, piecemeal systems into connected networks of considerable size.[49] Although it had the potential to
provide interprovincial television services, its early development in China
was largely bottom up, likely because of the way cable television was first
used in relation to other media and the territorializing logics that have
structured its development. Thus, in 1989, the first group of cable stations
in Guangxi Province were all in prefecture-level cities such as Yulin and
Wuzhou.[50]

The government began to systematically promote cable television in the 1990s, considering it a significant supplement to broadcast television for its capacity both to transmit broadcast television programs and to produce programs of its own.[51] In April 1990, the first province-level cable television station was established in the inland province of Hunan.[52] By the end of the 1990s, there were 21 such stations; with 161 stations at the prefectural or municipal level and 533 at the county level. The total number of cable television stations had grown to 715, covering a population of nearly 80 million.[53]

The development of satellite television in China parallels that of cable television; like cable, satellite television was first used to overcome the problem of poor reception of broadcast signals in remote, rugged provinces.[54] Since the mid-1980s, television stations in these provinces have been allowed to transmit their own programs and, more important, those from Chinese Central Television via satellite transmission, the most economical way to cover remote settlements in these provinces.[55] Satellite ground stations built by governments at multiple levels extended the coverage of Chinese Central Television into the farthest reaches of China. By 1985, construction had been completed on satellite ground stations at Ürümqi, Aletai, and Kashgar in the Xinjiang Uyghur Autonomous Region; that same year, ground stations in the Tibetan Autonomous Prefectures of Golog, Haibei, and Yushu in Qinghai Province also began to operate.[56] In 1991, the remote Yunnan Province began to transmit its television programs via the Asiasat 1 satellite, launched by China in 1990, which allowed wide coverage not only within that province, but also across other provinces and even to some South and Southeast Asian countries.[57] Ironically, owing to their special territorial conditions, peripheral provinces were the first to be allowed to make use of satellite television, a new technology that more affluent provinces jealously eyed and competed for in the 1990s in order to reach a wider audience.

In China, programs transmitted via satellite are mainly received through the cable system. In the 1990s, with the dramatic rise and expansion of local cable networks, television stations enriched by commercialization in developed provinces such as Zhejiang began to demand satellite transmission, citing as justification the location of some of their remote places in rugged terrain, even though their other, often more populous places were located on flat land.[58] The prospect of a powerful tool like satellite television for

advancing national influence certainly spurred this demand. The development of provincial satellite television was not smooth, however. Acquiring
"extraterritorial landing rights" (permission to transmit via satellite into
other provinces) was a major problem due to regional protectionism and
the capacity bottleneck of the local cable networks.[59] But, finally, by the
end of the 1990s, each provincial television station had been able to start
one satellite channel.[60] Now, instead of having to barter with central or
regional stations in order to have their programs known nationally or in
other provinces,[61] provincial television stations could access national audiences directly.

The rise of provincial satellite television had profound implications for
Chinese television and online video. On the one hand, national access to
content brought about by satellite television was later replicated by the
Chinese internet, and even today, most of online video companies' direct
competitors and collaborators from the television sector are top performing provincial satellite television channels. On the other hand, provincial
satellite television greatly challenged the monopoly of Chinese Central
Television in the national market and also intensified the interprovincial
competition for programming, audiences, and advertising revenue. In the
decade after 2000, provincial satellite television became an influential force
in the marketization of the television sector and the culture at large.

As we review the market-oriented restructuring of Chinese television in
the 1980s and 1990s, we need to keep in mind that, however extensive it
may have been, far from undercutting the status of television as an ideological state apparatus, the restructuring actually strengthened it. The party-
state generally succeeded in weaving its ever-changing political agendas
into commercial content produced by China's market-oriented television
stations during this period. By the late 1990s, many television dramas and
other entertainment programs had been outsourced to and produced by
the so-called makeshift troupes (*caotai banzi*) and private production companies, which were not officially recognized at the time.[62] But, even here,
the state managed to effectively police private productions through various
mechanisms into the 2000s, a theme I will return to in chapter 3.

In the commercial context, the state's ideological messaging arguably
became more sophisticated, powerful, and thus also more attractive to
audiences than the naive, crude mode of propaganda had been in previous
decades. In Wanning Sun and Yuezhi Zhao's words, it was "a reconfigured

regime of state control," which incorporated "more subtle techniques of discursive domination rather than blunt censorship."[63] This often involved the incorporation and redefinition of elements from outside the official cultural sphere, thereby causing its boundaries to shift. Moreover, the newly rich Chinese television stations now had more outlets and financial resources to fulfill their political obligations. In a strategic cultural and political move that may have surprised many, the party-state invited the market to join in its cultural governance. As media professor Jing Wang observes: "The state's rediscovery of culture as a site where new ruling technologies can be deployed and converted simultaneously into economic capital constitutes one of its most innovative strategies of statecraft since the founding of the People's Republic."[64]

Much scholarship has addressed the peculiar political economy of Chinese television—marketization, on the one hand, and ideological indoctrination, on the other—as well as its outcomes. Thus media professor Ying Zhu's pioneering study of Chinese television drama examines, from the perspective of both political economy and ideology, how dynasty dramas in the late 1990s and early 2000s held Chinese imperial rulers up as paragons of the Confucian ideal, thereby echoing the appeal to Confucian values embedded in the political ideology of the time: "building a socialist harmonious society."[65] Taking a similar approach, communications professor Anthony Fung shows how political ideologies were fused into state television's localization of Western television program formats during the same period. For example, Chinese Central Television's *Happy Dictionary* (2000), inspired by Independent Television's (ITV's) *Who Wants to Be a Millionaire?* in the United Kingdom, replaced the monetary awards in the original program format with home appliances and household consumables to downplay its materialistic tone and instead promote family relationships and social harmony.[66] Likewise, media professor Ruoyun Bai's research on televised corruption dramas, which have gained in popularity since the mid-1990s, and media professor Wanning Sun's study of representations of maids in Chinese television series both point to the role of these popular cultural products in supporting the party's political legitimacy.[67]

By emphasizing the continuing ideological relevance of Chinese television, I am not denying its significance as a discursive site of contestation. Bai has shown that, though the production of corruption dramas started off as part of the party's anticorruption campaign, it ended up creating a political and moral crisis the party had to deal with. Similarly, Michael Keane has found outbreaks of producer autonomy in the 1990s that made it possible to produce drama series that shunned "uplifting" socialist messages and instead portrayed social malaise and ennui.[68] But in stressing the "dynamic" and "polysemic" nature of Chinese television, to use Yuezhi Zhao's words,[69] for the purposes of this book, it is important to keep in mind that the state's ideological grip over television remained and remains to this day firmly in place.

These two decades also marked the increasing prominence of "small p" policy, which cultural studies professor Laikwan Pang defines as the administrative and regulatory side of policy, as opposed to its grand narratives and ideological principles.[70] Pang argues that, because politics directly determined everything, there was a weak sense of cultural policy in China before the 1980s. The reform saved China's popular culture from extreme politicization, leaving it as a site that needed to be managed administratively by the state through institutional arrangements, and it was in this context that "small p" cultural policies entered China's public discourse.

Piracy in the 1980s and 1990s

The development of an unofficial, alternative cultural sphere inevitably paralleled changes in state media from the very beginning of the reform, and its persistence in those decades before the reform paved the way for its postreform popularity. As Link documents, the beginning of the reform was characterized by a cultural efflorescence, with the resurgence of all kinds of popular arts, such as local operas, comedians' dialogues, and clapper tales.[71] In addition to the revival of indigenous popular culture, a flood of commercial culture from Hong Kong, Taiwan, and Hollywood entered the Chinese mainland, brought in by individuals traveling across the border and, on a larger and more organized scale, by private entrepreneurs. According to China scholars Nimrod Baranovitch and Andrew Jones, at the beginning of the reform, many ex-convicts, dropouts, and petty criminals, as well as those from other floating populations that were not absorbed into any government units (*danwei*), engaged in small private businesses and unofficial activities. These private entrepreneurs, known as *getihu* and numbering in the millions, accounted for the emergence of unofficial, alternative mechanisms of culture provision during these two decades.[72]

It is noteworthy that, even though private capital may have been officially recognized and permitted in peripheral cultural organizations and
functions before 2000, its operation in core content-related areas was generally forbidden. For the most part, private capital in media and popular
culture operated informally, outside the purview of "state policy, regulation, taxation and measurement,"[73] and, judging from current scholarship, it did so in roughly two different ways. In the first way, rental-seeking
activities by state media engendered an informal private media sector living in a symbiotic relationship with the state sector. Thus, as Yuezhi Zhao
explains, state publishing houses would sell ISBN codes, which served as
monopoly rights to publish books, to private book publishers, giving rise to
a secondary, unofficial book publishing (and pirating) industry.[74] Whereas
private capital for the official state-sponsored industry flowed through formal state institutions, another channel operated independently of the state
structure—through piracy. U.S. journalist and author Lisa Movius considers
piracy the most classic example of freewheeling capitalism in contemporary China.[75] It was through these two different ways and perhaps others as
well that unofficial culture, some of it local, but most of it overseas, began
to flourish.

Commercial popular culture from Hong Kong and Taiwan (collectively
known as "Gangtai culture," "Gangtai" being a contraction of the Chinese
names of the two places "Xianggang" and "Taiwan") penetrated mainland
China at the very beginning of the reform. The wide popularity of the then
officially banned Taiwanese crooner Deng Lijun (Teresa Teng) in the late
1970s, listened to on smuggled or copied tapes, symbolized the pervasive-
ness of Gangtai culture at the time. Low-cost cassette recording, a popular
technology of piracy in those years, greatly facilitated the spread of Gangtai music. Most Gangtai songs were soft and sweet and sung in breathy
styles to express personal feelings, particularly romantic love.[76] A number
of scholars have acknowledged the continuity between this Gangtai culture and its pre-1949 Western-influenced form in cosmopolitan cities such
as Shanghai during the 1920s and 1930s,[77] which, Baranovitch suggests,
emerged in the context of "the new modern, urban leisure culture of night-
clubs, cabarets, and dance halls"—precisely the culture dismissed by the
Communists in the 1930s.[78]

The audiovisual piracy that sprang up during the beginning of the reform
was another important part of China's unofficial culture, and it has evolved

over the last two decades alongside economic development and technological change. At the frontier of piracy in the 1980s, in some locations
in the southern province of Guangdong, adjacent to Hong Kong, people
defied the official ban on unauthorized reception of cross-border television
signals and set up fishbone antennas to receive Hong Kong television.[79]
Videocassette technology would extend the reach of the shady cultural
productions of Hong Kong, Taiwan, and Hollywood entertainment across
the country.

Video halls (*luxiang ting*) were a major mode of unofficial distribution
of audiovisual content between the mid-1980s and the first half of the
1990s.[80] As unregulated cultural spaces, video halls showed a considerable
number of comedies, crime and gangster movies, action thrillers, martial
art movies, and adult movies from outside mainland China.[81] Officially at
least, they were thought to be a breeding ground for criminality, promiscu-
ity, and immorality.

The network of video halls nationwide is estimated to have far exceeded
that of cinemas in those two decades.[82] And 1980s studies on piracy in
Latin America, Nigeria, and Saudi Arabia make us confident in arguing that
China's video halls were a constitutive part of a global audiovisual piracy
empire that had developed its own transnational routes.[83] In the following decades, piracy spread through digital reproduction—VCDs, DVDs, and
software—that was developed within the already existing network of the
informal cultural economy.[84]

But the distribution of video halls, although wide, was uneven and demonstrates the cultural hierarchy of Chinese cities and towns, central and
peripheral, elite and marginal. Thus video halls were a common presence
in my hometown of Xincheng, a small municipality in the port city of
Wenzhou in the southeastern province of Zhejiang, as they were in other
low-tier cities and towns, but they were less common in big cities like Beijing and Shanghai.

Attendance at video halls was also uneven, generally structured along
gender and class lines. As a young girl, I never went into a video hall, but in
my memory, their patrons were mostly adolescent and young adult males,
a memory supported by a few rare representations of video halls (see figure
2.1, for example). Thus video halls appeared to be masculinized spaces, and
the use of videocassette technology in postsocialist China did not seem to
foster a shift in cultural consumption from public to private places.

Figure 2.1. Video hall in Wenzhou, 2001.[85] Source: Yue Zhu, with permission.

The gendered character of video hall patronage further intersected with its class character. For example, as a Beijing native, my informant Hao, LeTV's copyright director, grew up when videos of pirated movies were widely consumed in his city and elsewhere, but the video hall was never part of his cultural experience. Born into a highly educated family, Hao lived in a *dayuan* (work-unit compound) of a research and educational institution.[86] Though he remembered video halls in Beijing, he never patronized them, instead viewing videocassettes in the privacy of his home. In primary school in the late 1980s, Hao used a Panasonic recorder and blank videocassettes to copy movies from his neighbors, who traveled abroad and returned home with popular culture items for their own enjoyment; his sources also included his scientist father. What Hao described was a relatively class-specific cultural practice at the time: few could afford to travel abroad easily and frequently.

With the expansion of popular culture toward the end of the 1980s, Hao admitted that the cultural privileges of being a *dayuan* kid were considerably more circumscribed than they had been a decade earlier. Even so, when Hao talked about video halls, he still appeared to consider them debased cultural spaces: "Video halls may really show something that harmed the mind and body."[87] With the further expansion of the market for popular culture into the 1990s, as a high schooler, Hao began to rent pirated videotapes from video shops, which later began to sell pirated VCDs.

Starting in the mid-1990s, the video compact disc format became a major method of distributing pirated movies, television dramas, and animes. Although an obsolete technology in the West, because of its low price and acceptable digital quality, the VCD format experienced an unexpected rebirth in Asia in the informal cultural economy. Visual and media arts professor Shujen Wang thus considers VCD development in Asia one of the most fascinating examples of a reterritorialized technological and cultural space mobilized by nation-states, local manufacturers, and consumers alike, and one countering the global audiovisual entertainment market order defined by transnational electronics corporations.[88]

When the VCD format was later supplanted by the DVD (digital versatile disc) format in the late 1990s, thanks to the DVD's higher storage capability, the price of pirated video discs decreased drastically from an initial ¥30–¥40 each (roughly $4–$5) to less than ¥10 (about $1.20) after 2000, which made the consumption of pirated movies affordable.[89] Even though internet use became more common in China after the late 1990s, DVDs remained popular, especially in the first few years of the 2000s. According to my informant GB, a fansubber of Japanese animes and a veteran internet user living in the port city of Hangzhou in Zhejiang Province, the black market was inundated with pirated DVDs from 1999 to 2001: "Even pirated discs had distinctions in quality. Feima [Flying horse] was a premium brand in piracy. Its products had nice packages and high image qualities."[90]

DVD discs came in different formats, based on different technologies and manufacturers' standards. Thus a DVD-5 was a single-sided, single-layered disc; a DVD-9 was a single-sided, dual-layered disc; a DVD-10 was a double-sided, single-layered disc; and a DVD-18 was a double-sided, dual-layered disc. The most common formats on the Chinese market were DVD-5 and DVD-9, abbreviated as "D5" and "D9." Feima was among a handful of well-recognized manufacturers producing pirated D5 discs with high-quality images, sound, and subtitles. Some of their discs even included original soundtracks, which earlier DVDs did not have. Piracy, Brian Larkin tells us, has distinct material qualities that influence the media being distributed under its regime of reproduction. Thus he finds that, in Nigerian pirated video, constant copying of discs has eroded their data storage, leading to blurred images and distorted sound and that the distortion creates a particular sensory experience for viewers, with a different sense of time, space, speed, and contemporaneity.[91] But media piracy in China shows that informal infrastructure is not always marked by a technology failure or breakdown, nor does it always constitute a mediating force that produces new modes of organizing sensory perception, time, and space. At its advanced stage, however, piracy infrastructure might replicate the capabilities of formal infrastructure to order, regulate, and rationalize society.

When sociologist Thomas Gold was in China in 1992, he was struck by the abundance and diversity of imported cultural materials. Some were certainly brought in by state institutions themselves or through joint ventures between the state and private enterprises, but many were brought in through piracy.[92] Whereas the officially provided cultural materials were significantly circumscribed, the pirated ones were apparently unrestricted in scope. Indeed, the comprehensive nature of piracy meant that almost anything could be pirated, including official imports, which made them available to a larger group of the population who, for various reasons, had no access otherwise to officially provided materials. The pirating of official culture thus serves as another instance of the indistinct boundaries between the official and unofficial cultural spheres.

The widespread presence of piracy immediately raises an obvious question. Why has China been so notoriously bad at regulating it? A number of scholars have attempted to explain the astonishing levels of piracy in the country. Legal scholar William Alford in his book *To Steal a Book Is an Elegant Offense* traces poor copyright enforcement in China to cultural factors, in particular, the Confucian and socialist legacies, both of which repudiate proprietary knowledge and instead hold that the repository of knowledge drawn upon in creating and inventing belongs to all members of a society. The effect of these cultural factors is reinforced by China's resentment toward the West for forcing it to join a global intellectual property rights (IPRs) regime. Although China has adopted major IPRs-related laws, it has done so reluctantly and has been unwilling to allocate the necessary time and resources to enforce them.[93]

Andrew Mertha, by contrast, contends that it is the complex, fragmented, and hobbled structure of China's IPRs enforcement bureaucracy that prevents it from having a real, lasting effect not only on piracy but also on ideological deviation. For, even though copyrights are not specifically designed to restrict freedom of expression, enforcing them could certainly become a means of exercising ideological control. But, embedded as it is within a cluster of more powerful bureaucracies concerned with value-laden media, including the General Administration of Press and Publication (GAPP) and the Ministry of Culture, the bureaucratic apparatus charged with copyright enforcement in China has suffered from personnel and budgetary constraints that have severely curtailed its independent action.[94]

As persuasive as Mertha's analysis is, an implicit explanation he suggests but does not develop may be more interesting—namely, that the Chinese state appreciates the social stability brought about by pirated consumption and is therefore unwilling to intervene excessively to regulate it. In close association with the state's antipiracy activities has been the semiregular government campaign against pornography and illegal publications (*saohuang dafei*). Since illegal pornographic and antigovernment works were by definition copyright infringing and thus pirated, the government's campaign against them often collapsed into antipiracy enforcement. But, according to officials Mertha talked with, some 80 percent of pirated items in China—books, audiovisual materials, computer software—were not pornographic or antigovernment in nature (although they were not necessarily politically neutral either), and were therefore generally accorded lower priority than that given to explicitly intolerable works, which the Ministry of Culture and others would actively pursue. In other words, as Mertha summarizes, with limited resources, there was a selective regulation of the publishing and audiovisual market in which only those pirated works that posed clear threats to the political status quo and to social stability were prohibited. Everything else was permitted, and the state apparently made no attempt to invest more resources to manage it.

This latitude led to what sociologist and documentary filmmaker Geremie Barmé calls the "grey zone of cultural tolerance," existing between the "red market of official culture" and the "black market specializing in overtly illicit dissident work"[95]—or, in Thomas Gold's words, the "zone of

indifference."[96] Scholars have speculated on the reasons behind this tolerance. First, as Barmé suggests, it was partly the economic imperatives that
allowed for a degree of liberalism in the cultural realm.[97] Second, it is commonly agreed that permitting a grey sphere may actually strengthen social
stability, at least in the short run. Such stability, Gold suggests, rests on an
implied agreement between the government not to engage in overt cultural
repression and the people not to turn their discontent into overt unrest.
Thus, it would seem, the state chooses not to intrude excessively into this
grey zone, finding "the costs [of such intrusion] outweigh the benefits."[98]

Conclusion

The coexistence of the "red" and "grey" cultural markets testifies to the
strategic nature of China's cultural governance in the 1980s and 1990s. It
would be a mistake, however, to regard state tolerance during this period,
even in the grey market, as random. Thus most popular music was permitted, but rock and roll was closely monitored.[99] And state media were
heavily regulated (as they always have been in China). In the 1990s, with
the introduction of satellite television, Chinese viewers in urban, coastal
areas increasingly watched foreign programs by using illegal satellite
dishes. Since people in the rural, remote areas were allowed to purchase
legal dishes to receive television programs, satellite dish manufacturing
soon became an industry.[100] Originally intended to overcome poor reception for television viewers in rugged, mostly rural areas, legal satellite dishes
soon exceeded their brief and were being used to receive forbidden foreign
programming.[101] To keep television screens clear of forbidden content, the
government painstakingly and effectively limited the use of satellite dishes
except where explicitly permitted by the state. Thus it allowed the installa-
tion of satellite dishes and the reception of foreign programming in hotels
and apartments serving foreigners, but, in rural areas, where satellite dishes
were more essential for television reception and restrictions regarding them
somewhat more relaxed, the government strongly encouraged residents
to use communal satellite dishes attached to local cable networks or relay
transmitters that it could manage.[102]

    What this tells us is that, if the Chinese state is seriously concerned about
particular television or video programs, for example, it will muster the necessary resources to attend to them, no matter how difficult that might be.

Thus there are good reasons to believe that the Chinese state was unwilling to come down hard on piracy. The existence of a cultural duality—of official and unofficial cultural spheres—in the 1980s and 1990s was clearly informed by a logic of zoning: whereas some content was under strict oversight, other content was tolerated or openly permitted. It was within this dual regulatory context that online video as a relatively independent medium developed in the 2000s. "There is no telling," Barmé opined in 1992, "what further mischief the practitioners of China's 'grey culture' will get up to in the future."[103] In that future, the "mischief" Barmé referred to was the internet culture, of which online video was an important part, a culture emerging in China in the first few years after 2000 and descended from the unofficial culture of the previous decades. Movies stored on physical discs began to circulate online; people growing up with pirated videos began to work for internet companies, bringing their independent sensibilities with them. I will cover all this and more in the following chapters. But before I turn to online video, I will first discuss the development of Chinese television in the 2000s.

3 Stay Left: Post-2000 Television Drama Production in China

Since the beginning of the new century, the state media and cultural sectors have been more significantly marketized. However, as in the 1980s and 1990s, the reform of state media was still largely contained within the orbit of the party-state, and their marketization remained far more controlled than that of the new media developing around the same time. This chapter first describes the "cultural system reform" (*wenhua tizhi gaige*) of the early 2000s and details changes in the television sector in response to it, focusing on television drama production and the frontier of marketization in television, and paying particular attention to the increased operation of private capital in that field. Although the chapter touches on a variety of government-sanctioned commercial developments in the field, its primary emphasis is on the ways the government effectively contained private television drama production, thereby preserving television's status as a politicized zone. The chapter concludes with a description of how two different generations of television industry professionals with unique histories made their careers in a fragmented industry. Those who could adapt themselves to the changing industry structure and multifaceted regulatory regime brought about by marketization survived, but those who could not were left struggling.

"This Is Savage Growth."[1]

Although state-controlled marketization has both enriched the state media and strengthened their political power since the 1980s, as Yuezhi Zhao is quick to point out, market-oriented restructuring has also led to their significant fragmentation and decentralization. In television, the proliferation of local stations, the spread of cable technology, the multiplication and rise of satellite channels, and the ferocious competition between stations and channels became matters of concern for the party-state.[2] In response, the government launched a campaign in the mid-1990s advocating media conglomeration to recentralize, manage the unintended consequences of media marketization, and prepare for Western competition after China joined the World Trade Organization.[3] In 2000, Hunan Province created the Hunan Broadcasting, Film, and TV Group, the first province-level broadcasting conglomerate in the country, which subsumed under its single control channels previously operated by different television stations. Major cities such as Shanghai and major provinces such as Shandong and Zhejiang quickly followed in 2001.[4] In this round of restructuring, stations as organizational entities in Chinese television disappeared, with channels becoming the major organizations responsible for both revenues and political objectives set by the conglomerates or "groups."[5]

But because, as communication and media professor Chin-Chuan Lee explains, the media conglomeration was organized by "administrative fiat," it resulted in bureaucratic competition, inefficiency, duplication, and waste.[6] The government intervened in the early 2000s with a more sweeping, systematic program of "cultural system reform" to accelerate the restructuring of the media and cultural sectors. As Yuezhi Zhao sees it, the immediate catalyst for cultural system reform was the unsatisfactory pace of marketization of the state media and the stumbling conglomeration of organizations.[7] By contrast, emphasizing the global context, Michael Keane looks at the reform in relation to China's objectives of "cultural security" and "soft power." In particular, upon entry into the WTO, China needed to build a stronger national media culture to successfully compete with foreign media; to that end, its government more actively pursued the promotion of China's cultural industries, a key component of cultural reform in the 2000s.[8]

Central to cultural reform this time around was a more radical separation of media components that served public/political interests and entailed state subsidies from media components that were less pertinent to those interests and could be more readily exploited as commodities. The former were categorized as "public interest–oriented cultural undertakings" (*wenhua shiye*), which were protected from market relations,[9] and the latter, as "cultural industries" (*wenhua chanye*), which were carefully opened to varying degrees of marketization. This distinction entailed a separation both of public/political interest–oriented and market-oriented media institutions and of public/political and market-oriented functions within a particular institution.[10] Thus the editorial function of Chinese Central Television was categorized as a "public interest–oriented cultural undertaking" (*wenhua shiye*), whereas its activities in providing entertainment, leisure, and other cultural services were subsumed under the rubric of "cultural industries" (*wenhua chanye*). This distinction allowed the state to pursue its core interests in the cultural realm and served as a powerful discursive basis for inviting market forces to reengineer state media, at least to some extent.

Cultural system reform formally began in June 2003 with a national work conference in Beijing, followed by the announcement by the central government that pilot work would begin in selected media groups.[11] In broadcasting, although the mother groups would remain public interest–oriented entities, their business operations, advertising, and production of less ideologically oriented programs such as television dramas, categorized as "cultural industries," were to be spun off and turned into shareholding companies. These would absorb state capital from nonmedia sectors and private capital from domestic enterprises—and even from foreign investors in some cases, provided the state held a controlling interest.[12]

Private capital was not only encouraged in the restructuring of state broadcasting groups, but also allowed to establish purely private production companies. Unlike in previous decades, when private capital, though present in the cultural realm, was generally not officially recognized by the state, private investments in production companies were largely permitted in the mid-2000s, conferring many advantages, the most important being legitimacy. In August 2003 and June 2004, the State Administration of Radio, Film, and Television (SARFT, which would merge with GAPP to become the SAPPRFT in 2013) twice issued a long-term television drama production permit to twenty-four private companies, sending a strong political message to formalize the position of private capital. By 2005, there were more than 2,000 private companies of various sizes across the country, and they accounted for some 80 percent of the total investment in television drama production.[13]

By contrast, although private production companies, whether jointly or individually owned, proliferated outside the state sector, the state reserved the right to censor their programs and to decide whether to air them.

Thus, even though the production of entertainment programs including television dramas was included within the (ostensibly private) category of "cultural industries," distribution remained within the purview of the government. The state monopolization of distribution outlets fragmented the flow of private capital—and, as I will show, constituted a major mechanism through which television drama production, though pushed into the market, was still effectively politicized. Indeed, as Yuezhi Zhao argues, the party-state's use of the term "non–publicly owned capital" as an alternative to "private capital" in official documents reveals its reluctance to fully embrace privatization.[14]

When it came to investment in its television sector, China treated foreign capital much more cautiously than it did domestic capital. For a short period of time, there were signs that the party-state might lower the threshold for transnational media corporations to enter the field of television program production. In 2003, the SARFT issued its Opinions on Promoting the Development of the Radio, Television and Film Industry, which allowed both foreign and domestic capital to participate in producing nonnews television programs and films; in particular, influential overseas production companies would be allowed to establish joint ventures with state television production units and film studios in China as long as the studios held a controlling interest.[15] And, in 2004, the Provisional Regulations on Sino-Foreign Joint and Cooperative Ventures in Radio and Television Program Productions, jointly issued by the SARFT and the Ministry of Commerce, further extended Chinese participation beyond state entities to encompass private media organizations.[16]

Very quickly, however, this good news (which thrilled global media giants like Sony and Viacom) was followed by bad news. In early 2005, in its Notice on Implementing the Provisional Regulations on Sino-Foreign Joint and Cooperative Ventures in Radio and Television Program Productions, the SARFT stipulated that each foreign company would be allowed to set up only a single joint venture in China.[17] A few months later, bad news was followed by worse news when Opinions on Introducing Foreign Capital to the Cultural Realm, jointly issued by the SARFT, the Ministry of Culture, the General Administration of Press and Publication (GAPP), the National Development and Reform Commission, and the Ministry of Commerce, further restricted foreign investments in television program production.[18] Although the SARFT would still allow foreign investments in single projects with its approval, it would not allow any foreign television program production companies to participate in joint ventures with Chinese companies. When all was said and done, Chinese television was to be protected against excessive marketization.

Building on its two-year pilot program, the government brought cultural reform to new heights in the next five years. Thus, in 2009, the State Council, the highest organ of state administration in China to which ministries and ministry-level agencies like the SARFT report, announced the Plan to Revitalize Cultural Industries,[19] the country's eleventh revitalization plan after those addressing the steel, automobile, and textile industries, among others. Clearly recognizing the strategic importance of cultural industries for the national economy, the State Council's plan proposed two substantial moves. First, it called on central and local governments to provide bailout funds in the form of discount loans, project subsidies, and capital injections to develop cultural industries. And, second, it called on banks and financial institutions to lend active support to the cultural industries by coming up with, guaranteeing, and reguaranteeing new instruments and services oriented to those industries.[20] Both state-controlled and privately owned cultural enterprises were encouraged to launch domestic IPOs in response to the plan's moves.

To that end, local governments accelerated the development of cultural industries by nurturing promising local enterprises and actively pushing them into the stock market. It should be noted here that, alongside its cultural reform, the party-state delegated central power to local authorities—in the case of television, to the local SARFT bureaus—as part of its national administrative and legal reform from 1998 to 2003 to rationalize governance by withdrawing from direct intervention while retaining political authority.[21] Decades of media reform had given rise to self-serving provincial media and other corporate entities outside the state sector (though still intricately related to it), making it imperative for ministry-level agencies like the SARFT to decentralize their power and invite their local bureaus to participate in cultural governance. Moreover, the explosive growth of private television drama production companies and the considerable growth of their drama outputs made it extremely difficult, if not impossible, for the SARFT to handle censorship of those outputs centrally, again making decentralization of power essential. Although the delegation of administrative power did not always create more space for provincial governments to participate in national policy making, it did allow them greater discretion in implementing national policies.[22] Since they regarded the development of cultural industries to be an important aspect of their political achievement (*yeji*), local governments made every effort to move the project forward, and their greater discretionary power helped them further that development. On the one hand, local administration facilitated the creation of private companies, allowing them greater space for innovation and negotiation. On the other hand, it gave rise to a network of vested interests involving government officials (indeed, television drama production was for years rumored to be a way for government officials to launder money),[23] which acted as an incentive for local authorities to support cultural industries.

Thus the Huace Film & Television Company (henceforth "Huace"), a major private studio in Zhejiang Province, whose stock was the first to be listed in television drama production, had an entrenched local establishment. Its CEO, Yifang Zhao, was the former deputy director of the local SARFT bureau in Dongyang, a county-level city in Zhejiang. Zhao quit government service and moved to the province's capital city, Hangzhou, to do business in the early 1990s, at a time when a large number of other government officials were leaving China's bureaucratic system (*tizhi*) for private business, a trend later known as *xiahai*, which literally translates as "jumping into the ocean" in English. Many of these former officials, including Yifang Zhao, have become influential businesspeople in various sectors of the Chinese economy. They are called the "'92 school" for having emerged after Deng Xiaoping's southern tour in 1992, but, unlike the businesspeople who emerged from the grassroots in the 1980s, they have benefited from their close ties with the government.[24]

When the SARFT's Zhejiang bureau made a determined effort to speed up cultural reform within its jurisdiction, Huace became a key recipient of government support. As an icon of Hangzhou's cultural industries, the company received numerous awards, subsidies, and other forms of support such as consumer vouchers from the local government.[25] The Zhejiang provincial government and the SARFT also played an important role in prodding Huace into the stock market. A former project manager at Huace, my informant Wei recalled a lunch he had with a retired deputy director of the SARFT's Zhejiang bureau:

In that lunch, he told us that they at the time wanted to take three cultural enterprises to the stock market, Huace, Huayi Brothers [film], and Zhongnan Cartoon. ... So the government was quite consciously pushing it. Of course, personal [corporate] willingness was also a factor. But in China, like many things, while it may appear to be a personal matter, it turns out to have deep connections with the government.[26]

Wei's recollection was confirmed by an official source. In the press conference held by the SARFT's Zhejiang bureau in 2010, its spokesman reviewed the broadcasting reform in Zhejiang: "In recent years, the Zhejiang provincial SARFT nurtured a group of influential private film/television production companies including Great Wall, Huace, Zhongnan Cartoon. ... It supported and facilitated Huayi Brothers' stock market launch. ... Now it is supporting [the efforts of] Huace, Great Wall, and Zhejiang Time Cinema to launch IPOs."[27]

Huace's successful stock market launch in 2010 brought considerable personal wealth to Yifang Zhao. The billions of yuan that she made, however, might have belonged to her former business partner, Zhongfu Lou, a rich old entrepreneur from Dongyang with businesses primarily in construction and real estate. In the early to mid-2000s, he several times missed the chance to own stock in the first listed shareholding company in Chinese television drama production. Now what he got was Zhao's New Year gift every Chinese Spring Festival.[28] In Wei's version of the events, it was a Bentley in 2013: "Zhao is grateful to Lou for his help in early years. She once promised that whatever car she would buy, she would buy one for Lou's wife. She bought a Bentley last year, so she also bought one for Lou's wife."[29] Nevertheless, it was said that, for a long time, Lou was regretful every time he saw Zhao. It was probably beyond his imagination, and the imagination of many other Chinese as well, that the party-state could—and would—transform popular culture, one of its ultimate sources of legitimacy, in such a powerful way.

Huace's public listing, supported by the government, seemed to mark a newer stage in China's cultural reform of television. The lucrative prospect of Chinese television drama production attracted many investors and led to the large-scale expansion of the sector, or its "savage growth," as Wei called it. The risks of investing in cultural production in China were indeed high—but so were the rewards. As Wei summarized it: "The rate of profit is astonishing. Well-performing companies can turn a profit for one production cycle within a single year, and the profit rate is more than 100 percent, which is unimaginable elsewhere. ... For businessmen, the interest rate of money stashed in banks is low. Even the usury interest rate [for money lent out] is only about 20 percent." "Hot money" (private capital seeking short-term high returns) began to pour into the field in the late 2000s. Meanwhile, as the impact of the 2008 global financial crisis was felt across China's economy, companies and individuals began to withhold or withdraw their investments from other sectors and place their capital in the cultural market. By late 2010, the television drama production industry had already received large investments from other industries such as real estate, energy, and manufacturing. These industries and individuals invested in single projects, and profits were distributed to them as dividends. Wei entered the television production industry right at the moment of its ferocious growth. His first job was in the Great Wall Film and Television Company (Changcheng), another long-established firm in Zhejiang Province. As he recalled, "Immediately after I joined the company in 2009, I felt its expansion. One could feel it expanding every day."

Inspired by Huace's public listing, interest in investing in shareholding companies instead of in single projects also began to grow. Wei witnessed that kind of heightened interest in Changcheng as well: "People from commercial banks and various financial institutions visited the company every day. They were less interested in investing in single projects than in buying shares. They wanted to make another listed company." Of particular interest were the private equity (PE) funds, mainly Renminbi (RMB) private equity and venture capital funds registered in China, which invested in and incubated production companies that culminated in stock market launches, mergers, and other promising business outcomes. In 2012, there were twenty-two cases of private equity investment with a total amount of $212 million. Among them, iFirst Capital (Yingfeng chuangtou), DT Capital (Detong ziben), Ray Stone Capital (Leishi touzi), and Seven String Investment jointly invested more than $30 million into Hairun Film and Television, one of the largest television production companies in China and a leading IPO hopeful.[30] These investors waited to receive their payouts when Hairun successfully entered the stock market.

The influx of hot money into the field drove up both the production cost and the selling price of television dramas considerably. Nevertheless, state television stations/channels, especially those of provincial satellite television, made increasingly rich by ever-higher advertising revenues in the 2000s, were still able to buy into those expensive productions. In fact, to some extent, it was the ongoing commercialization of state television stations/channels and their growing buying power that both assured the unprecedented amount of interest in television drama production and contributed to a steady—and in recent years a sharp—increase in the production budgets of television drama series. Buying drama programs from private production companies, a common institutional practice for state television nowadays, was a product of commercialization during the reform. Commercial slots were not as expensive in the 1980s and early 1990s as they are today. My informant Shao, a television producer, told me that, much like the bartering arrangement between Chinese television stations and foreign media companies, it was common practice for television stations to trade commercial breaks within the show schedule (*suipian guanggao*) in exchange for the productions of domestic private content providers, who then solicited advertisers for themselves.[31] Eventually, however, as commercial slots became more valuable with accelerated commercialization, programs would be acquired by monetary exchange rather than bartering.

In 2004, the tremendous commercial success of *Super Girl,* a talent show along the lines of *American Idol* produced by Hunan Satellite Television, ushered in a decade's worth of cut-throat competition for audiences and advertising revenues among television channels with national reach, including those of Chinese Central Television and provincial satellite television, especially channels in the first tier. Since then, the commercialization of state television stations/channels has accelerated at an unprecedented rate, a trend directly reflected in their soaring advertising revenues, whose growth rate peaked at about 49 percent in 2007.[32] The increasingly rich television stations/channels inevitably focused on acquiring quality dramas. Indeed, as Ruoyun Bai notes, television drama has become the dominant and most important genre in generating advertising revenues for most channels.[33]

It was this explosive growth—of television stations/channels, on the one hand, and of private investment in them, on the other—that pushed up the production cost of Chinese television dramas. According to my informant Han, also a television producer as well as an investor, in the early 2000s, it cost an average of ¥3 million (about $400,000) to make a television series, depending on the genre.[34] That cost was to increase tenfold over the next decade. Wei believed that cultural production had been reduced to a game of capital: "It is such an age," he sighed, "an age of crazy capital markets. If the changes I felt in those years at Changcheng were just early signs of this trend, now it is just crazy. It shows no signs of retreat."[35] Drastic as these changes were, we must keep in mind the mixed role of the Chinese state in this process. Thus, even as it created space for domestic private capital to grow in the television sector, the state also fragmented the flow of that capital by excluding it from program distribution as an effective mechanism to police cultural production. I will now turn to this point.

"They Must Be from Television Stations."[36]

Despite an influx of private capital into the field, television drama production was still subject to a multifaceted regulatory regime, one that included heavy postproduction censorship at various levels of the SARFT or its successor, the SAPPRFT. The state's firm grip on distribution outlets, specifically, state television stations/channels, constituted another central mechanism through which the SARFT, using these stations/channels as its intermediaries, exerted political constraints on private television drama production. Thus, private production companies are not allowed to own television channels; they must rely on state television stations/channels for distribution. But since these stations/channels were managed with a heavy hand by the SARFT, they had to prioritize their political obligations over their economic interests. More important, their monopoly over the life-and-death resource of distribution has allowed them to impose their political obligations on private television drama producers and constrain their productions in many ways. Private production companies in the new century thus still function largely as the "supply factories" of state television, as they did in the 1990s, despite the dazzling market developments since then.

In 2004, the Television Drama Regulation Section under the SARFT's General Editorial Department was upgraded by one administrative level to the Television Drama Regulation Department (*Dianshiju guanli si*), which has since become a fully developed regulatory unit for television dramas within the SARFT. State intervention in private television drama production first began with a regulation on topic (*ticai*) selection. Periodically, to promote its political and moral agendas, the SARFT issued guidelines regarding a mandated theme of television drama production and scheduling. Thus, in early 2008, in keeping with the celebration of the thirtieth anniversary of the reform and opening up, television drama producers were required to produce "realistic" leitmotif dramas (*xianshi zhuxuanlu ticai*) that would positively represent the impact of the reform on Chinese society and praise it, the Communist Party, and socialism more generally.[37] And then, in 2014, according to my informants Wei and Xin, a distributor at the Beijing Television Art Center, producers were required to center their productions around the "Chinese dream," an evolving political ideology developed by the new leadership under Xi Jinping.[38]

The SARFT's involvement in shaping topics was more substantially realized through television drama topic planning (*ticai guihua*) and project establishment administrative approval (*lixiang shenpi*). From 2001, as part of the SARFT's efforts to plan drama production and keep television screens clear of forbidden content, it required producers to submit project proposals with an abstract of 150–200 words and a synopsis of no fewer than 1,500 words for topical approval and preproduction planning. Depending on the subject matter of the drama (for instance, foreign affairs, religion, or crime), the proposal also needed to be approved by the corresponding government agency.[39] Perhaps in light of the delegation of administrative powers to local levels and the need to develop cultural industries, beginning in 2006, the SARFT decided to decentralize and streamline the topic approval procedure. According to the revised procedure, except for those dramas concerning "large and important revolutionary historical subjects" (*zhongda geming lishi ticai*), which had to go through a separate procedure, producers (except those from centrally administered organizations such as Chinese Central Television) were allowed to register their intent to produce dramas with provincial SARFT bureaus, provided they submitted, for each drama, a 1,500-word synopsis stating the theme, main characters, historical background, and storyline, with a clearance from relevant government agencies in the case of a special topic drama.[40] Although the revised procedure was intended to both decentralize and streamline the original topic approval procedure, industry professionals still referred to it as *lixiang*, that is, "project establishment," a term carried over from the previous period, revealing just how limited the increase was in their autonomy as a result of this particular procedural change in the larger multifaceted regulatory regime.

Industry professionals believed that most of the proposals were able to get through this first stage, except those deemed obviously inappropriate by the state's political and moral standards. Even so, according to Ruoyun Bai, between May 2006 and May 2012, out of a total of 6,797 proposals submitted for ratification, 1,493 (nearly 22 percent) were rejected. Proposals receiving local approval had to be submitted to the SARFT centrally each month and posted on its website, where the SARFT publicized its concerns about "unhealthy" trends it discerned from those proposals during particular time periods, for example, a concentration of crime dramas in 2007.[41]

Once a project received final approval at the central level, it moved to the stage of script creation, although, in most cases, script development was already underway. As the most important phase of content development, writing the script or screenplay entailed the greatest amount of censorship, mainly self-censorship, in television drama production. Screenwriters tried to avoid potential problems by paying close attention to current censorship regulations. In 2010, The Rules on Television Drama Content Regulation banned content that

> violates the basic principles of the Constitution, foments resistance or induces infringement to the Constitution, laws, administrative rules and regulations; endangers national unity, sovereignty and territorial integrity; discloses national secrets, jeopardizes national security, and harms national reputation and interests; foments ethnic hatred and discrimination, threatens ethnic customs, hurts ethnic feelings, and destroys national unity; violates the state religious policies, publicizes religious extremism, heresy, and superstition, discriminates and insults religious beliefs; disrupts the social order and damages social stability; publicizes pornography, gambling, violence, terror, and drugs, induces crime or imparts criminal knowledge; insults or defames others; endangers social virtues or national cultural traditions; infringes the rights of the minor and harms the physical and mental health of the minor; all the other content forbidden by the law, administrative rules and regulations.[42]

In addition to this seemingly exhaustive list, there is also an incomplete list of unofficial, unwritten rules circulating widely among producers. Compared with the relatively vague guidelines stated publicly, these unwritten rules, compiled by producers over time, are more specific and clear-cut. One such rule prescribes the desired political correctness of the main character in a drama, which is to be consistently close to Communist Party ideals. For example, the novel from which the drama *Too Late to Say I Love You* (*Laibuji shuo woaini*) is adapted, is a love story between a warlord and a woman from a noble family during the Republic of China (1912–1949). In the dramatic adaptation of the novel, the second half of the warlord's life is characterized by his active involvement in the Anti-Japanese War led by the Chinese Communist Party. In dramas set during the Republic of China, it is a common practice to depict a major character such as a gang member or a wealthy playboy as someone who eventually experiences an awakening of political consciousness, joins the Communist Party, and participates in the Anti-Japanese War. Other rules cover the depiction of crime, such as avoiding detailed representations of criminal behaviors, the obligatory inclusion of scenes depicting the arrest or sentencing of the criminal and positive representations of the police. When a drama portrays suicide, responsibility for the act must be attributed to the individual rather than to society. It is also unwise for script writers to humanize criminals or historical figures who have already been defined as negative or controversial in the party's master narratives of modern Chinese history.[43] These unofficial, unwritten rules spell out in concrete detail what the producers believe is meant by the abstract generalities in officially announced policy documents forbidding content that damages social stability.

After a production concluded, it had to go through postproduction/predistribution censorship by the SARFT in order to obtain a "television drama distribution permit" (*dianshiju faxing xukezheng*), a process that has been in place since 1998. As with decentralized topic approval, most dramas were censored by provincial SARFT bureaus except those produced by centrally administered organizations such as Chinese Central Television or by coproductions.[44] To conduct the censorship of a drama, local SARFT bureaus would organize a small ad hoc committee consisting of four to five members, who reviewed the drama and wrote down their recommendations: accept, reject, or revise. Although this appears to be a civil board of censorship, committee members were normally members of political and social elites such as incumbent or retired SARFT officials, university professors, and experts. The SARFT considered these people to be equipped with the necessary political literacy to make correct decisions about what should be shown and what ideas should be taught, decisions characterized by elitism and paternalism. According to Wei, postcensorship was mainly a political and moral check: "For example, good people in the drama must have good endings, whereas bad people must be punished; mistresses must have bad endings, and traitors cannot be overhumanized." Producers were required to respond to the comments of the committee reviewers by making corresponding changes; through postproduction censorship and feedback, they gained knowledge of the SARFT's unspoken rules that they needed to form unwritten rules of their own. Comments provided by the SARFT, especially those from decisions recommending rejection or revision of a drama, were widely disseminated and shared in the industry. Producers and screenwriters studied them as meaningful precedents in order to avoid making similar mistakes.[45]

According to Wei, postproduction censorship did not usually result in rejection of a project, but only in its revision. This suggests that self-censorship and feedback from censor-reviewers had a chilling effect on the production of works that might challenge the political or moral norms of the party-state. Or, as Wei more concisely put it: "In fact, everyone has a balance in mind. These [political or moral things] are propagated every day. We all know [them]. When it comes to creation, no one is as stupid as to challenge these things."[46] Although, as a liberal-minded person, Wei seemed not to genuinely believe in and was sometimes even critical of the ideological pronouncements by the party, it was his survival strategy to freely comply with the regulatory regime in order to gain the benefits this entailed, such as career advancement.

If a drama was meant to reach nationwide audiences through satellite television channels, it had to go through another round of censorship by the central SARFT. As Bai notes, television dramas aired during prime time on Chinese Central Television and provincial satellite television were more heavily censored because of their national reach than were those aired on broadcast television channels or stations.[47] Dramas on subjects the state considered to be important were also more strictly censored by the central SARFT.[48] Taken together, these examples show that cultural zoning was exercised not only according to media form (television versus online video) and within a particular media form, but also according to technology (satellite versus broadcast or ground-based television), time, and genre. But, most important, as Chinese studies professor Xiaoling Zhang concludes: "it is [largely] the perception of the leaders on the reach of the media that decides the level of control to be exercised."[49] Being the most accessible and family-oriented medium in China, television is certainly more strictly controlled than online video is. And, because of their larger audience, prime-time television programs are more heavily monitored than those in other time slots. In fact, it is almost a universal practice to impose different regulations on prime-time and non-prime-time programs, which, based on the reach of television, is an implicit method of social control.

According to Bai, the less rigorous supervision of dramas shown on broadcast television is also a necessary consequence of the decentralized nature of the censorship regime, with censors at the provincial level tending to apply looser censorship criteria. Bai suspects that another reason is the market-friendliness of local bureaucrats who do not want to discourage local cultural industries with rigorous censorship.[50] Moreover, the provincialization of administration tends to breed interest networks at the local level, which can breed bribery as well, potentially undercutting the censorship regime. Censorship committee members were paid by production companies to review dramas, or as Wei put it more plainly, "censorship is done by humans ... and the censorship fee is paid by us, so they, of course, can be bribed."[51] Although it is still unclear to what extent those practices of corruption challenged the censorship regime, the SARFT made repeated attempts to discipline its provincial bureaus.

After a drama made it to the television screen, the SARFT implemented a strict monitoring system, which, according to Michael Keane, consisted both of officials designated to watch programs and of complaints and reports lodged by the audience.[52] In extreme instances, the SARFT would ban the airing of particular dramas or genres. In late 2011, for example, the agency issued a special administrative order to restrict the airing of historical dramas about imperial court politics, time-travel dramas, shows involving crime and the law, and copycat shows using foreign formats on prime-time satellite television. Orders such as this were handed down to the stations but then relayed to production companies, which adjusted their production plans accordingly. Indeed, companies and producers made a point of staying in close touch with state television stations throughout the production process—for instance, by sending scripts to television stations/channels for review well in advance of actual production.[53] The state's monopoly on distribution was another mechanism through which it shaped the production of television dramas. Media studies scholar Nicholas Garnham, referring to media generally, observes that it is cultural distribution, rather than production, that constitutes the key locus of power and profit.[54] His observation clearly holds true for Chinese television.

Possible obstacles to the effective regulation of China's television drama production industry are the increasingly flexible structure of that industry and, with the rising presence of freelance, casual workers, its elusive labor practices. For example, after working for a few drama production companies, including Changcheng and Huace, Wei embarked on his own career as an independent screenwriter and has contracted projects from these two and other production companies. Experienced producers also began to establish their own studios, and production companies now hire them on a project-by-project basis. A network of subcontracted studios and individuals arose as a result, which makes the drama production industry appear decentralized, open, and dispersed. The question is how does the SARFT adapt to this increasingly flexible industry and manage to pass down its messages to those outside formal organizations, when their relationship with the system becomes attenuated, at least superficially? This question also involves the organizational communication apparatus of the government and its affiliates. Those producers, in order to survive in a system where the state monopolizes distribution, have actively accommodated themselves to the multilayered regulatory regime from topic planning to postproduction censorship, a regime that has already inculcated in them its rules, whether explicit or unspoken. Yet there are also other mechanisms working in support of that regulatory regime that incorporate outlying individuals.

When screenwriters, whether affiliated with a private television drama production company or self-employed, embarked on a project, they worked closely with producers, project managers, responsible editors (*zebian*), and others who acted as gatekeepers of script development in or on behalf of the production companies. As a freelance screenwriter, Wei sent completed scenes out to production companies for review and continued with his screenplay when the scenes were approved. Through this back-and-forth process, Wei avoided content that was likely to be censored. Veterans of production companies, many of whom originally worked in state television stations, were occasionally called to attend briefings, seminars, lectures, workshops, and training sessions organized by the SARFT, where they learned about new rules and imparted them to their colleagues either within their organizations or through temporary associations with freelancers.[55]

In order to reach content producers beyond the production companies, the state contacted freelance industry professionals through networks of social or civic organizations (*shehui tuanti*) such as the China Radio and Television Association (*Zhongguo guangbo dianshi xiehui*), supervised by the SARFT. According to law professor and legal scholar Karla Simon, the political and legal framework for civil society in China has historically allowed the following types of social organizations: mass organizations (such as labor unions), social welfare service organizations, art and literature groups, academic research organizations, religious organizations, and other organizations compliant with the laws of the government.[56] Social organizations, considered by political scientist Jude Howell to be the "transmission belts" (to borrow a Leninist term) between the Chinese Communist Party and the people, provide indirect channels through which the party communicates and penetrates society at large.[57] In the field of television drama production, SARFT-led associations that could potentially be categorized as "art and literature groups" worked to bridge divisions between the SARFT and industry professionals. Today, during the process of marketization, associations as such have increasingly labeled themselves as "industry guilds" in order to emphasize their professional identity and to downplay their political function, which nevertheless remains.

Each year, these industry associations organize industry-wide conventions, trade fairs, and workshops. They invite SARFT officials to attend and give speeches at the beginning of these events, and the official speeches on those occasions are interpreted as important political guidelines for media content. As the industry boomed, industry associations proliferated, and each of them organized its own conference for profit and self-promotion. Currently, there is at least one major industry conference in every month of the year, which allows for frequent exchanges of information. These associations also hold training workshops, which provide another opportunity for the state to make its wishes known to the industry. For example, in 2013, the China Radio and Television Association, authorized by the SARFT, organized training workshops for producers across the country. My informant Xin, a distributor at the Beijing Television Art Center who attended these workshops, recalled that the head of the Television Drama Regulation Department of the SARFT gave a lecture concerning politics and policies.[58] In this context, the current industry structure is characterized by a vertical network of flexible corporate entities and individuals, mediated through horizontally distributed, politically charged social organizations. Moreover, whereas the industry is becoming increasingly flexible, as noted above, the state remains *in*flexible in terms of key resources such as distribution. In this way, regardless of how dispersed the industry appears to be, industry professionals always orient themselves toward the sole center of power.

The ways in which the government communicates with industry professionals, both company employees and the self-employed, have been transformed by digital technologies. First, as I said earlier, the SARFT used its website to convey its position on industry trends, announce which projects have been approved, and disseminate news, regulations, and other relevant information. Industry professionals paid close attention both to ensure that their projects were within SARFT guidelines and to gather information for planning future projects. As Wei told me, "I often visit the SARFT website. ... I study the news, rules, regulations, and announcements of newly established projects, and speculate about the possible trend based on them. For example, when a lot of anti-Japanese dramas are approved, you should avoid the topic." For Wei, visiting the SARFT website, which most Chinese people would not, is a survival strategy.[59]

The rise of social networking sites has also transformed the dissemination of information in the industry, mainly among professionals themselves. "Information in this industry travels very quickly," Wei explained. "When there is news, my friends publish and forward it through WeChat [a Chinese messaging app]. Then everyone knows it overnight."[60] Indeed, WeChat has become a crucial element of the new social fabric in China. In the field of television drama production, industry professionals heavily relied on WeChat for social networking, information exchange, and professional development. I added the industry professionals I interviewed to my WeChat account, so I know that Wei did not exaggerate the speed of information flow in that context. Mediated social circles are so influential that they sometimes render traditional institutions irrelevant. Wei admitted that social media have today become one of his primary ways to acquire information.

The limits set by the state have established a lopsided relationship between production companies and state television stations that was enacted through many industry practices. First, this relationship can be seen in television drama trading. Since state television stations monopolized distribution outlets, production companies needed to pursue them and win their favor in order to sell their dramas. State television stations were the unassailable "Party A" (*jiafang*), a term that producers have borrowed from legalese to mock them in private conversations. The asymmetry of the relationship between producers and stations has worsened since the crisis of overproduction in the industry. At the Thirteenth Beijing Television Program Market and Exhibition I attended in March 2014,[61] members of one company brought a large bag of iPads and iPhones to the trade fair and gave away these devices to people they encountered from television stations. This practice was only a small part of the corruption going on between television stations and production companies. Bribery has become an open secret in the industry. An exception may be quality dramas produced by highly reputable companies, but, in general, to facilitate the selling of their programs, production companies must bribe the director of program purchasing in television stations or higher-level officials in charge of program buying. Euphemistically called a "broadcast supervision fee" (*jianbo fei*) in the industry, such a bribe accounted for at least 1 percent of the purchase price of a drama.[62]

But illicit transactions occur not just in the marketing of dramas. The asymmetrical relationship between television stations and production companies is also reflected in how—or whether—the stations decide to pay. When a television station decides to purchase a drama, it pays the production company 30 percent of the full price on delivery and the remainder depending on the actual rating of the drama when it airs. If its rating is not satisfactory, the station delays payment of the remaining amount or even refuses to pay it altogether. Payment delays are common in the industry. "This is an industry where contracts don't work," Xin sighed. "Television stations can break the contract anytime and refuse to pay the money, yet you cannot sue them."[63] Indeed, in order to secure distribution opportunities for future projects, most of the companies cannot take any legal action at all. Money for bribes is thus an essential part of production companies' budgets, not only to sell their productions but also to secure early scheduling, receive their entire fees from sales of their television dramas, and smooth the way for all aspects of the process.

To conclude this section, a story from the industry illustrates well the asymmetrical relationship between television stations and production companies. In June 2014, my informant Han, a veteran industry professional, and I both attended the Twentieth Shanghai Television Festival, he to publicize his new business in company registration and financial/taxation services. I offered to look after his booth at the festival and get business for him as part of my participant observation. But when I tried to stop people passing Han's booth and hand them the company leaflets, they simply ignored me. "They must be from television stations," Han said with a laugh. "People from television stations look different than people from production companies," he told me. "They have different styles. People from television stations appear to be elegant ... and relaxed. They don't carry things ... [and] are often crowded by several attendants." My experience supported Han's observations and gave me a taste of what it is like to participate in the asymmetrical relationship between powerful television stations and drama producers.

"I'd Rather Be the Ferryman in the Gold Rush."[64]

It is estimated that only about one-third of all television dramas in China make it to state television, and only 10 to 15 percent of them can make a profit.[65] Moreover, private production companies, although supposedly on an equal footing with their state-originated counterparts, are considerably less privileged when it comes to market competition. Lenders favor these counterpart companies, perceiving them to be stable institutions or, in industry discourse, companies that "won't run away" (buhui pao) because of their state origins.[66] Underlying this perception, common among players in the industry from bankers to freelance producers, is a profound and prevalent belief in an eternal state and therefore in that state's "permanence and immutability," a belief anthropologist Alexei Yurchak found to be widely held in the Soviet Union as well.[67] Moreover, the perceived stability and permanence of state-originated production companies gain them special privileges not only in fundraising, but also in sales: they are virtually guaranteed sales to their mother stations, if nowhere else. And, in some cases, television stations are virtually obligated to back them up and purchase their productions.[68] In an industry that has been increasingly plagued by overproduction and problematic distribution, this is a huge advantage.

Hot money, entering the field with a view toward earning immediate high returns, is typically withdrawn after one or two failed projects or simply after investors see the less romantic side of the industry, and newer, less knowledgeable investors take their place. There are some individuals and production companies who choose to stay in the industry for various reasons. To avail themselves of the opportunities that cultural system reform has brought about, they are prepared to live with the disillusionment and frustration that so often ensue when they do. Even though most people are flexible enough to deal with the political side of television drama production, survivors must also adapt to the industry's rapid technological and structural changes.

My informant Han is one of those survivors. We first met in March 2014 at the trade fair in Beijing, and again in June of that year at the Shanghai television festival. As a man in his fifties, Han appeared slightly out of place among the mostly young people in their twenties and thirties attending the two events, but his ruddy complexion, loud voice, energetic manner, and great willingness to talk to people all belied his age. He entered the world of television drama production in the late 1990s from the periphery of the cultural industries, as an employee in the advertising and marketing department of one of the largest state-owned pharmaceutical companies in China. After years of effort, the pharmaceutical industry had finally persuaded the government to allow over-the-counter (OTC) drug advertising. Han's job was mostly to plan and place OTC drug commercials mainly on Chinese Central Television. At the time, his company's advertising budget for cydiodine buccal tablets (*huasu pian*) was about ¥100 million (about $12 million). Although, as provided in an "all-in" package, the drug company paid Chinese Central Television (CCTV) both to produce the commercial and to arrange its placement, CCTV diverted some of that money to fund production of a television drama. "Television drama was not expensive to make at that time," Han explained. "One drama cost only about two to three million [yuan]. ... It was really easy to get two to three million out of it [the commercial's budget]. ... The production of the commercial only took a little time, probably just overnight. But they [CCTV] said it took two months to produce and another two months to air. In these four months, they used the money to produce a television drama." In return, the drug company's commercial was placed in the "preroll" ad slot when the drama aired. What Chinese Central Television had created here was a mixed operation of sponsorship and advertisement, and the benefit to Han from this arrangement included free trips to filming locations, an introduction to the field of television drama production, and possibly even kickbacks.

Han witnessed the spinning off and incorporation of production units that had been affiliated with state television stations. By the mid-2000s, it was obvious that the state was promoting the development of cultural industries. With the "golden age" of the pharmaceutical industry coming to an end, Han turned to the more promising cultural industries, where he leveraged his experience in marketing, advertising, and media planning to gain a foothold. But, at the same time, he did not resign from the pharmaceutical company, apparently wanting both the security of the state system and the benefits of the market economy, without entirely exposing himself to its precariousness. As an incumbent employee of a state-owned enterprise, Han was not allowed to register private production companies. To work around this restriction, he used an alias. As a calculating, creative, and resourceful individual, Han was able to identify opportunities and challenges, which allowed him to survive and succeed in both the state and market systems. Though he remained evasive about personal details of his past, likely because of its unlawful nature, he was quite cynical and outspoken about the shady side of the television production industry: "Government officials did much more than I did. Half of the companies here [exhibiting at the Shanghai television festival] might be run by governmental officials or heads of television stations." Han called these "dummy companies" (*yingzi gongsi*).

Han first began to operate a production company with his business partners in Beijing, but the company was later abandoned when its slipshod invoicing, chaotic tax situation, and a variety of lax practices prevented it from growing into a larger business. After that, Han and his partners registered project-based production companies in places like Shanghai, Xi'an (the capital of Shaanxi Province), and Haining (a county-level city in Zhejiang Province), selected because they could grant policy or financial favors or tax breaks, or because at least one of the partners had previously established relationships with local SARFT bureaus and television stations. For one of Han's most recent projects, based in Xi'an and (at least nominally) run by a locally registered production company, the Shaanxi Culture Industry Investment Group (SCG), a state-owned investment fund established by the Shaanxi provincial government in 2009, was willing to offer a ¥10 million (about $1.25 million) loan, provided the project was run by a local company. Registered in Xi'an in 2011, the project's production company, together with two of its joint producers, eventually raised ¥40 million (about $5 million) from various sources, including bank loans—and, it was said, even from one of the officials at the local television station/channel that eventually broadcast the project's show.

Han's companies have likely followed the development trajectory of most companies in the Chinese television drama production industry, which Bai describes as first producing no more than one drama series every one or two years.[69] Because Han and his business partners started with personal funds, it took a few years before they saved enough to produce a drama series. Given the low production costs at that time, Han was still able to manage his projects using his own money and with small-scale, workshop-style operations. The expansion of the industry since then, however, required a new model—the "Xi'an model," as Han called it. Responding to skyrocketing production costs with a greater ability to organize resources and operate projects, Han's new model was at first a success, but, in an industry that increasingly favored big companies, it faced increasing challenges. "There comes a point," reflected Han, "where we cannot afford the investment again. When the production cost rose from two to three million to 40 million [yuan], I partnered with others. Now we cannot afford the investment even through partnerships. ... Times have changed."[70] If Han had not been able to push his company onto the stock market, he might have had to repeat the process of making a production every one or two years and using the money earned to make the next production forever. But, even as a shareholding company, financing productions was becoming more difficult.

Having identified opportunities and limits presented by shifts in the market, Han decided to embark on a new and different business, one that aimed to provide complete services from company registration to financial assistance to newcomers in the industry. He aptly referred to his new business as a "whole value chain service," where profits would be made by charging service and annual membership fees and where the principal asset would be Han's firsthand knowledge of an industry whose many rules were opaque to most outsiders. As he had done for himself, Han compared regional policies to find the most favorable terms for his new clients, registered companies for them, and provided subsequent financial support as well as consultation services (on taxes and invoicing, for example). Upgrading urban China's entrepreneurial features was an integral part of the cultural system reform, with cultural industry clusters carved out by local governments to attract capital and professionals.[71] In this context,

Han's new service business could act as a broker between willing cultural entrepreneurs and local governments, by encouraging its clients to register businesses with cultural industry clusters. These locally incubated cultural enterprises could then be counted as the political achievements of local governments.

Han's cynicism about the corrupt system did not seem to dampen his enthusiasm for profiting from it. As a businessman, what he cared about most was locating potential market opportunities. Despite his setbacks in television drama production, Han firmly believed that cultural industries would remain the new engine of China's economy for the next decade. At the 2014 Shanghai television festival, while he was promoting his new business, he was also, as he put it, "feeling the market," that is, identifying new developments in order to adjust his services accordingly. As we walked out of the exhibition hall on the last day of the festival, Han told me he planned to remain in the industry. But, as soon as his new business became stabilized, he would withdraw from investing in television drama production. In his anticipation of future possibilities, I saw an unusual combination of optimism and pragmatism.

Han's most recent base was in Zhejiang Province, in the county-level city of Yongkang, whose government hired him in early 2014 because of his reputation in other cities. By the time of our conversation in June of that year, he had introduced more than fifty clients to the local government. As Han saw it, Yongkang was probably the best policy environment for his new business at the time, requiring neither an operational site (i.e., office), nor local employees, nor other local concessions from newly established companies. Indeed, since all his new clients had to do was "carrying a company registration certificate in their briefcase," Han considered the "briefcase company" (*pibao gongsi*) to be an advanced business model because of its exceptional flexibility. To justify his transition from production project manager to business service provider, he would often tell a story about the California Gold Rush, one that has been widely circulated and recycled in China, especially in self-help books teaching readers how to succeed in business. Many of these popular books tout successful entrepreneurial and management experience from advanced capitalist countries—above all, the United States. The ferryman in the Gold Rush story, instead of directly profiting from mining gold, makes money by taking miners across the river for a fee. Although this story is most likely apocryphal and, indeed, does not figure largely, if at all, in popular historical accounts of the Gold Rush, the ferryman's wisdom impressed Han and others who were looking to find niche markets. "Other people rush to mine the gold," Han explained, "but I will just help them cross the river. Other people exploit mines, but I will just sell them shovels. If I can make money from selling shovels, why should I go for mines? This is the most primitive U.S. model, isn't it?"

Wei shared many of Han's traits—his calculation, creativity, and pragmatism. As a digital video and movie lover in college, he entered television drama production in late 2009 after working in an advertising agency for a few months and as a freelance producer for over a year. He then hired on as a producer at Changcheng and later as a project manager at Huace. Although Wei made only a short, amateur digital film at school before he began his career in the industry, lacking the appropriate professional background did not seem to have been a significant disadvantage for him, which testifies to the industry's low entry requirements at the time, especially after its rapid expansion. As Wei recalled, when he was hired by Changcheng, the company had only a few dozen staff workers, most of whom were making documentaries, and was in desperate need of new employees. But Wei's success despite his lack of media education and training also testifies to his resourcefulness as a fast learner, which paved the way for his later advances in the industry.

At Huace, Wei's revision of a project script revealed a certain native ability. And when the script for another project was not ready in time for the scheduled shoot, because of his previous experience in screenwriting, however brief, he was made understudy to the original screenwriter. Stepping up in his new role, Wei wrote the script during shooting and worked effectively with the crew under immensely challenging circumstances. "I worked as a producer," Wei told me, "so I know how television crews and shooting work. I had directing experience, so I know how to manage a team. I know exactly how what I write will look like when it is put into shooting ... so the scripts [scenes] I sent out were very accurate. ... Everything was pushed forward smoothly."

The drama was aired on two broadcast television stations, establishing Wei's credentials as a screenwriter. And with this incident, Wei came to realize not only the scarcity of screenwriters and scripts in the industry, but also what that scarcity meant. As he put it, "scarce resources are always worth money." Meanwhile, Huace was slowly transforming itself into a project investment and management company, acquiring projects from outside instead of incubating original scripts. Wei was not against this model. Indeed, he believed that Huace's model was a more modern, scientific way to proceed than Changcheng's in-house operations because it freed its founders to engage in higher-level operations such as financing and thus to create greater value. But Wei also knew that investment was not a game for low-ranking professionals like himself. To survive and succeed in the industry, he needed to develop the professional skills that would make him competitive and indispensable.

Wei also referred to the California Gold Rush story Han so often told: "The situation now is very much like the Gold Rush moment. ... Very few people could actually find gold, and currently I don't have the ability to mine gold ... but I can ferry people across the river and make money from it. Once I accumulate a certain number of points, I can bargain with people. ... [One] must find opportunities amid changes." Thus industry professionals from two different generations, Wei and Han, turned to a similar strategy in navigating the increasingly monopolized television production sector. Identifying both the limit of career development at Huace and opportunities emerging beyond it, Wei decided to embark on his career as a freelance screenwriter in 2013. He called it a "well-considered decision," made with the same awareness and calculation that had informed his previous decision to leave Changcheng when it decided to produce a welter of projects all at the same time in order to build a record for its public listing. Immediately sensing that Changcheng was veering out of control, he moved to Huace for a better chance at personal development.

Wei knew himself well: "I am evaluative, able to shift identities according to situations." In fact, even though he had been a freelance screenwriter for only a short time when we spoke in April 2014, he had already developed new ideas about his future development. Most recently, he contracted projects from production companies and vetted the plot and content of each episode with them. After that, he created scene-by-scene outlines for each episode and delegated the writing of them to his less-established freelance collaborators to fill in the content. In this way, he shortened the time for writing a script from some seven to three or four months, without, he believed, compromising its quality. Happy with his model, Wei planned to expand. Part of his plan was to look for someone who could perform his own role in the whole process. By finding such a person, Wei said: "I could further free myself."

Clearly, Wei's practices were informed by a conception of screenplays as standardized products that could be mechanically assembled much like automobiles. Indeed, elsewhere in our conversation, he described the screenwriter as "a factory, a machine." Wei was fully aware and disapproved of the cutthroat commercialism prevailing in the industry. He admired those old-generation screenwriters who spent years in developing and revising a script. Although Wei used to think that his field involved "artistic creation," these idealistic sentiments did not hinder him in his pursuit of market-oriented projects. Such is the peculiar paradox of Wei's and Han's lives in the industry. Although both men were committed to cultural quality, they both also understood the importance of keeping pace with the market. As Wei remarked, almost as if reminding himself, "In recent years, those [industry professionals] in their fifties and sixties are dying out very quickly. They don't update their ideas, so they are washed out."

My informant Shao is probably one such person who failed to update himself in response to the constantly shifting market. Born in 1964, Shao graduated with a degree in Chinese literature from a university in the Xinjiang Uyghur Autonomous Region in the late 1980s. Shao's parents were both members of the Xinjiang Production and Construction Corps (Xinjiang Shengchan Jianshe Bingtuan), a collection of distinctive, mainly Han Chinese–populated military-agricultural settlements, created on Mao's orders in the 1950s to develop and guard China's vast western region—and a central element of China's ethnic frontier governance.[72] Like Shao, most of his friends and classmates would work for the government or for state-owned enterprises after graduation. But, unlike him, they would do so in Xinjiang, whereas Shao would be brought by his teacher to Beijing, where he would work in a production unit affiliated with the party organ *People's Daily*. And, though he called himself an "outlier," Shao would remain largely in the state cultural sector. Indeed, he never worked for private production companies, nor was he interested in them, even though he admired some cultural entrepreneurs from Zhejiang and Jiangsu Provinces who he thought had good taste (*you shuiping*). Since the early 1990s, Shao has successively worked for production units affiliated with *People's Daily*, the Young Communist League of China, and the Ministry of Culture. His main job has been to plan special topics programs (*zhuanti pian*), mostly public interest oriented, for these units. One of the programs he planned and proposed for broadcast on Chinese Central Television cleverly echoed the message of the national West China Development (*Xibu da kaifa*) project and was warmly supported by local governments in the western provinces. In light of the accelerated pace of cultural reform, Shao recently became a self-employed producer and screenwriter, but he retained his interest in "serious" themes such as ethnic minorities and customs in the western region and worked closely with various levels of local government.

It was this interest that put Shao in a difficult situation in the market economy. To be precise, his problems arose because he failed to package his work according to market principles. When we met, he was struggling to sell one of his television drama projects on ethnic minorities to television stations. He complained that the people in charge of drama acquisition at the stations were "lacking quality" (*suzhi cha*): "They do not know how to appreciate good topics and good scripts," he grumbled. "They like those lousy, noisy, eye-catching ones ... the so-called commercial ones. They don't want artistic productions that reflect national history and 'main melody' themes."[73] Shao scorned them as "rural women" (*nongcun funv*), a group considered to have poor taste. As a cultural worker for the party-state, he resisted marketization and upheld the tradition of what Yuezhi Zhao calls the "state socialist high culture" that aims to enlighten and uplift the masses' aesthetic sensibilities;[74] he was obsessed with grand narratives of the revolutionary past, of national unity, history, and culture. Shao felt deeply that the party-state was abandoning its ideological principles or, in his words, the "main melody" during the course of marketization. But, in fact, the party-state has shown no desire to abandon its principles. Instead, it has made perceptible official attempts to redefine the socialist core value system by incorporating universal values, including capitalist and traditional Confucian values. According to Han, the party-state would never reject its "main melody." Instead, it was simply adapting it to market forces. In doing so, the party's cultural system reform has created an entirely new vision of culture, but Shao was unable to grasp this change. To him, there appeared to be an irreconcilable conflict between ideological doctrine and commercial entertainment.

Shao also lamented the declining quality of cultural producers. To him, it took years or even decades to cultivate a good screenwriter with rich life experience, literary accomplishments, and a distinct personal style.

He yearned for those days when writing a script was an art or craft, when screenwriters were all properly trained at state art institutions such as the Beijing Film Academy or in literature programs at reputable universities, and when, as a community, they exchanged their own works for comment and careful, little-by-little improvement. Shao was referring to a time when cultural production was centralized in a few state-owned units. Currently, because art school graduates alone cannot fill all the positions opened up by the rapid privatization and expansion of the cultural industries, extra hands are needed. But in Shao's view, the young people flooding into the field from various backgrounds were all unqualified. To him, the mass production of culture first started with the mass production of cultural workers. The hastily and poorly trained industry professionals, like Wei, for instance, were themselves products, not much different from the ones they produced.

Conclusion

Shao's bewilderment and grievances contrasted sharply with Han's and Wei's enterprising, pragmatic spirits. Although Shao and Han belong to the same generation, Han was much more aware and adaptable than Shao, whose confusion resulted to a large extent from his failure to recognize the fundamentally political nature of television drama production in China and its cultural industries in general. He was perpetually alarmed by dazzling market-oriented developments in the field, and even by the designation "cultural industries" per se, which he saw as a contradiction in terms. A few years after China's official agreement on "cultural industries" was announced, another international term, "creative industries," began to gain currency in the country. Michael Keane offers an interesting account of the political divide between conservatives and reformers behind the discursive work of "cultural industries," on the one hand, and "creative industries," on the other, noting that "creative industries" stood as an alternative to "the more political and highly regulated cultural industries." As Keane rightly predicted, the Chinese party-state has exploited cultural industries to "provide content for propaganda campaigns, much as socialist culture has done for the past several decades."[75] This is the point Shao missed. Certainly, the expansion of private capital coupled with strong state endorsement was a primary growth model for television drama production in the

2000s. But what Shao failed to see is that the operation of private capital, as shown in this chapter, has been heavy-handedly managed by the state through a multifaceted regulatory regime subject to state politics. The cultural zone constituted by this political economic relationship is thus political in nature. It is in this sense that I describe the milieu of television as politics as usual in contrast to online video, whose development is more readily and strongly shaped by the logic of the market or capital. I will turn to this alternative cultural zone in chapter 4.

4 Early Online Video: A Political Economic Perspective

In the new millennium, the market-oriented reforms taking place in China's cultural realm could not be fully realized without considering the impact of digital technologies—above all, the internet. The internet as we know it today entered China's blueprint for reform in the 1990s, when China underwent a market-driven rupture and, as media professor Yu Hong argues, when it ardently embraced a version of modernity defined by Western capitalist economies, leading to China's accession to the World Trade Organization in 2001 and its comprehensive integration into the global economy.[1] An imminent economic slowdown following the 1997 Asian financial crisis convinced the Chinese state to embark on an economic restructuring and at the same time to cultivate new industries with sustainable market demand.[2] In this context, the internet, booming in Western countries, became attractive to China, despite the challenges its introduction would inevitably pose to the government's ideological endeavors, challenges that led some of China's top leaders even to suggest a domestic "intranet" as an alternative.[3] But, ultimately—and even though the Chinese state would not relinquish its ideological grip over it—the great economic potential of the internet's emerging technology seemed to triumph over ideological concerns.

From the very beginning, the state's decision to focus more on market relations set the tone for how it would govern the internet sector, including online video. Whereas foreign capital was unwelcome in the television sector, it would be freely permitted in the Chinese internet sector through specially designed financial structures for entrepreneurial development known as "variable interest entities" (VIEs). Because it was largely and most directly attributable to the protracted rivalry among multiple bureaucratic actors to determine which should have the authority over online video, the lax regulatory regime for online video content before 2007 requires an extended discussion. An examination of that regime in relation to the inter-ministerial rivalries also reveals the state's unwillingness to censor online media as it had traditional media. Early online video as an alternative zone to television in China developed within this political economic context, which I will return to shortly. But first we need to review the state-led con-struction of telecom infrastructures in China, upon which the internet and online video depended to emerge and thrive there.

Telecommunications Infrastructure, Internet Data Centers, and Bandwidth

China's experiments with computer networks began in education and research institutions, which replicated the pattern of data network con-struction in the United States and most other technologically advanced countries. The first computer network in the country, the China Academic Network (CANET), was set up in 1987, followed shortly by a few regionally based educational networks.[4] In the early to mid-1990s, China began to build its first national education and research network with international links—the China Education and Research Network (CERNET)—developed using lines leased from the Ministry of Posts and Telecommunications (MPT), which at that time was both the regulator and monopolist operator of China's telecom services.[5] The dependence of national educational net-works on the telecom sector points up its essential role in shaping China's internet development. Indeed, since internet services, including online video, are largely laid over telecom networks, the formation of both online video and the internet in China cannot be understood without mapping the links of both to the telecom sector.

The Ministry of Posts and Telecommunications began to build China's first commercial backbone network called "ChinaNET" in the mid-1990s, when the commercial potential of data communication became widely recognized in the West. Operated by the MPT-affiliated telecom enterprise China Telecom, ChinaNET acted both as a wholesale provider of band-width, leasing its lines to regional telecom branches, and as a brand name, allowing these intermediaries to provide retail services. Soon other inter-net service providers, both telecom offshoots and privately owned com-panies, began to provide internet services after securing licenses from the

Ministry of Posts and Telecommunications or its local representatives. Early subscribers to ChinaNET included state-owned enterprises, private companies, and wealthy individuals who were able to afford the expensive connection fees.[6]

The MPT's data network soon faced a series of competitors. Deng Xiaoping had clearly recognized the economic value of telecom when he identified it as a strategic sector at the very beginning of the reform era. The guiding principle of telecom reform in China has been to break up the existing monopoly and introduce competition to a sector where the mentality characterized by China scholar Barry Naughton as a "command-bureaucratic economy" persisted.[7] But, instead of inviting external, foreign players, China fueled competition within the state-monopolized telecom sector by creating new state enterprises. Adding an element of bureaucratic rivalry to profit from the liberalizing trend, Asian studies professor Eric Harwit tells us, only furthered that competition.[8] In the early 1990s, for example, the Ministry of Electronics Industry (MEI), which supervised electronics and computer manufacturing and was interested in adding telecom services to its brief, joined forces with the Ministry of Railways and the Ministry of Power to pursue the possibility of restructuring telecom networks once reserved for railway, power, and military purposes and redirecting their excess capacities to social or commercial uses. Although their endeavor was opposed by the Ministry of Posts and Telecommunications, with higher-level support, it eventually led to the creation of the telecom enterprise China Unicom in 1994.[9] Sixteen ministries and state enterprises outside of the MPT family invested in the new company, which began to compete with the MPT's China Telecom in providing telecom services, thereby ending its long-standing monopoly over public communications services, and soon the company introduced a data network of its own.[10] Around the same time, another newly launched telecom enterprise, Jitong, backed by the Ministry of Electronics Industry, built a series of national economics and finance data networks, collectively known as "Golden Projects," and began offering internet services to the public in 1996.[11]

In 1998, as part of China's first serious attempt to introduce institutional reform in response to digital convergence, and reflecting the increasingly prominent role of information industries in the national economy, the Ministry of Information Industry (MII) was established by merging the Ministry of Posts and Telecommunications and the Ministry of Electronics

Industry in the administrative restructuring of that year.[12] This restructuring led not only to the separation of telecom from postal services, but also, and more important, to the separation of China Telecom from the Ministry of Posts and Telecommunications, leaving the Ministry of Information Industry solely responsible for regulating the telecom sector. In the ensuing years, the newly formed ministry continued to introduce new competition: first by splitting China Telecom into several entities, and second by creating new telecom companies through mergers.[13] In 2001, for example, in light of China's impending entry into the World Trade Organization, China Telecom, which had just gone through a split in 1999, was further divided into a new China Telecom and a second new company called "China Netcom," both of which competed in areas beyond fixed-line—above all, internet services. The new China Telecom took control of networks in twenty-one provinces in the South and Northwest of China and dominated 70 percent of the networks' assets, and China Netcom, which merged assets from other telecom enterprises, was given facilities in ten northern provinces.[14] The physical division of the telecom sector into northern and southern structures, as discussed below, both necessitated the development of "content distribution networks" (CDNs), essential for today's video streaming, and shaped the layout of those networks.

This frequent restructuring, notes political scientist Chung-min Tsai, was partly to accommodate the intricate, conflicting interests among different bureaucratic factions, all of which were eyeing the remunerative telecom sector.[15] Thus, it would seem, the telecom infrastructure in China is bureaucratic politics in material form. Eric Harwit argues that the convoluted bureaucratic rivalry inherent in the competition for resources ironically turned out to be a powerful engine for breaking up the telecom monopoly in China and for leading its communications networks to new heights of efficiency and consumer accountability.[16] In this period, the looming prospect of competition from foreign companies following China's entry into the World Trade Organization also served as an impetus for internal restructuring in the late 1990s and early 2000s.[17]

The development of the Chinese internet took off as the Chinese government accelerated liberalization of the state-owned telecom sector and construction of its networks. By early 2001, there were 238,249 registered websites in China, and more than 80 percent of them belonged to the private, corporate domain.[18] As in the United States, where heavy users of the telecom infrastructure mainly come from the business sector,[19] state telecom enterprises in China at the time made most of their profits from corporate clients rather than from residential consumers.[20] The government also encouraged millions of enterprises in traditional sectors to adopt the internet; its national Enterprises Online (Qiye shangwang) campaign, together with its Government Online (Zhengfu shangwang) and Households Online (Jiating shangwang) campaigns, promoted e-commerce across the country.[21] Yu Hong observes a striking similarity between the state-led development of an internet economy in China and in South Korea, where each country waged "a systematic social-engineering campaign to create IT-based governments, business, and even citizenship."[22]

The growth of e-commerce and web-related companies made outsourced data services desirable since the traditional virtual server and server hosting solutions offered by internet service providers could no longer meet growing business demands for network resources (especially bandwidth), management, and security.[23] In this context, "internet data centers" (IDCs), based on a concept of outsourced data solutions imported from the United States, became something telecom carriers and internet service providers began to invest in and sell. As a scarce resource, bandwidth was the primary factor that drove internet companies' demands for internet data centers, which could provide much more bandwidth. Looking back, the overall scale of internet companies and indeed the total number of internet users at the time was far from adequate to sustain a robust IDC industry, as it would do a decade later. Moreover, the functions of internet data centers at the time were also rather basic, compared to what they would later become. Nevertheless, the growing business need for infrastructure and network performance still constituted the primary driver for the first, brief IDC boom in China.

As an outsourced data solution, internet data centers offered space and associated facilities to house servers and other components of internet companies in a controlled physical environment, and they connected their servers to backbone networks at high speed.[24] In addition to this service, commonly referred to as "colocation," the data centers also provided dedicated and shared web hosting, leased-line services, and virtual private networks (VPNs), as well as other web solutions and management services.[25] Of the total cost of IDC service provision, 30 percent went to bandwidth.[26] Because, as direct operators and wholesalers of backbone networks, telecom carriers and internet service providers owned the bandwidth essential to the services the data centers provided, it made the most sense that they invested in them. Telecom carriers, in particular, had inherent advantages in network resources, given both their control over telecom infrastructures and facilities nationwide and their direct connection to the global internet.[27] Considering the telecom-dependent nature of internet data centers, players from other industry sectors needed, at the very least, to have close ties with the telecom sector.

As infrastructure for media, internet data centers are not just conduits to telecom facilities or a product of a set of political and economic relationships. They are also, media scholars Lisa Parks and Nicole Starosielski contend, a "complex material formation" that operates on multiple scales.[28] For example, properly functioning internet data centers depend on land, raw materials, and energy, and all these material factors are bound up with issues of political economy. A medium-size internet data center in China at the time, which could host roughly 3,000 servers, required, in addition to internet bandwidth, a land area of 2,000 square meters (about a half acre), transformer-rated power of about 1,000 kVA (kilovolt-amperes), cooling equipment, security and surveillance systems, firefighting facilities, and maintenance and repair staff.[29] But above all, it required a reliable power supply. Indeed, in their contracts with IDCs, internet companies would stipulate that the centers' electricity supply be at least 99.99 percent reliable.[30] Spending on these nonbandwidth requirements accounted for at least 40 percent of the total investment in constructing an internet data center.[31]

The cost of building internet data centers was at least ¥25,000 (about $3,125) per square meter (or about $300 per square foot) in the late 1990s in China, which brought the minimum total cost of building a medium-size data center to ¥50 million (about $6 million),[32] and which meant that only state-owned telecom enterprises and large internet service providers could afford to invest in IDCs. At the time, most internet service providers were struggling because the revenues they collected from a fledging retail market were insufficient to cover the high leasing fees charged by the Ministry of Posts and Telecommunications.[33] In fact, even in the IDC business, internet service providers had a difficult time. The need to build and maintain a deep relationship with the telecom sector often tied internet service providers to a particular local or regional telecom administration, thereby limiting their capacity to expand into national markets.[34] Meanwhile, as downstream resellers of bandwidth, internet service providers had fewer resources than telecom carriers did and were generally unable to compete with them. As a result, some turned to niche markets by providing IDC value-added services.[35] And some simply resold data centers built by telecom carriers.[36]

Though much less known than telecom companies and internet service providers, real estate developers were also IDC providers. Because building an internet data center required a huge amount of storage space to house servers, real estate companies that owned land and buildings used this advantage to enter the IDC market. The real estate company Andi, for example, constructed a 5,000 square-meter (roughly one-and-a-quarter-acre) internet data center on its Kingdom Garden (Jin dian huayuan) property in Beijing.[37] Developers' entry into the IDC market through the resource of land foregrounds the materiality of internet data centers as media infrastructure. Indeed, property companies and engineers saw IDCs differently. To real estate companies, the internet data center was a particular type of property or property facility. Yi Chen, a Guangzhou-based veteran real estate professional, viewed the internet data centers as a way to bring added value to properties: thus, if an office building was furnished with server racks, the rental of just one floor would outperform that of the entire building. Similarly, after the IDC market was hit by the dotcom crash in 2001, Chen's team used the same heavy-handed tactics they had used to sell real estate properties to sell internet data centers in Guangzhou.[38] The imperfect regulatory system was partly responsible for developers' involvement in IDCs since it not only enabled them to enter the IDC market but also allowed them to withdraw without any political cost. These developers could easily convert their data centers into normal real estate properties if regulators should ever intervene and disqualify them from operating IDC businesses.[39]

With investments from both telecom and other industry sectors, IDC businesses boomed. By early 2001, there were at least fifty, mostly in major cities such as Beijing, Shanghai, and Guangzhou and in surrounding areas where telecom resources were concentrated.[40] In Beijing, major players included Beijing Telecom (China Telecom's Beijing bureau), Unicom, Netcom, 21ViaNet, Tsinghua Wanbo, and Feihua. Shanghai Online's servers were at the time connected to a 1 Gbps (gigabit per second) dedicated line out (dedicated bandwidth), providing fast data transfers for its clients such as the web portal Sina and the e-commerce site EachNet.[41] For IDC providers, 2000 was the best year. Reflecting the high-investment, high-return nature of internet data centers, small and medium-sized IDC businesses could make a profit simply by developing and relying on one or two long-term large clients.[42]

Optimism about internet data centers soon waned, however, as the insalubrious side of the industry's development showed itself. Monopolies became an immediate trend. In 2000, the full-year revenue of Beijing Telecom reached about $25 million, 60 percent of the IDC market in Beijing.[43] Replicating its dominance over telecom infrastructures, China Telecom's internet data centers controlled 70 percent of the national IDC market by mid-2001, with other data centers of various sizes dividing up the remaining 30 percent.[44] Professionals in the IDC sector began to question whether there was an IDC market at all, given the extent to which the sector was telecom dominated. At the very least, that market appeared to be significantly overestimated considering the limited development of the Chinese internet at the time. When massive investments flood into a limited market, it almost invariably leads to oversupply. Some internet data centers in Beijing reported having only 20 percent of their server racks rented out.[45] And, as internet companies impacted by the dotcom crash had to close down, enthusiasm for internet data centers all but disappeared. In a sense, the internet data center industry was another bubble on top of the dotcom bubble. Its prosperity in the late 1990s and early 2000s lasted only a few years. Between 2001 and 2003, the telecom and internet industries were laboring under the shadow of a shrinking market and rapidly growing layoffs.

Internet data centers began to enjoy a second life from late 2003, as the internet industry slowly recovered from the dotcom crash and with the emergence of newer online entertainments such as multiplayer gaming and video streaming. Online video streaming was particularly data consuming, and service providers relied more heavily on telecom resources, especially bandwidth, than on others. Critics of media industries tend to explain power relationships by analyzing the structure of control over crucial industry bottlenecks, in this case, access to scarce resources.[46] If copyright was a crucial bottleneck for video companies in the later period of their market development, bandwidth represented the first bottleneck in determining the distribution and redistribution of power in the early days of online video's market development when telecom infrastructure in China was not as developed as it would later be and when bandwidth was more restricted. Understanding bandwidth as a technological constraint is crucial in revealing the early relationship between the telecom sector and the online video industry. As an engineer from a prominent video portal, Wen Man, told me in April 2014, in the eyes of internet engineers, online video is a telecom/tech business, not a cultural industry even today.[47] The importance of bandwidth to video streaming likely motivated telecom companies' ambitions to provide online video services in the early 2000s, although those attempts, turned out to be futile, as I will show in chapter 5.

Online video assumed a more definite presence in public discourse in the mid-2000s. When venture capitalists revived their enthusiasm for the internet after the dotcom bust, they focused on Web 2.0. First, P2P live streaming service providers appeared, and YouTube-style video-sharing websites followed. Whereas the former relied on localized P2P networks in delivering video streams, thereby significantly shrinking content providers' bandwidth usage,[48] most YouTube-like websites based on the client-server model were bandwidth hungry. Mostly backed by venture capital, these YouTube-like companies spent much of the investment they received on IDC services/bandwidth. Videos normally stream at a rate of approximately 350 Kbps (kilobits per second). At this rate, a bandwidth of 1 Mbps (megabit per second; 1 Mbps = 1,000 Kbps) would be needed to allow three users to stream a video simultaneously without clogging, and a bandwidth of 1 Gbps (gigabit per second; 1 Gbps = 1,000 Mbps) would be needed if there were 3,000 users streaming a video simultaneously. In 2007, online video companies needed at least a 2 Gbps bandwidth plan to start and, with a growing number of users, this could easily run up to 10 Gbps or even as much as 100 Gbps.[49] Given the price of bandwidth at the time, the most immediate issue facing online video startups was to find cheap telecom resources/bandwidth across the country and to determine in which internet data center to locate their servers.

The price and quality of bandwidth were marked by distinct regional differences, depending on the telecom resources and the level of marketization in a specific area. The dedicated bandwidth of 100 Mbps provided by Shanghai Telecom (China Telecom's Shanghai bureau), for example, was priced at about $4,000 per month in 2007.[50] Their counterpart in Beijing charged about $2,500. Bandwidth prices in these cities were generally higher than in the rest of the country. In places like Wuhan, one of China's key inland cities, the counterpart rate for bandwidth could be as low as $400 per month, although the quality of bandwidth there was not as high as in Beijing or Shanghai. Telecom service providers in Beijing could deliver from 90 to 96 percent of the dedicated bandwidth their clients purchased.[51] Online video companies' decisions regarding server location were informed by all these factors and, most important, by where their ties to the telecom sector were strongest. For instance, the bandwidth price in Shanghai could be reduced to about $1,250 if the client had ties (*guanxi*) with Shanghai Telecom, which meant that video companies only needed to pay about $150,000 for 1 Gbps bandwidth per year.[52] Nevertheless, this was still an exorbitant price to online video companies at the time. In 2006, even when the founder of an early major video-sharing website Ku6 was able to negotiate a price of $150,000 per year for a dedicated 1 Gbps bandwidth from Beijing Netcom, that price was still prohibitive. In the end, after exhausting their personal networks, startup entrepreneurs would finally find cheaper bandwidth from Maoming, a coastal city located in southern China's Guangdong Province, and from Harbin, the capital city of Heilongjiang Province in northeastern China.[53]

The regional differences in telecom resources demonstrate the uneven development of marketization in China. Online video companies from more developed regions were dependent on telecom resources from less developed ones to optimize their infrastructure solutions, and they did not rely on telecom resources from any one place. Although small startups tended to place source files on servers in one particular location, growing companies whose server cluster handled a large number of nationwide user requests soon had to find ways to redistribute online video traffic across the country so as to prevent their primary server from crashing and to improve their users' streaming experience. In a country as vast as China, geographical reality is a crucial factor affecting when the transmission of data speeds up or slows down. In 2007, it took between 4 and 5 milliseconds for users in Beijing or Shanghai to ping servers in their own city, yet it took about 20 milliseconds for Shanghai-based users to ping servers in Beijing, and twice as long in the reverse direction.[54] The geographical hindrance was further exacerbated by a fragmented telecom infrastructure. As shown earlier, bureaucratic infighting in the telecom sector that manifested itself through infrastructure changes led to a multitude of telecom networks that were disconnected more often than they were connected. Because of the North-South divide of China Telecom's backbone network, for example, internetwork data transmission took much longer than intranetwork transmission.[55] All these factors necessitated the redistribution of video traffic on a national scale, and the technology of content distribution networks demonstrated its value in this context.

To redistribute traffic strategically, online video companies began to deploy servers in multiple data centers across regions, often across multiple backbone networks. These servers were connected through the content distribution network system, which identified the geographical and network origins of user requests and then algorithmically directed each request to a server that was closest to the user making that request or optimal for data transmission. Designed to manage traffic, optimize usage of network resources, and therefore improve content delivery performance, a content distribution network system could help reduce the total bandwidth cost for online video companies, but construction of a CDN system required a high investment in servers and bandwidth. Thus Youku, an active early market player, reportedly spent up to 70 percent of the funds it raised on servers and bandwidth in 2007.[56]

To develop a content distribution network system, most online video companies, especially those which had already developed strong ties (*guanxi*) with telecom administrations, chose to identify appropriate internet data center locations by themselves and then either to build up their own content distribution network or to purchase partial CDN services from dedicated providers. Although building an in-house content distribution network system was cheaper than relying entirely on outsourced CDN services, it required that video companies not only procure cheap network resources from the telecom sector, but also, and more important, know how the national telecom infrastructure worked and how to strategically capitalize on that knowledge. For example, in 2007, the optical fiber system in Nanchang, the capital city of Jiangxi Province in southeastern China, was not yet connected to Guangdong Province, although these two places are geographically close to each other. Knowledgeable CDN system designers would realize the futility of trying then to redirect user requests from Guangdong Province to Nanchang.[57]

From infrastructure resources (i.e., bandwidth) to knowledge of infra-structure, operating as "soft" infrastructure, the development of online video was heavily reliant on the liberalizing telecom sector, but probably less reliant in recent years since China's continuing investment in internet infrastructure has brought about a gradual decline in the price of band-width. Although we should acknowledge the crucial role of the telecom sector in the development of the online video industry, we should not over-look the fact that telecom carriers, internet data centers, and later, CDN service providers were the greatest beneficiaries of the economic upsurge in that industry. It is ultimately the state-dominated telecom sector that profited from the online video boom when most video companies were still losing money. As Yu Hong argues, there exists a symbiotic relation-ship between telecom operators and internet companies.[58] Indeed, know-ing the telecom sector's economic stake in internet industries has served to strengthen my informants' conviction that the state would not let the online video industry down.[59]

Foreign Capital, Variable Interest Entities, and Their Controversies

As we have seen, online video was an expensive business, considering the enormous investment in infrastructure required. Like internet companies in general, most online video companies in China were backed by foreign venture capital (VC) and private equity (PE), especially in the early years. Although domestic investments from provincial governments, private investors, and universities were growing in the 1990s and early 2000s, those funds were generally marginal owing to the immature, illiquid domestic capital market of the day.[60] Global venture capital made a notably identifi-able appearance in the late 1990s; between 1997 and 2001, leading Ameri-can investment firms such as the Carlyle Group, Draper Fisher Jurvetson (DFJ), and Redpoint Ventures assumed a prominent presence in China.[61] In these few years, the Chinese internet experienced its first boom as the telecom infrastructure took shape and different kinds of internet content providers (ICPs) emerged and rapidly developed. Among these was the country's leading commercial web portal, Sina.com, creator of a financial structure known as a "variable interest entity" (VIE), which, as I will show, was of vital importance to decades of internet development in China.

Sina received foreign investment from its very beginning as a company. Founded in May 1996 as an online subsidiary of the "Sino-foreign" computer software company Beijing Stone Rich Sight (BSRS), Sina was then called "SRSnet.com," offering news, information, and community services such as a bulletin board system.[62] In 1997, BSRS/SRSnet received $6.5 million from early investors led by Walden International.[63] In March 1999, SRSnet merged with a U.S.-based Chinese-language internet content company, SinaNet.com, which resulted in the formation of Sina as we know it today.[64] Finally, in May of 1997, Sina acquired financing of $25 million from Walden International, Goldman Sachs, and Flatiron Partners among other investors.[65]

After the merger and other fundraising by Sina, foreign capital owned 80 percent or more of the company. This raises a question regarding the regulation of foreign investment in China's technology, media, and telecom industries, traditionally considered to be ideologically sensitive. In the 1990s, foreign capital was generally prohibited from operating in those industries, with restrictive policies on foreign investment there replicated across different ministries. For example, the Chinese government's *Guiding Catalogue of Industries for Foreign Investment,* periodically updated in the 1990s by a number of relevant ministries, placed telecom in the category of industries in which foreign investment was prohibited. And policies announced by the Ministry of Posts and Telecommunications in 1993 and 1995 also prohibited foreign investment in the telecom sector.[66] Thus the massive presence of foreign capital in early internet content provider companies such as Sina seemed in clear violation of those rules. Although such a violation could have been overlooked as a result of weak policy enforcement, considering the policy trajectory that became obvious in the late 1990s, it was more likely overlooked because of a regulatory loophole: since the newly emerging internet sector was not yet explicitly defined as a telecom-related industry, it was therefore not subject to regulation by the telecom administration. But, to venture capitalists who ultimately aimed to recoup their investment in Chinese internet content providers through IPOs, regulatory ambiguity meant nothing but risk. Obviously, these would-be investors needed clarification from the relevant ministries.

It is worthwhile to digress here by noting that, even apart from the internet, the telecom sector in the 1990s was not entirely free of foreign investment. Absent overt objection from the State Council, China Unicom was allowed to innovate a joint investment scheme known as the "Chinese-Chinese-foreign" (Zhong-zhong-wai) or "CCF" scheme in 1995, which allowed the company to absorb foreign funds and survive the regulatory scrutiny of the Ministry of Posts and Telecommunications. In the CCF scheme, the foreign company ("F") would form a joint venture with a Chinese company (the second "C"), which was usually a satellite company of one of Unicom's shareholders, with the foreign company holding a majority stake in the joint venture. The newly created joint venture would then sign a contract with a local Unicom branch (the first "C") to provide it with services and support, and, in return, foreign partners received a share of the revenue. Such a contract-based arrangement allowed foreign capital to establish an indirect and invisible connection with Unicom, thereby circumventing the official ban on direct foreign investment in China's telecom sector.[67] This sub rosa "near equity" investment plan enabled Unicom to create more than forty CCF joint ventures in the years to come, attracting an investment of nearly $1.4 billion.[68] Lacking explicit approval from the Ministry of Posts and Telecommunications, however, the CCF scheme existed in a regulatory grey area, and it was officially banned by the MPT's replacement, the Ministry of Information Industry (MII), in 1998. Following the government's cancellation of the CCF contracts, China Unicom settled with foreign companies by offering them varying degrees of compensation, and those refusing to accept cancellation of their contracts were threatened with being banned from any future participation in the Chinese market.[69] Even though it existed only for a short period of time, as a cleverly designed foreign fundraising practice originating from the telecom sector, the CCF scheme preceded and indeed inspired other internet content providers seeking to launch IPOs on NASDAQ in the late 1990s.

Companies like Sina came under the regulatory spotlight in the late 1990s when internet content provision was officially and publicly recognized as a telecom value-added service (VAS) by the MII minister, Jichuan Wu, in September 1999[70]and would be more formally defined in the Telecommunications Act passed by the State Council the following year.[71] Internet content providers like Sina would now be required to conform to state policies that forbade foreign investment in the telecom sector. Indeed, as Minister Wu declared in September 1999: "Whether or not it is an ICP or an ISP, it is about value-added services. In China, that area is not open [to foreign capital]."[72] Although some speculated that the hard stance by the

Ministry of Information Industry on foreign investment was simply a tactic designed to gain more bargaining leverage in China's ongoing WTO negotiations,[73] it was still the biggest obstacle to Sina's IPO plan because, as an internet company mostly funded by foreign capital, it would be considered illegitimate and denied a license to operate, under regulations being drawn up by the ministry that would be formally written into the Measures on the Administration of Internet Information Services (the "ICP rule") one year later.[74] Sina had to find ways to spin off its content services and assets from its public listing vehicle, as advised by the ministry.[75]

However, toward the end of 1999, the prolonged U.S.–China bilateral negotiations over China's accession to the World Trade Organization were reaching a crucial stage and were likely to lead to new agreements regarding foreign investment in the telecom sector, a sector the United States was eager to pry open.[76] Everything became uncertain during that period of regulatory transition. The old restrictive policies appeared to be suspended, but, at the same time, Sina was advised by the Ministry of Information Industry to postpone its IPO launch.[77] The U.S.-China negotiations led to agreements for a gradual opening that would eventually allow 49 percent foreign ownership of basic telecom services nationwide six years after China joined the World Trade Organization and 50 percent foreign ownership for value-added services including internet services and content provision, two years after its accession.[78] As a retired telecom bureaucrat recalled in a media interview, the opening up of value-added services was one of the major disagreements in the negotiations, with Chinese negotiators, especially conservatives, insisting on a maximum of 49 percent foreign control, whereas the United States demanded 51 percent. In the end, the Politburo decided to concede an additional 1 percent, allowing a maximum of 50 percent foreign control.[79] The smooth path of the Chinese government toward a relatively drama-free WTO agreement in 1999, even as the Chinese embassy in Belgrade was being bombed (an event that had angered domestic conservatives), can be largely attributed to top-down decisions that bypassed bureaucratic wrangling, and also to minimal media coverage of the negotiations.[80] These decisions, in some respects, were a triumph of the reform-oriented State Council and its minister, Zhu Rongji, over the conservative Ministry of Information Industry and its minister, Jichuan Wu, who was famous for his opposition to opening up China's telecom sector to foreign investment.[81]

The additional 1 percent China ceded for value-added services is crucial to an understanding of the zoning logic China applied to old and new media. Whereas foreign capital was allowed to acquire up to a 50 percent stake in the internet in China, investment in the television sector was mainly restricted to domestic private capital, with foreign capital being treated much more circumspectly and tentatively there. Certainly, the lack of a clear, transparent legal framework in China could have meant that a 50 percent foreign investment in China's internet would be subject to the wide range of discretion exercised by various levels of government authorities at a later stage.[82] But what the largely symbolic 1 percent change in capital structure really meant was that, without surrendering to foreign control, the Chinese state was willing to assume the risk of ideological challenges and open up its internet to the utmost extent for the sake of economic growth.

Minister Wu's resistance to foreign capital seemed driven less by ideology and more by a desire to protect the domestic market. In fact, on a few occasions, the minister appeared to have acknowledged the need for foreign investment in a developing high-tech industry.[83] It was in this context that Sina, whose foreign ownership share far exceeded the 50 percent cap stipulated in the U.S.-China agreements, was allowed to reconstruct itself by using a CCF-like structure called a "variable interest entity" to indirectly absorb even more foreign capital than the 50 percent. Thus, it would seem, the Ministry of Information Industry or the Chinese government was not unwelcoming to all foreign capital, just to "ungovernable" foreign capital. As long as the Chinese state could reign over foreign capital rather than the other way around, it seemed open to creative ways of bringing in more foreign investment to the internet sector, and the variable interest entity was such a way.

Sina began to design its VIE structure in September 1999. It weathered a series of complications including the ongoing WTO negotiations, and eventually received at least indirect approval from the Ministry of Information Industry in April 2000. Sina's CEO Zhidong Wang was said to have spent a great deal of his time in the ministry's meeting room in early 2000, repeatedly explaining the corporate structuring and restructuring of the company to telecom bureaucrats and making revisions in response to their feedback.[84] In the VIE structure that was finally given indirect approval, Sina removed content services and associated assets from its parent software company

BSRS, which was almost a wholly foreign-owned enterprise (WFOE), and set up two new Chinese-owned companies to incorporate its internet content provider components. The newly created subsidiary, Beijing Sina Internet Information Services Co., Ltd. ("the ICP company"), ran the content provision and was entirely Chinese owned and thus eligible for an ICP license that could not be legally owned by or transferred to BSRS under the foreign investment restrictions. Beijing Sina Interactive Advertising Co., Ltd. ("the Ad company"), in which BSRS owned a 25 percent share, was also incorporated in China and would purchase all the advertisement banner space of the ICP company at cost and sell advertisements from that space to third parties under its advertising license. BSRS then entered into an agreement with the ICP company to provide it with technical services, license to it intellectual property associated with www.sina.com.cn, and transfer to it BSRS's equipment and leased line in exchange for fees or payments in kind. Similarly, BSRS provided consulting services to the Ad company in exchange for a fee. In this way, virtually all of the economic benefits of the two Chinese companies were transferred to BSRS through a series of contractual arrangements, and the actual NASDAQ-listed Sina Corporation operated as an offshore shell company, registered in the Cayman Islands, which directly owned BSRS.[85] Foreign investors could buy shares in the shell company once it was listed overseas, but because its stocks would then become foreign stocks, Chinese investors would be precluded from becoming shareholders.[86]

In 2000, the VIE structure devised by Sina was indirectly approved by the Ministry of Information Industry, which issued an opinion to the State Administration for Industry and Commerce, recognizing the spinoff of Sina's content businesses and granting permission for the newly created ICP company to be issued an ICP license. These actions, according to telecom industry attorneys, were likely the closest the ministry ever got to formally approving the VIE structure at the time.[87] On another occasion, the investment banker Fan Bao, one of the brokers who worked for Morgan Stanley, which prepared Sina's public listing in 1999–2000, offered a personal account of an interaction when Minister Wu was invited to a teleconference with investors and analysts from Wall Street, answering their concerns about the variable interest entity.[88] This served as a significant gesture of support from the government, despite the unofficial status of the variable interest entity. In fact, the China Securities Regulatory Commission

(CSRC), another ministry-level agency from which internet content providers like Sina needed to get approval for their overseas listing, was working to mitigate overcontrol of the industry and had no plans to curtail the business of these companies.[89] Although the VIE structure was never formally approved, it was seen by industry professionals as operating under the tacit approval of the state, and its success was considered to foreshadow China's loosening grip on its restricted telecom sector, coinciding with its WTO accession.[90]

Although conceived as a temporary means to clear the way for Sina's IPO launch in the early 2000s, the variable interest entity has since been widely adopted by other internet companies to solicit foreign investment and to list overseas, bringing about a golden decade of internet development in China. In 2011, the first time that the VIE structure was exposed to public scrutiny, Richard Liu, founder of the Chinese e-commerce company JD.com, claimed online that, as far as he knew, all Chinese internet companies with venture capital investments, including his own, adopted the VIE structure.[91] It is noteworthy that even though the VIE structure was originally designed by internet companies, since 2006, companies from traditional and asset-heavy industries such as auto retailing and coal trading have also begun to exploit it to gain contractual control of other domestic companies in China. Moreover, the VIE structure also enabled these industries to avoid increased regulatory surveillance by the Ministry of Commerce of mergers and acquisitions of domestic companies by foreign investors.[92]

As a CCF-like workaround method allowing foreign investors to gain a controlling interest in China's internet businesses, the key feature of the variable interest entity is for the wholly foreign-owned enterprise to gain actual control over domestic enterprises through contractual arrangements, rather than through equity interests that would trigger restrictions. Ultimately, a properly working VIE structure relies on a binding contract, without which the listed foreign enterprise would be unable to merge the financials of the domestic enterprises, and its financial reports would suffer accordingly. This contractual control was recognized by securities regulators in the United States, enabling the offshore listed enterprise to consolidate the financial reports of the domestic entities into its overall financial statements. The term "variable interest entity" (VIE) is, in fact, a U.S. generally accepted accounting principles (GAAP) term, describing a financial entity consolidated in this way.[93] Various agreements have been designed to align common interests of the wholly foreign-owned enterprises and variable interest entities and to minimize the temptation for domestic legal owners to take self-interested actions to the detriment of foreign investors, making use of a variable interest entity a more sophisticated method than use of the CCF joint investment scheme.[94] Still, as Sina warned its investors in its SEC registration statements filed in March 2000, the contractual arrangement may not be as effective as direct ownership in providing control over variable interest entities.[95] The biggest risk stems from political uncertainties. The Chinese government could at any time determine that the VIE structure violates existing Chinese laws and regulations concerning foreign investment in China's internet sector and ban use of the structure, just as the Ministry of Information Industry banned use of the CCF scheme in 1998. The design of the VIE structure "avoids binding constraints so as to retain political initiative and room for policy revision."[96] Moreover, the fact that the Chinese government never formally approved the use of VIEs allows the government more flexibility to ban or indirectly regulate use of the structure (for instance, through the exercise of discretion in refusing to issue relevant licenses to the domestic ICP company in a VIE structure) if it decides to do so. The VIE's very presence in a regulatory grey area enables the government to take a guerrilla-style approach to regulation, with enough flexibility to allow it to pursue its goals without the constraints of official policy.

A review of regulatory incidents associated with use of the variable interest entity in the decade after 2000, however, seems to show only minor attempts to tighten control over use of the structure. In 2006, for example, in a notice concerning foreign investment in telecom value-added service businesses, the Ministry of Information Industry required assets crucial to those businesses, such as domain names, trademarks, and servers, to be held by the license holders rather than leased or licensed from third parties.[97] Internet industry attorneys interpreted the notice to mean that, in a VIE structure, the variable interest entity needed to hold these key assets, instead of leasing or licensing them from the wholly foreign-owned enterprise. The notice demonstrates the ministry's attempt to strengthen the bargaining power of variable interest entities and lessen foreign control over them.[98]

The last time the variable interest entity was under the regulatory spotlight was in 2011. In the year before, the People's Bank of China (PBOC) had issued the Rules on the Administration of Payment Services Provided by Non-Financial Institutions, which required all third-party payment service companies to apply for a license. Although the rules did not explicitly refer to the VIE structure, China's leading third-party online payment company, Alibaba's Alipay, which submitted its license application, claimed that it had received an inquiry from the bank asking it to declare its foreign controlling interests, including indirect contractual foreign ownership. Alibaba's CEO Jack Ma stated that the PBOC inquiry amounted to a ban on the use of variable interest entities, and thus he had no choice but to end Alipay's contractual relationship with its foreign shareholders Softbank and Yahoo in order for Alipay to receive the license it needed.[99] Since other third-party payment service providers, some reportedly under a VIE structure, were able to obtain licenses from the PBOC, Jack Ma's move was widely seen as self-interested scapegoating of regulators to conceal his own desire to terminate variable interest entities and internalize Alibaba's most valuable asset.[100] Although Alibaba settled the dispute with Yahoo and Softbank over the terms of the spin-off of Alipay in July 2011,[101] the Alipay incident still exposed variable interest entities to more significant scrutiny than they had received since their inception, causing industry-wide uncertainty and anxiety among internet companies about prospective regulation of VIEs and the companies that made use of them.

On July 5, 2011, two researchers from the Chinese Academy of Social Sciences published an editorial titled "The Government Should Attend to Foreign Control of Internet Companies" in *Study Times*, an organ of the Communist Party School. They warned against the VIE's potential threat to China's national and political security and called for stringent supervision of the financial structure of Chinese internet companies and their business operations. Their warning came at a time of resurgent nationalism in the country. A popular book, *The Historical Truths 99% of Chinese Don't Know*, published in the same year, stated that more than 85 percent of the shares in leading internet firms in China such as Baidu, Sohu, and Tencent were owned by Americans, Japanese, and South Africans.[102]

Liberal observers, however, were quick to counter that foreign control of the Chinese internet was an illusion. In comments posted on his blog on July 7, 2011, Donald Clarke, a professor of law at George Washington

University, argued that it was far from clear whether and to what extent the contractual relationship between foreign investors and their onshore companies was even enforceable under Chinese laws. Clarke further pointed out that the offshore enterprises were not necessarily owned by foreigners and that, even when foreigners did own most shares in these companies, ownership was largely dispersed, with no single shareholder having a controlling interest, and thus foreign ownership of more than 50 percent did not necessarily constitute foreign control, much less absolute foreign control.[103] An intriguing way to rethink our notions of boundary and citizenship in a global economy and a challenge to an essentialist understanding of transnational capital, these counterarguments show us another side of the ideological debate over capital, ownership, and politics surrounding variable interest entities.

In August 2011, the Ministry of Commerce released its measures to implement the Circular on Establishing Security Review Mechanism for Mergers and Acquisitions of Domestic Companies by Foreign Investors, issued by the State Council earlier in the year. The ministry's measures decreed that foreign investors could not use any means, including but not limited to nominee ownership, trusts, multilayer reinvestment, leasing, loans, contractual control, and overseas transactions, to avoid the security review of their mergers and acquisitions. Explicit reference to the VIE structure (i.e., contractual control) caused widespread concern about its possible prohibition and about the overall climate for foreign investment in China. This concern was heightened in early September when rumors spread about an internal report submitted to the State Council by the China Securities Regulatory Commission, recommending tighter regulation of the VIE structure. Later that month, however, the *Shanghai Securities News* revealed that the "internal report" was in fact neither an official report nor submitted to the State Council, but only a research note, and suggested that the now-discredited rumors were likely a sign of the bureaucratic turf war being fought for jurisdiction over variable interest entities.[104] Nevertheless, despite the *Shanghai Securities News* article, clouds of suspicion still hung over the internet industry. The 2011 regulatory strife subsided somewhat in late September when the Ministry of Commerce clarified that its new measures would target only a few merger and acquisition practices that could affect or might even threaten national security in areas such as military-industrial and related enterprises or key energy resources, infrastructures, and equipment manufacturing.[105] And, as an internet industry attorney argued, since the national security review specifically targeted sectors essential for securing core national interests, it was not surprising that regulators would explicitly disallow all forms of indirect control, including variable interest entities, designed to escape that review.[106]

The relatively lax regulation of the VIE, a structure that would endure for years after 2011, has been an exception in the regulatory history of foreign investment in China's technology, media, and telecom sector and thus a significant product of the Chinese state's flexible governance in the reform era. No one knows when a complete ban on the use of VIEs in the internet industry might occur, but the more important message from intermittent regulatory interventions over the years seems to be that regulators including the Ministry of Commerce were fully aware of the use of the VIE structure and could have taken action against it if necessary. And, as the philosopher Giorgio Agamben reminds us, whether something is necessary clearly entails a subjective judgment, a moral and political evaluation, which overrules any laws.[107]

"Nine Dragons Governing One River"

Lax financial regulation of the Chinese internet was accompanied by equally lax content regulation, which benefited most Chinese internet companies including online video companies from the very beginning. Such a regime was the product of different factors, operating under different circumstances at different times. But acknowledging the complexity of the factors behind China's lax internet content regime should not prevent us from seeing one of its most defining aspects, especially in the early days, specifically, the overlapping of fragmented jurisdictions that resulted from bureaucratic politics and power struggles. These were endemic in China's administrative system and have become more noticeable in the new media context, where technological, institutional, and regulatory boundaries have become blurred. Prior to media convergence, different media sectors and tangentially related services such as education and health care were subject to different regulatory bodies. Whereas traditional media technologies had clearly defined regulatory boundaries, newer media technologies blurred the regulatory boundaries between different media and cultural forms. Complicating the new regulatory environment, almost every internet form could be seen as a version of its traditional counterpart or at least as intersecting with it, which potentially involved both regulators of the internet and the respective traditional counterparts. This regulatory reality was further complicated by the build-out of newly created agencies, a situation that industry professionals, borrowing a metaphor from ancient Chinese mythology, aptly called "nine dragons governing one river" (*jiulong zhishui*).

Taking a closer look at this regulatory fragmentation, we note that, although the Ministry of Information Industry has managed the general and operational aspects of the telecom, internet, and software industries since the mid-1990s, different government bodies have been authorized to manage different aspects of the internet content that came within their respective jurisdictions, and some indeed have fought to extend their authority into the operations of the internet itself in order to share in its development. The State Council Information Office (SCIO), for example, has been responsible for online news publishing, and the Ministry of Culture has drafted regulations to extend its jurisdiction over online gaming. Under these circumstances, multiple regulatory bodies coexisted in specific areas, and their functions overlapped and sometimes contradicted one another. In this context, internet sectors were very likely to find themselves in regulatory limbo until the bureaucratic disputes were resolved. And, at the same time, regulatory fragmentation reduced the legitimacy and effectiveness of the regulatory bodies involved. In contrast to overregulation of some of the more important online sectors, other marginal ones simply lacked any regulators, and responsibility for regulating them was passed from one ministry or agency to another.[108]

The online video sector was marked by such a fragmented regulatory regime from the very beginning. Early online videos were dispersed across different platforms and lacked a relatively identifiable form of industry operations. As I will show in chapter 5, the emergence of video on demand (VOD) websites in the early 2000s, which quickly became service/content providers for telecom companies' own value-added service portals, roughly signaled online video's earliest form of industry operations. Before that, in the narrowband period (dial-up internet connections), despite technological restrictions, web portals offered online video services among their variety of businesses. Although only a constituent of portal services, and thereby lacking independent status, portals' video operations continued into the broadband era, and, together with VOD, they were two prominent sources of online video before YouTube-like video-sharing platforms and peer-to-peer (P2P) live streaming services took over in the mid-2000s. At the beginning, most of the content these online video services provided consisted of television programs aggregated from television stations and audiovisual content, both copyrighted and pirated, originally stored on VCDs or DVDs. Later on, service providers began to experiment with online shows and webcasts and to incorporate digital video productions from small studios and professional creatives, although the number of productions was rather limited compared to how many there would be only half a decade later. Around the same time, numerous amateurs and professional or semiprofessional creatives were exchanging their works in online forums, which only surfaced in the mid-2000s, when video-sharing platforms ushered in the upsurge in user-generated content (UGC).

There were many early regulatory interventions targeting China's emerging online video. As a crossover medium straddling telecom, the internet, television, and film, online video found itself subject to claims of authority from the Ministry of Information Industry, the SARFT, and the Ministry of Culture. The Ministry of Information Industry considered online video a form of telecom value-added services, which fell within its jurisdiction, as outlined in the Telecommunications Act and the ICP rule of 2000. Designated regulator of audiovisual products (*yinxiang zhipin*) before 2008, the Ministry of Culture could exercise its regulatory authority over online video and could therefore claim authority over the internet as well because audiovisual content was reproduced online. In the traditional scenario, the regulatory divide between the SARFT, as regulator of radio, television, and film, and the Ministry of Culture seemed to be based on the difference between instantaneous communications through electronic signals (as with live television) and communications on demand through recording and playback (as with video).[109] Indeed, given the continuity between analog video and online video in challenging television's cultural status as a live, immediate medium, the Ministry of Culture seemed to be a more logical regulator of online video than the SARFT. In 2003, the ministry issued the Provisional Rules for the Administration of Internet Culture, which delineated online audiovisual content as its regulatory subject and required service providers to apply for an "internet culture operating permit" (*wangluo wenhua jingying xukezheng*).[110]

But, even though the Ministry of Information Industry and the Ministry of Culture both signaled their ambitions to include online video within their respective regulatory jurisdictions, the SARFT was the most invested and hardline participant in the jurisdictional rivalry. The SARFT's interventions began as early as 1999; in the next few years, it continued to announce new policies concerning online video. The agency's regulatory actions seemed to be rooted in the recognition that some of the content circulating online consisted of programs from television stations and other content that exhibited features of a television show or film. However, the SARFT's early policy discourses seemed to be plagued by uncertainty about the blurred boundaries of the emerging media.

In 1999, the SARFT issued its first known and somewhat amorphous policy statement on online video, the Notice Concerning Strengthening the Administration of Quasi–Radio, Film, and Television Programs Communicated to the Public via Information Networks.[111] In 2000, the agency issued a second policy statement on online video, the Provisional Measures for the Supervision and Administration of Quasi–Radio, Film, and Television Programs Communicated via Information Networks, to add specifics to its 1999 notice.[112] And, in 2001, the SARFT released a third policy statement to guide the implementation of the 2000 measures, targeting online communication instead of information networks. In all three policy statements, the SARFT defined online video content as "quasi–radio, film, and television programs," which included "continuously moving images or continuous audible sounds" that in terms of form, "resemble radio, television programs, or films," indicating its awareness that online video content and television content were not quite the same. But by naming its regulatory subject "quasi–radio, film, and television programs," the SARFT revealed its reserved way of viewing online video, associating it with television instead of acknowledging it as an independent medium, and this had immediate regulatory implications.

Seen as similar in form to television, online video was, at least at first, regulated in a similarly restrictive way. For example, news-related programs circulating online were restricted to those which had already been broadcast on a province- or higher-level radio or television station, and which had received prior authorization from the broadcaster. Soft content such as television dramas and films, as stipulated in the SARFT's 2000 policy statement, was restricted to program types listed in a special catalogue (*zhuanyong mulu*) monitored by the SARFT and narrowed down, in its 2001 policy statement, to programs broadcast on province- or higher-level radio or television stations. Content from overseas pirated online or recorded from overseas television was forbidden. Thus, in general, the internet was considered to be a redistribution outlet for traditional content, rather than a nascent generative field. But, despite their old-fashioned approach to online video, an approach soon to be replaced, those policy statements established the permitting and licensing system as an enduring regulatory regime for the emerging new medium.

The SARFT first recognized online video as a legitimate medium in its 2003 Measures for the Administration of Audiovisual Programs Communicated via Information Networks Including Internet (known as "rule 15"),[113] where it used the term "audiovisual programs" to replace "quasi–radio, film, and television programs." This change was likely made in the light of the rapid growth of online video services and content as a result of improved internet conditions, especially the increasing number of shows produced solely for online distribution. Rule 15 appeared to have been hastily drafted, with a changed subject name yet largely unchanged regulatory details, and it was superseded in 2004 by an elaborated version under the same title, which came to be known as "rule 39."[114] This newer rule was the policy statement industry professionals and observers most frequently referred to when tracing the earliest regulatory history of online video. Rule 39 defined audiovisual programs as "composed of continuously moving images or continuously audible sounds recorded by cameras, recorders, and other audiovisual recording devices," a definition that fully recognized online video as a moving-image medium, and the changing policy language seemed to parallel the changing regulatory regime at the same time. Although restrictions largely remained on news-related programs, soft content, and overseas content, service providers' self-made content, such as online specialty-topic shows, was no longer restricted to programs already broadcast by radio or television stations, as previously stipulated in rule 15. What rule 39 required instead was the establishment of a self-censorship mechanism as a prerequisite for service providers to apply for a permit, a requirement that would define the SARFT's regulatory approach to online video in the decade after 2004.

Because of unresolved bureaucratic disputes among relevant ministries, however, especially between the SARFT and the Ministry of Information

Industry, most of the SARFT's policies were not well implemented at the time. To some extent, its frequent policy-making activities with regard to online video might be seen as a way of staking claims to this territory and warning off competitors rather than actually regulating content. Indeed, compared to the making of the 2007 foundational rule 56, formulated after prolonged research and deliberation, the SARFT's policy making during this period seemed cursory and arbitrary.

The rivalry between the SARFT and the Ministry of Information Industry was, to a large extent, rooted in the three-network convergence (*sanwang ronghe*)—the integration of telecom, broadcasting and internet networks—that the Chinese state had been advocating since the early 2000s, with the project of IPTV (Internet Protocol television) at the forefront. Although the convergence and IPTV are not the focus here, the bureaucratic politics surrounding their development had implications for the early regulatory limbo in which online video found itself. Ideally, with the three-network convergence, the SARFT could exploit its national cable networks to provide internet services, and the Ministry of Information Industry could exploit its telecom networks to deliver audiovisual content.[115] This would require that the two converge their regulations or at least collaborate by sharing resources and offering access to each other's markets. But what happened instead was that each ministry or ministry-level agency fought to guard its areas of jurisdiction and prevent the other from entering its markets.

The disadvantage for the SARFT in developing Internet Protocol television lay in the lack of a well-established infrastructure under its authority. To offer interactive television services, the SARFT needed to upgrade its existing cable networks to high-speed two-way communication networks, which called for a long-term effort.[116] The Ministry of Information Industry seemed to have everything ready—everything, that is, except an access to the end users and their living rooms. Over the years, the three-network convergence has turned into a digital marathon, with the Ministry of Information Industry trying its best to facilitate the IPTV project, and the SARFT trying to thwart it in every possible way. In issuing its rule 39, for example, the SARFT was not simply targeting online video. The rule's all-encompassing definition of the regulatory subject signaled the SARFT's ambition to claim authority over all Internet Protocol–based audiovisual services transmitted through all kinds of information networks including mobile, cable, and satellite networks, as well as the internet, to all kinds of end-user devices including computers, televisions, and mobile phones. This certainly included IPTV, an Internet Protocol–based audiovisual service delivering content through computer networks to home screens. Having subsumed IPTV within its jurisdiction, the SARFT stipulated that only provincial and municipal radio stations, television stations, and their parent groups would be eligible to operate IPTV services. If this announced policy were put into practice, no IPTV permits would be granted to applicants from the telecom sector, which, to have a share in IPTV, would have to team up with license holders, mostly content providers from the broadcasting sector.

The SARFT's announced policies incurred resistance from the Ministry of Information Industry, from whose perspective, IPTV was a typical telecom value-added service, and service providers who possessed a proper value-added service permit from the Ministry of Information Industry were perfectly well qualified to run IPTV businesses.[117] Simply put, the whole SARFT-MII debate originates from the problematic reality that SARFT-regulated content travels on MII-regulated networks, which raises the question of which ministry/agency should regulate the service providers, that is, the "market entities" (*shichang zhuti*). The regulatory dilemma around the development of IPTV also plagued online video in the same way that the crossover nature of online video mirrored that of IPTV. Thus, the early regulatory history of online video in China needs to be viewed within the context of the long-standing bureaucratic rivalry surrounding the three-network convergence, and IPTV in particular. Emerging media forms such as online video, developing around the same time as IPTV, appear to have intensified the ongoing opposition between the SARFT and the Ministry of Information Industry.

The MII's challenges to the SARFT's rule 39 mainly focused on the question of its legitimacy. As a ministry-level agency under the leadership of the State Council, the SARFT derives its authority from the council, as do other ministries or ministry-level agencies including the Ministry of Information Industry. In the 1998 administrative restructuring, the State Council stated that the SARFT's role was "to supervise and regulate broadcasting programs, satellite television programs, and audiovisual programs communicated to the public via information networks." This statement allowed the Ministry of Information Industry to challenge the SARFT, by arguing that the agency was only authorized to regulate audiovisual programs per se (content), not the providing of such programs (service provision and providers) and that the SARFT's rule 39, which claimed authority for itself over online audiovisual services, was simply a "ministerial rule" (*bumen guizhang*), lacking the imprimatur of the State Council and thus invalid as a regulation.[118] The Ministry of Information Industry further argued that authorities higher than ministries had already issued regulations concerning online audiovisual services, which were, first and foremost, telecom value-added services. The Telecommunications Act and the internet content provider (ICP) rule of 2000, by which the Ministry of Information Industry exercised its authority over value-added services, for example, were administrative regulations (*xingzheng fagui*), approved by the Standing Committee of the State Council and announced in the form of State Council decrees. Therefore the SARFT's rule 39 was not only invalid as a regulation, but also in conflict with existing regulations.[119]

And, as a form of internet culture, in the MII's view, online video ought to be subject to regulation by the Ministry of Culture, under its Provisional Rules for the Administration of Internet Culture, rather than by the SARFT. Even though the provisional rules were also ministerial rules and therefore at the same hierarchic level as the SARFT's rule 39, the Ministry of Information Industry appeared to be seeking a strategic alliance with the Ministry of Culture against the SARFT. Indeed, when the Ministry of Culture was drafting its provisional rules, the Ministry of Information Industry was said to have advised it to define "internet culture" as including not only the provision of internet culture online, but also delivery of that content over the internet to all kinds of end-user devices, from computers and mobile phones to televisions.[120] Because this would mean delivering content to end users over IPTV as well, the MII's advice revealed both its long-standing rivalry with the SARFT and its desire to ally itself with the potentially less-threatening Ministry of Culture.

According to China's 2000 Legislation Law, regulatory matters falling within the jurisdiction of two or more ministries or ministry-level agencies either require the State Council to formulate an administrative regulation, or the ministries/ministry-level agencies concerned to jointly formulate an interministerial rule. Before this happened, the SARFT was unable to establish its role as a legitimate regulator of online video, and its announced policies were only partially implemented (mainly within the broadcasting system) before mid-2004.[121] For example, http://enorth.com.cn (*beifang wang*), which was approved by the SARFT to provide online audiovisual services in early 2003, was in fact a regional web portal affiliated with the state-owned Tianjin Radio, TV, and Film Group.[122] Indeed, in the first few years after 2000, although in its official publications, the SARFT chronicled a series of regulatory interventions, including its joint endeavors with the Ministry of Public Security to crack down on illegal audiovisual services,[123] very few such interventions were mentioned in industry discourses. This discrepancy between official and industry sources reflects a gap between the SARFT's regulatory ambitions and their curtailment in practice. In this context, numerous online video websites of various sizes, at the time mainly telecom value-added service portals, VOD companies that were also value-added service content providers, and other private web portals, were offering content that "played edge ball" (*da cabianqiu*), skirting the regulations by a very narrow margin.[124]

The SARFT's efforts to win higher-level support for fully establishing its authority as the sole or at least the primary regulator of the online video industry met with initial success in 2004, when the General Office of the CCP's Central Committee, directly serving the party's Central Committee and its Politburo, issued document 32, Notice Concerning Further Strengthening the Administration of the Internet, which designated the SARFT as the authority over online audiovisual services.[125] In light of this support, the SARFT was initially able to incorporate audiovisual service providers with telecom backgrounds within its jurisdiction. Negotiations with Netcom led to a 2004 agreement that the SARFT would acknowledge the legitimacy of telecom enterprises such as Netcom in providing VOD services provided these companies accepted the SARFT's leadership. In May 2004, the SARFT issued an online audiovisual program transmission permit (*wangshang chuanbo shiting jiemu xukezheng*) to Netcom's value-added service portal 116.com.cn (*tiantian zaixian*), the first market player outside the broadcasting system to receive this permit.[126] In the same year, the SARFT expanded its jurisdiction by inviting other private service providers to apply for online permits, and it issued forty-one permits to major web portals, including Sina and Tencent.[127]

Despite these signs of its increasing dominance, the SARFT still seemed to have a long way to go before it would be able to remove major bureaucratic impediments and create a new regulatory order. Thus, in May 2005, only a few days after the SARFT announced its Measures on the Implementation of the Notice Concerning Further Strengthening the Administration of the Internet on its website, detailing the SARFT's plan to investigate illegal audiovisual service provision on a nationwide scale, the poster measures disappeared from the agency's website for reasons unknown, though most likely related to interministerial rivalry.[128] The second wave of online video developments, the Web 2.0–inspired video-sharing websites and P2P live streaming services, emerged within this regulatory limbo. Also in 2005, the founder of one of China's earliest video-sharing websites, Tudou, complained to the press that, though the website was applying for a permit, the ministries/agencies concerned had provided neither a sound regulatory framework nor sound implementation measures.[129]

Without definite state involvement, whether and to what extent the online video industry would perform self-censorship varied, depending on the political sensitivity of service providers. It is important to remember, however, that industry self-regulation was by no means solely motivated by political concerns. As my informant Peng, an early staff member of the live streaming service provider PPS recalled, its editors, who at first only wanted to check technical details of the videos PPS was going to stream, found themselves offended by overtly violent, bloody, or sexual scenes in some of them and began to excise those parts, based on personal judgments prior to any formal intervention by the SARFT. Comments left by viewers also hastened that process. Peng described the company's early self-censoring practices in this way: "When the company began to have social impacts, [it also needed to have] social responsibilities. ... [Censorship was] not entirely because of the SARFT."[130] Censorship here was first a social construction rather than a political regulation, a construction that relied on the audience being seen as social and moral subjects rather than political ones. When this happens, censorship transforms itself from an external, repressive force to what law professor Robert Post calls "a positive exercise of power."[131]

Trade discourses were filled with rumors about the SARFT's escalating regulatory interventions starting in mid-2006. Thus it was rumored that the SARFT would release new rules governing online video that October.[132] At the national SARFT officials' meeting earlier in 2006, the head of the SARFT, Taihua Wang, emphasizing that audiovisual services were the new media counterpart of broadcasting, not just value-added services of the telecom sector, declared that the SARFT should justly seize control of the audiovisual services and strengthen its regulation of them.[133] Indeed, since late

2005, the SARFT has become noticeably more aggressive in asserting its jurisdiction over these services.[134] Invoking its rule 39, the agency penalized seven online video websites for providing services without permits and engaging in illegal news reporting, and its provincial bureaus took the lead in closing down illegal online video websites within their respective jurisdictions. And it also prevented regional telecom bureaus/companies from providing unauthorized IPTV services.[135] Although some of these regulatory interventions met with strong industry resistance, possibly supported by the telecom sector,[136] they collectively seemed to signal the SARFT's victory in the ongoing bureaucratic turf war with other ministries/agencies.

Nevertheless, compared to half a decade before, the industry that the SARFT faced now had gone through a sea change, with more diversified online video services, a much larger number of service providers and, most important, a far greater amount of user-generated content. Various opinions concerning how to regulate online video within the context of a rapidly changing media environment were circulating among industry professionals, and those opinions were likely all communicated to the SARFT and in some way reflected in its contested process of policy making. For example, for a short period, the SARFT was holding symposiums (*zuotan hui*) to solicit opinions from industry professionals, and the PPS was one of the participants.[137]

Ultimately, the debate over regulating online video centered on how to find a balance between political necessity and industry development. This debate was most intense when it came to the regulation of content created and uploaded by users. In the mid-2000s, video-sharing websites emerging amid the rush to Web 2.0 enabled amateur videographers and independent creatives to share their work directly with the public. Among these alternative productions were short parody videos and works shot on digital video. Hu Ge, amateur producer of the seminal video spoof "A Murder Caused by a Steamed Bun" (*Yige mantou yinfa de xue'an*, which I will discuss in chapter 5), released another eye-catching production titled "Terrorists of the Birdcage Mountain" (*Niaolongshan jiaofei ji*) in 2006, which got caught up in the ongoing regulatory debate. Industry professionals speculated that the SARFT might require users who disseminated personal content to obtain distribution permits, especially for short videos and digital video works that used the plot from a television drama or film.[138]

That the SARFT might require online works to be individually licensed, though only a possibility at this point, was immediately questioned by industry professionals as infeasible. Shaofeng Gu, founder of the audiovisual sharing platform podlook.com (*boluo wang*), argued that the government would have to establish a colossal office of censorship if it were to require all audiovisual content online to be precensored.[139] And many others argued that the lengthy process of prescreening and licensing user content by the SARFT would likely dampen users' enthusiasm, shrink video websites' user base, and eventually cripple the entire industry, which put great stock in the new medium's interactivity.[140] A compromise solution arising out of the debate suggested industry self-censorship, followed by government monitoring and, where needed, postcensorship. Taking an approach called *qiuhou suanzhang* in Chinese, which literally means "Square accounts after the fall harvest," the compromise solution would have the government assess and, if need be, censor online content *after* it was published.[141] This *qiuhou suanzhang* approach echoed the governing philosophy of the telecom bureau in Guangdong Province—experiment with new methods, then adapt their regulation to technological and industry developments.[142]

And, judging from the Regulations on Internet Audiovisual Services jointly issued by the SARFT and the Ministry of Information Industry in late 2007,[143] it was an approach the SARFT adopted as well. This epoch-making policy statement established the SARFT as the primary regulator of online video or, to be exact, of "online audiovisual service provision," with the Ministry of Information Industry providing supplementary support, and with responsibility for online audiovisual censorship delegated to the video companies. Its removal of before-the-fact regulatory limitations applied not only to user content, but to all nonnews programs, including television series and films, shown online. Around the same time, the Outline of the Cultural Development Plan during the National Eleventh Five-Year Plan Period, promulgated by the CCP's General Office and State Council in 2006, called for establishing the norm of "industry self-regulation" to "strengthen the regulation of new media communication" in general. Indeed, China's policy makers now considered self-regulation to be a necessary alternative for managing the internet without compromising its development.[144]

The promulgation of the 2007 regulations, commonly known as "SARFT rule 56," marked the easing of hostilities in the year-long turf war between the SARFT and the Ministry of Information Industry. The Central Propaganda Department was said to have played a key role in the interministerial reconciliation.[145] Almost concurrently, the SARFT created the Online Audiovisual Program Regulation Department (Wangluo shiting jiemu guanli si), specifically tasked with regulating online video, a job originally assigned to the Online Communication Regulation Office (Wangluo chuanbo guanli chu) of the SARFT's Social Management Department (Shehui guanli si). An institutional change like this reflected the agency's clear desire to formalize its online regulation by putting its hard-won authority to immediate use. As part of the process, the SARFT began to institutionalize industry self-censorship, just as it had done with its censorship of television, although taking a rather different regulatory approach.

In contrast to earlier voluntary self-censorship in the industry, which had tended to be uneven and random, the SARFT began to hold self-censorship training sessions (*peixun ban*). It organized two such sessions in April and December 2008, educating more than 300 SARFT administrators and top-management staff members from major online video companies.[146] Industry participants in these sessions were expected to pass on the principles to their companies and to organize internal self-censorship according to what they had learned. Video companies began to build or expand self-censorship units in order to fulfill the censorship prerequisite for being licensed. Major venture capital–funded video companies began to receive operating licenses from the SARFT in 2008, the first SARFT licenses having gone mostly to applicants from the state sector earlier in the year.[147] Included in the second, private group of licensees was Tudou, which had been warned for distributing programs that contained obscenity and violence or endangered national interests in the SARFT's first wide monitoring of online video content in early 2008.[148]

A well-functioning post hoc approach to regulating online video required the SARFT to develop effective ways of gathering information in order to stay informed about industry practices and online content and to know what needed to be censored, so that it could intervene as necessary. Knowledge, or the capability to know, is of foremost importance in exercising strategic censorship. Over the years, the SARFT had been building and continually updating a monitoring system for audiovisual programs. And, in 2006, it began to operate its monitoring center.[149] According to my informant Tao, a government public relations representative from Sohu

Video, the center was connected to video companies through a specially built communication system to inform them, by posting notices to a "program information database" (*jiemu xinxi ku*) it maintained, to remove any harmful content the SARFT detected.[150] The agency also relied on its reporting (*jubao*) system to hear from whistle-blowers and to learn of complaints about online programs lodged by the public.

Among the SARFT's intensive activities to provide a coherent regulatory regime during this period was its first, formal intervention in the online video industry after years of laissez-faire development. Using information gleaned from months-long monitoring of online content, particularly in early 2008, the agency closed down dozens of websites that clearly crossed the party-state's ideological bottom line and warned numerous others for posting daring content.[151] Although intervention like this certainly constrained websites from posting content that would have been allowed online in the earlier, laissez-faire period, in selecting websites for elimination and warning, the SARFT focused on liberal content at the extreme end of the broad ideological spectrum, content intolerable to the Chinese state. The authorizing of industry self-censorship, a more permissive mechanism, as its name suggests and as censorship practices in the following years demonstrate, still resulted in a much wider range of ideological content than had appeared in traditional media. Indeed, as an anonymous industry insider said in a 2006 interview, the SARFT would silently tolerate most online video content as long as it did not involve counterrevolutionary topics or pornography.[152]

Thus, as this section shows, the lax regulation of online video content in the early days of the online video industry was generally but not exclusively a product of regulatory fragmentation. But, if there had been a single regulatory body and a comprehensive regulatory framework, free of infighting between different government agencies, would the lax regulation of online content that the Chinese internet enjoyed have existed? A look at the evolution of regulation to this point, especially the government's allowing the online video industry to self-regulate, seems to suggest that, yes, it would have. In the early to mid-2000s, the Chinese state was mostly incapable but also unwilling to impose comprehensive, strict regulation of the internet/online video, and this lack of will, once obscured by jurisdictional disputes, became manifestly clear after the SARFT became the primary authority of online video.

Conclusion

Although, in the history of online video in China, it was not the state but rather the market that appeared to be a more direct and powerful force in shaping the formation of the online video industry and the Chinese internet, this does not mean that the state was absent from this process. Like the broadcasting sector, which developed within the context of heavy oversight from state agencies, especially the SARFT, in the case of online video, we should acknowledge the constitutive role of the state in making possible the industry's development, noting that state intervention occurred in a manner that foregrounded the role of the market. Beyond construction of infrastructure, this came down to a lax regulatory regime over foreign investment and online content that would prove to be a blessing to the industry in the years to come. In this lax regulatory regime, some significant arrangements, like those made regarding foreign capital on the Chinese internet, in particular, the use of variable interest entities (VIEs), were not formally documented. This should warn researchers studying the Chinese internet and media against relying overmuch on traditional policy analysis in the form of a literal or critical reading of formally documented policies.

An examination of the early history of China's online video industry exposes at least two myths about its internet governance. The first myth holds that the rapid development of the Chinese internet took place largely if not entirely because state agencies were too slow to respond to what was happening. But, as this chapter shows, the Chinese state's attention to the internet was not late in coming; indeed, its recognition of the strategic importance of the internet guided the policy making of its ministries and agencies from the very beginning. However, there is widespread evidence of intense bureaucratic rivalry between competing government agencies/ ministries, especially in earlier times, and that rivalry clearly appears to have impeded internet governance in China, at least for a short period of time. But this should not obscure the balance and consensus soon reached within the regulatory system, often as a result of higher-level interventions overriding bureaucratic politics, which lends us the confidence to argue for the collective will of an informed (more often than not), agile, and calculating Chinese state.

The second myth, espoused in many liberal accounts, casts the Chinese state and online video/the internet as irreconcilable antagonists and holds that internet censorship in China was and is externally imposed. But, as this chapter shows, the relationship between the two is closer than previously imagined, though it cannot simply be characterized as collusion, as some critical scholars have argued. The state and the online video industry have not always had common goals, but this does not exclude the possibility of shared interests. A more accurate description would be that the state and the industry have certain entrepreneurial goals in common, and in support of those goals, they engage in continuous negotiations and compromises.

5 Piracy, Internet Culture, and the Early Online Video Industry

In early 2006, a video spoof titled "A Murder Caused by a Steamed Bun" (*Yige mantou yinfa de xue'an*) went viral on the Chinese internet, traveling widely online as a downloadable file through forums, e-mails, and instant messenger (IM) programs. In the same year, numerous YouTube-like video-sharing websites came into public view, carrying a growing number of video spoofs and other works created and uploaded by internet users. These platforms were also used to share a vast number of pirated videos from physical and digital environments. Much of this content came from fansubbing communities.

When asked to recall this period of China's internet history (which was much more vibrant than many have assumed), most people I spoke with had a vague impression that the development of the country's early online video industry was intertwined with China's internet culture in general from the early to the mid-2000s. But it was not completely clear, either to them or, at least at first, to me, how all those internet communities and practices such as P2P downloading, fansubbing, forum culture, and spoofing related to one another and to early online video platforms. Like my informants from the industry, I was an early Chinese internet user, and from the perspective of online video's industry formation, I was unsure of each of those cultural forms' times of appearance and their interrelationships. In China, the internet's rapidly changing context has altered our sense of time and challenged our memory of contemporary cultural life. Although early milestones in the development of the Chinese internet occurred within the last two decades, they already seem like the remote past to many. A more precise and accurate account of this short period of history is essential not only because the early internet culture in China has been overlooked, but also because it is key to understanding the development of online video and its culture.

This chapter reconstructs early Chinese internet culture upon which the online video industry developed. Video sharing was only one popular form of early online video. Depending on different online video technologies and the business approaches under which they were organized, early Chinese online video forms also included video on demand (VOD) and peer-to-peer (P2P) live streaming. Although the chapter contextualizes each of these within the larger cultural milieu of the Chinese internet, largely shaped by piracy at that time, its main focus will be on video sharing, which involved the widest range of online user practices at the time. In considering two vernacular sharing practices in the early to mid-2000s—"video spoofing" and "fansubbing"—led by amateur enthusiasts and intimately associated with the legacy of preinternet piracy in China, I will identify and explicate the social energies that encouraged the formation of these practices, the trajectories of their development, and, finally, how the two eventually became assimilated within a nascent online video industry—with attention also paid to the counterhegemonic ethos that emerged in the industry's noncommercial productions. Ultimately, this chapter will show how—unlike television—China's online video as a cultural zone was not only constituted by political economic relationships (as shown in chapter 4), but shaped by social and cultural ones as well.

Online Video in the Early 2000s

As we saw in chapter 4, the online video industry and, indeed, the entire internet sector in China, took off in the late 1990s and early 2000s when the Chinese state, telecom infrastructures, and transnational and local capital went through interrelated and profound changes in conjunction with popular demand. The development of internet data centers provided infrastructure and networking solutions to numerous fledgling internet companies, and lax financial regulation, characteristic of the Chinese internet from the very beginning, created a permissive environment for internet companies to attract foreign investments—all of which has fueled development of the Chinese internet since the late 1990s. And it was in this specific political and economic context that China's online video industry began to take shape.

Arguably, online video's earliest identifiable industry form was VOD. The website bbvod.net (*jiuzhou mengwang*) established by Success Multi-Media in August 2000 was one of the earliest VOD service providers. The trajectory of VOD development was shaped by the commercialization of the state-owned telecom sector. Following settlement of "last mile" residential broadband access,[1] rapidly commercializing telecom operators began to get involved in value-added services. Through a project initiated by telecom carriers in the late 1990s, broadband service had been provided to nearly 6.6 million internet users by the end of 2002.[2] Use of the ADSL (asymmetric digital subscriber line) access model, in particular, had spread to most of the telecom user market and experienced exponential growth in some provinces in 2002.[3] The rapid development of that market lured telecom carriers to try value-added services. China Telecom, for example, after experimenting with its value-added service portal, vnet.cn (*hulian xingkong*), commonly called "VNET," in Guangdong Province in 2002, officially put the portal into commercial use in September 2003.[4]

Soon after, VOD companies were quickly transformed into service/content providers for value-added service portals developed by major telecom corporations.[5] The portal VNET, for example, fostered hundreds of service/content providers, whose wide array of services included information, entertainment, and education during the first half of the decade after 2000.[6] By the end of 2005, the number of service/content providers cooperating with that portal had grown to more than 500.[7] Providers specializing in video entertainment contracted with telecom companies to build and maintain the VOD system and divided revenues from user subscriptions with them.[8] Because, far from creating original content, these providers aggregated others' content mainly through illegal, though occasionally legal, means, this collaborative mode of doing business produced what is likely the first generation of distributors of copyrighted digital works in China. And this collaboration also played a major role in paving the way for China's online video development. One of the later online video monopolies, LeTV (*Leshi wang*), exactly began its career as a service/content provider, first for wireless value-added service portals and then for telecom operators' VOD services. Unlike that of other market dominators, LeTV's unexpected rise after 2008 (as I will show in chapter 6), sprang from its strategic control of the biggest bottleneck in media industries—copyright.

Despite China's foray into managing digital copyright, much of content provided by service/content providers to telecom value-added service portals was copyright infringing; indeed, small service/content providers appeared more active in supplying pirated content.[9] An internet user under the pseudonym "Qianshan Muxue" commented online: "The 'Star Theatre' channel of the VNET carries numerous Chinese and foreign blockbusters. These are obviously pirated movies. Although I download movies from online every day, I at least delete them after watching, not to mention not using them for commercial purposes. But this website shamelessly sells stolen stuff to innocent users. I really despise it."[10]

What this comment tells us is that VOD companies, which deployed pirated content for profit, were acting online much like pirated video retailers in the physical environment. It is interesting to note that, whereas piracy was welcomed as a way to enrich cultural life in the physical environment, "digital piracy" like VOD was considered intolerable in the internet's free online culture.

The story of VOD shows us that the early online video industry, which did not yet identify with a professional mode of cultural production and lacked the resources to do so, was mainly sustained and inspired by piracy, a point I will return to throughout the chapter. Like those behind YouTube-like video-sharing websites who invoked the "safe harbor" rule to shield themselves from liability for copyright-infringing video clips uploaded by users, China Telecom put out a statement on VNET disclaiming any responsibility for the legitimacy of the content provided by service/content providers.[11] Most of these providers were small companies headed by people who had less to lose in the larger internet economy than big companies did, which made them fearless in providing copyright-infringing materials and later even pornography, and the nonchalant attitude of telecom carriers made them even more fearless. Although the copyright regime in China has undergone a top-down tightening since 2000, the "hands-off" position of China Telecom, one of the largest state-owned enterprises at the center of the wide network of state interests, shows us that the many institutions affiliated with the state were far from working toward a common goal, and, indeed disagreements among them were at least in part responsible for China's weak enforcement of copyright laws.

Early Internet Culture, Piracy, and P2P File Sharing

Alongside commercial, proprietary VOD services, a prosperous user culture was developing on the internet in China. Most notably included in that culture was the practice of P2P file sharing, which was associated with pre-internet piracy to varying degrees and which laid down a sociocultural basis for sharing-oriented online video forms emerging in the mid-2000s. Before broadband access and, later, the "unlimited monthly broadband" (*kuandai baoyue*) plan introduced by telecom carriers, early users of the internet mostly browsed websites and visited online forums. According to my informant GB, a fansubber of Japanese animes and a veteran internet user living in Hangzhou, the best he could do in using the internet to access popular media at the time was to occasionally download music using download-managing software such as FlashGet and NetAnts, which cost him considerable time and money.[12] Thus, when he downloaded a 5 MB (5-megabyte) mp3 audio file at a speed of 10 KB/S (kilobytes per second) from one of the online forums in 2000, it not only ran up his traffic-based charges; it was also "slow as hell." Under these conditions, it made little sense to download or stream movies online.

But, however limited its technology may seem to us today, early internet culture in China was both rich in content and quite varied in forms. Indeed, as Guobin Yang recognizes, it was even vibrant, with forms and practices that ranged from online forums, short text messaging, and web hacking to Flash culture and, later on, blogging.[13] On its online forums, for example, early Chinese internet users would exchange information and form online communities, and a wide range of expression emerged. A longtime gamer, GB found information on games, animes, and associated original soundtracks on mop.com (maopu), created for game lovers and one of the oldest online forums in China. As part of the popular cinema culture that developed with film piracy in the 1990s, online forums became a continuation of traditional cinespaces such as unofficial film societies and cineclubs, in the digital context.[14] As I will later show, forum culture also laid the foundation for the development of both P2P file sharing and fansubbing.

Online forums also facilitated a boom in online writing and literature,[15] which was to influence online video a decade later. The result of popular participation in the production and sharing of literary works in the digital environment, internet literature dates back to the mid-1990s, when BBSes (bulletin board systems) appeared on the Chinese internet as platforms for sharing opinions and personal writings, including literary creations.[16] In the years to come, online forums and literary portals would become the main sites where internet users shared their literary works, works later assimilated into a private publishing industry that operated independently of state-run publishing houses. Today, as I will show in the next chapters, internet literature serves as a convenient creative engine for the online video industry, with video companies acquiring massive numbers of online novels and adapting them into "web soaps."

Flash culture was another important constituent of the early Chinese internet. The Flash technology introduced by Adobe inspired a group of enthusiasts in the late 1990s, who came together through forums, exchanged knowledge, and used Flash to create two-dimensional motion graphic animation. Offering a new possibility of visual narrative storytelling in a limited technological environment, Flash works satisfied internet users' desire to watch moving images online before the arrival of online video. Indeed, through the website FlashEmpire.com, established in 1999, Flash animation soon became an influential internet practice, attracting much attention even from mainstream media such as Chinese Central Television.[17] A new online form recognized by many as a means of "unofficial, alternative popular expression,"[18] Flash could well be considered a forerunner to video spoofing, to which we will soon turn.

Internet use and culture went through a decisive change around 2003, when technological developments brought about a wide diversity of internet services. Following on the heels of the early online forms just described, blogging and Flickr-like photo sharing functioned as more idiosyncratic extensions of online forum culture. The most important development at this stage, however, came with the popularization of P2P file-sharing technology. Combined with improved net-surfing conditions enabled by greater access to broadband services, P2P technology made free internet downloading of movies possible. Bram Cohen's invention of the BitTorrent (BT) protocol in 2001 revived the spirit of P2P after Napster's demise. In China, different types of P2P file-sharing networks building on different networking protocols, possibly BitTorrent's at the very beginning and, later on, the protocols of eD2k and vagaa (originating from China), emerged around 2003. Internet users had ample choices in P2P file-sharing programs. Applications such as BitComet and BitSpirit were Chinese versions of BitTorrent that specifically supported the BitTorrent protocol. VeryCD was a local application that incorporated resources from eMule and thus specifically supported the eD2k protocol. There were still numerous local download-managing applications such as FlashGet and Thunder (Xunlei) that began to support BitTorrent beyond the traditional Hypertext Transfer and File Transfer Protocols (HTTP and FTP).

The emergence of P2P networks enabled a shift in piracy practices from disc burning to free internet downloading. As a veteran internet user who experienced this shift, GB recalled that, in the early days, consumers of pirated VCDs and DVDs compressed pirated content in the form of physical media into RealMedia Variable Bitrate (RMVB) video files. In BitTorrent downloading, for example, after users compressed a disc into an RMVB file, they then created a small torrent descriptor file using BitTorrent programs that contained metadata about the file and folder to be distributed. The torrent file was commonly referred to as "seed," and users published it in online forums or seed-sharing websites. Again, with the assistance of BitTorrent programs, their peers could start downloading the publisher's folder/content after finding and downloading the seed. Online forums, as suggested earlier, played an important and long-lasting role in the development of P2P file sharing. The Chinese state eventually carried out a series of crackdowns on BitTorrent communities, especially after 2009, but, even though large-scale websites providing seed resources were eliminated, users can still find seeds if they search deep into online forums.[19]

The consumption of pirated videos through P2P networks, a noticeable trend in 2003, would become a cause for alarm throughout the entire intellectual property rights establishment in the following years. On the heels of P2P technology's debut, niche magazines like *Computer Weekly* and *China Computer Education* began to teach readers how to optimize the torrent downloading experience. By the end of 2005, nearly 30 percent of Chinese internet users, more than 30 million people, were using BitTorrent software.[20] In early 2006, P2P file sharing accounted for 60 percent of the data exchange taking place on the Chinese internet. Those years were probably the heyday of P2P sharing practices. People could find the most recent movies and television dramas, both domestic and foreign, on P2P platforms.[21] GB reported using NetAnts the most to download large-size files such as movies. As he fondly recalled, when he wanted to download a movie, he would let his computer and P2P application run for an entire day, and check them after returning home from school.[22]

The development of P2P file sharing largely reduced the attractiveness of VNET to users during the same period. Although telecom value-added service portals like VNET gained momentum between 2003 and 2005, they failed to attract new users. Growing up with mostly free content, Chinese internet users were generally unwilling to pay for it, even in the form of subscriptions. Moreover, to many, the VNET portal appeared to be a hodgepodge of various services and content without a guiding brand, making it difficult to use. According to a staff member of China Telecom's Sichuan branch, quoted in *Telecommunications Weekly*, even by 2005, most broadband subscribers were unfamiliar with VNET and unsure how to navigate it.[23]

Commercial online video services (i.e., VOD) developed only slowly from 2000 to 2005. In contrast, free P2P downloading rapidly spread to meet the vast social demand for video consumption; P2P file sharing—a form of digital piracy—would become a central part of early internet culture in China. In fact, in many ways, all aspects of internet culture during this period were informed to different extents by the legacy of preinternet piracy. As he admitted, the audio and music files GB downloaded from online were "certainly pirated."[24] And, before P2P file sharing became common, online film societies had to rely on physical piracy for materials to aid in the production of film reviews. Thus sustained by piracy, Chinese internet culture developed and prospered in the first half decade after 2000. Two specific user practices simultaneously grew out of and constituted this piracy-informed internet culture: "video spoofing" and "fansubbing." As video-sharing websites outmaneuvered VOD in the mid-2000s, these two user practices became an important part of content provision for user-produced videos, thereby sustaining the online video industry's early operation.

Video Spoofing

After the 2001 dotcom crash, venture capitalists renewed their interest in the internet in the mid-2000s by investing in a new wave of web startups—known as "Web 2.0"—that focused on user participation and sharing. Following the popularity of MySpace, Flickr, Facebook, and YouTube in the

United States, the Chinese internet rode the trend of Web 2.0 closely, moving from the first-generation portal business model, which used centralized websites to provide gateway access to the internet's vast content, to a focus on internet communities networked by subjects, interests, and niches. Possibly the first Web 2.0 product introduced into China, blogging was quickly outmaneuvered by e-magazines, e-publishing, podcasting, and social networking sites. In 2005 and 2006, venture capitalists injected more than 400 million U.S. dollars into forty-four Chinese internet companies, and most of these investments were energized by the concept of Web 2.0.[25]

In this context, after the VOD model came into public view, newer commercial video services emerged as YouTube-style video-sharing platforms. Technologically, in addition to improved residential access to broadband, the application of Adobe Flash technology around the mid-2000s also contributed to the development of video-streaming businesses.[26] With the Adobe Flash Player preinstalled on most computers, users no longer needed to download media players or install plugins to stream online video. The first video-sharing website in China, Tudou.com (*Tudou wang*), was founded in 2005, when startup entrepreneurs, venture capitalists, and researchers crowded into industry forums and conferences to discuss the prospect of Web 2.0.

Tudou's founders, Gary Wang, a former managing director of Bertelsmann Online China, and Marc van der Chijs, a Dutch partner in a consulting company in Shanghai, were inspired by the idea of podcasting, then getting popular in the United States, to create a local equivalent that would allow people to go beyond the capabilities of blogging, to produce and publish multimedia content in the most economical way. Given that becoming a podcaster in China in 2005 meant having to rent a server, set up a personal website, and pay for bandwidth, and since not everyone had the digital literacy, financial resources, and dedicated time to do so, podcasting was confined to a niche community. The Tudou website, originally intended to reproduce the podcast tool iPoddler for the Chinese market, was eventually launched as an audiovisual hosting and streaming portal in April 2005.[27] Right around the time Tudou was released, podcast hosting websites also began to emerge in China.

Gary Wang represented a type of Chinese internet startup entrepreneur characterized by a cosmopolitan temperament, a liberal outlook, and idealistic goals. Having earned an M.B.A. from the Institut Européen d'Administration des Affaires (INSEAD), he was more practical than his more bohemian peers. But he was not as shrewd as competitors like Victor Koo, the founder of Tudou's longtime rival Youku, in China's now relatively unfettered capitalist system. Among the throngs of entrepreneurs in the Web 2.0 gold rush, Wang was probably the one who most sincerely believed in the beauty of free expression, as evidenced by Tudou's inspiring logo: "Everybody is a director of life." Early on, he envisioned that Tudou would foster shows like *The Dawn and Drew Show* in the United States that would attract hundreds of thousands of listeners/viewers willing to support them. Wang believed that someday, when many such shows appeared, Tudou would be able to survive without advertising.[28] At least at the very beginning, making profits seemed to be a means instead of an end to Tudou's founder.

Unlike VOD websites, which stood in opposition to user-generated internet culture, video-sharing platforms like Tudou responded directly to users' needs for video expression. Arguably, the most sophisticated form of such expression in China's early internet culture was video spoofing, which had developed slowly before 2005 but broke out as video-sharing websites became popular. In some respects, video spoofing can be considered part of what film scholar Zhen Zhang and anthropologist Angela Zito call China's "DV [digital video] culture," to be found in the independent documentaries, narrative features, and avant-garde media experiments that emerged from the personal use of new media tools and outlets.[29] But, even though all these moving-image practices feature an alternative, grassroots ethos outside the purview of mainstream cinema and state television, they differ from one another in their ambitions, the sociocultural contexts from which they developed, and their relationships with the public. Most important, as film and media professor Paola Voci notes, practices such as video spoofing are located outside the intellectual discourse surrounding "auteur cinema" and avant-garde digital art.[30]

Online video spoofs are best considered as the subjective expressions of a younger generation that grew up in a piracy-filled cultural milieu. The consumption of pirated films had a significant impact on expanding the cultural repertoire of this generation, cultivating particular kinds of aesthetics and nurturing a desire for creative expression. In the early 2000s, these factors would eventually lead some members to get involved in video making when digital technology made it affordable. Hu Ge (henceforth

"Hu"), the amateur producer of "A Murder Caused by a Steamed Bun," told me that the development of his interests in cultural expression and online creativity were intertwined with his history of media consumption.[31] Born in 1974, Hu spent his time as a youth in one of China's key inland cities, Wuhan. From the 1980s, when he recorded the pop songs of Michael Jackson, Madonna, and ABBA using a tape recorder and a blank cassette, to the early 1990s, when he listened to the music of Western rock bands such as Pink Floyd; and when he occasionally visited video halls, to the early 2000s, when he purchased pirated DVDs and used BitTorrent downloading, Hu's reminiscences form a narrative pastiche that reflected the popular cultural landscape of China in the 1980s and 1990s, shaped, above all, by piracy.

When Hu moved from Wuhan to Shanghai in 1999, he became aware of the uneven pattern of cultural consumption in different parts of China: "When Shanghai people were listening to Michael Jackson, people in Wuhan were still listening to Gangtai music. Places like Wuhan were still backward in this regard." He saw himself as different from other young residents of his hometown because he had listened to Western pop music right from the beginning. He reminisced about his experiences learning to breakdance in the 1980s with no small amount of pride, which appeared to be a product of his distance from mainstream culture in the China of his youth and his closeness to Western and especially U.S. pop culture, then and now. His video spoofs and later video works were permeated with this nonmainstream ethos. Hu was particularly influenced by Hong Kong comedy movies such as those of Stephen Chow, a Hong Kong director known for his nonsensical humor imbued with cynicism, whose movies are not parodies, as video spoofs are, but simply broad comedies: "I like the ones that are really funny; [when] people in them are stupid." His favorite Stephen Chow productions, *Out of the Dark* (*Huihun ye*) and *From Beijing with Love* (*Guochan 007*), were nevertheless not officially imported into mainland China.

Although a comedy fan and friendly, Hu never smiled. A journalist from *Xinmin Weekly* who interviewed him immediately following the fever over "Steamed Bun" confessed in his feature that he had only one word to describe the man sitting in front of him: "dull." Though prepared by this article before I met Hu, I was still surprised by the contrast between the hilarious works he produced and his personal reticence. According to anecdotes in celebrity magazines, friends of Stephen Chow and people who interviewed him were often baffled by the same inconsistency. Some of Hu's traits, however, seemed to fit in well with the stereotype of an eccentric, geeky enthusiast obsessed with hobbies of his own.

Loving music and movies, Hu was first a self-taught digital music maker. He held many different jobs after graduating as a student of engineering in 1997, but he never flagged in his pursuit of making music. The rise of personal computers and the internet played a decisive role in enabling Hu's avocations. With the personal computer his family purchased in 1998, he perfected his skills in composition using keyboard and wavetables. Later, he delved into multitrack audio software and joined communities of music amateurs in online forums. His interest in making videos developed alongside his audio endeavors. This again, Hu told me, was tied to technological developments making access to the necessary tools easier and more affordable. He bought his own computer in 1999. The next year, he purchased a cheap webcam, with which he produced a 30-second video mocking television commercials. In 2001, he spent ¥3,000 (about $375) on a Panasonic digital video camera. With the new tool, he began to film moments of everyday life. His digital video of a friend's cat won him a second prize in a contest organized by Samsung, an accomplishment Hu was clearly proud of. All these events occurred between 2001 and 2003, but because of the technological constraints of the day, Hu was limited to saving his works on his computer rather than sharing them with friends. Occasionally, he edited clips he was particularly satisfied with into video files and uploaded them to a music forum he maintained for his friends to download.

In December 2005, Hu went to a local theater in Shanghai to see the fantasy film of the year, *The Promise* (*Wuji*), produced by Chen Kaige, an award-winning director known for epic storytelling. Although Hu disliked the movie, as he did most Chinese-language films, this time, he felt a strong urge to do something with this big-budget blockbuster. He bought a pirated copy of the movie on the black market and ten days later, he had created "A Murder Caused by a Steamed Bun," Hu's first video spoof of a fictional film, his previous ones having been based on nonfiction footage. As he had done with his earlier works, Hu uploaded this 20-minute piece to online forums.

Set in ancient China, the original film, *The Promise*, begins with a starving orphan girl, Qingcheng, who agrees to become the slave of a warrior's little son in exchange for a steamed bun (*mantou*), but breaks her promise and runs away. She encounters the Goddess Manshen, who promises her a life of luxury but at the price of never finding true love. Years later in the Imperial City, Qingcheng, having grown into a beautiful woman, becomes the King's concubine. The Imperial City is besieged by the traitorous Duke Wuhuan, the little boy Qingcheng had stolen the *mantou* from. Loyal General Guangming and his soldier Kunlun set out to rescue the King and Qingcheng. But, in the battle, Kunlun accidently kills the King, and in the ensuing fight against Wuhuan, both the General and his soldier fall in love with Qingcheng, which pulls them into the complex web of fate.

The movie contains grand narratives on choice, love, fate, revenge, and, most of all, promises. Appropriating video clips from the original for his video spoof, Hu turns Qingcheng into a migrant worker and wife of a night club manager, murdered by an urban-management policeman (Guangming) and his deputy (Kunlun).[32] Wuhuan becomes a spurned admirer of Qingcheng, who frames her for the murder out of revenge. Hu modeled the voiceovers for his spoof on the narrative style of Chinese Central Television's legal program *China Legal Report* (*Fazhi baodao*).

"Steamed Bun" deconstructs the elitist myth that the original film establishes through grand narratives, epic style, and allegorical design, subverting its cultural authority.[33] It satirizes Chinese Central Television and the official media culture it represents by mimicking the standardized tone, ideologically laden language, and propagandistic reporting style of *China Legal Report* so familiar to Chinese audiences; it lampoons the ongoing process of commercialization by continually interrupting the spoof with commercial breaks; and it even addresses larger social issues such as domestic migration and urban police brutality.[34] Whether deconstructing the authority of original texts and being nonconformist, or engaging in social and political critiques, video spoofs like Hu's emerged as an alternative political discourse online.[35] With the opening titles of "Steamed Bun," Hu states that the work is for personal appreciation only and not to be disseminated, but his friends were highly entertained by it and sent it on to others. The spoof immediately went viral among internet users and brought Hu instant fame. In early 2006, Tianya BBS, one of the most popular online forums in China, conducted an interview with Hu that attracted numerous internet users, who posted comments and questions. Many expressed their fondness for his work and their unconditional support for Hu in the lawsuit they expected Chen Kaige to file against him. Quite a few also asked Hu if he planned to make more video spoofs on social issues of concern to ordinary people such as education, health care, and housing reform.[36]

In the history of contemporary China, there are many such stories where unofficial cultural consumption inspired amateur media making. For example, the formation of China's early rock music scene, marked by a sense of amateurism, was shaped by the lovers of Western rock. What is believed to be the first rock group in China, Wanlimawang, whose name was a combination of the members' surnames, was formed by four students at the Second Foreign Language Institute in Beijing.[37] According to the fragmentary evidence available, its core member, Xinbo Wang, serendipitously encountered the music of the Beatles in the early 1970s when the cultural environment was still dominated by revolutionary model plays. Obsessed with a rock genre he did not understand at the time, the young man searched in any way he could for musical knowledge related to it and learned how to design his own musical instruments and electronic devices.[38] Wang also shared his musical skills with his friend Xiaoyi Ma, a teenager living in the *dayuan* of the Ministry of Foreign Affairs, and came to know the other two band members through Ma.[39] Wang, Ma, and the others shared a passion for music and musical instruments, and frequently gathered to exchange ideas and perfect their self-taught skills. Ma later entered the Second Foreign Language Institute and persuaded the secretary of the institute's Youth League Committee to finance the band in the winter of 1979.[40] Thus the first local rock band in China was created out of amateurs' enthusiasm for foreign music, despite its elitist origins.

Although no further sources are available to pinpoint how Wang encountered the music of the Beatles during the Cultural Revolution, it is unlikely that the official network of audiovisual publishers was the source. However, the dissemination of foreign rock music through unofficial channels had a huge impact on the development of early rock in China. Nimrod Baranovitch documents the increasing presence of foreigners in China's cities and at its universities, especially in Beijing during the 1980s, and the pivotal role they played in this process. Foreigners, mainly but not exclusively Westerners, not only introduced foreign cassettes into China but also participated in the local performance and production of rock music. Indigenous rock bands developed through their interactions with music from outside the country.[41] Although it is likely that local professional musicians participated in the early rock music scene in China, we cannot ignore the greater role of amateur music makers sustained by the enthusiasm of the youth culture of the day. Rock music, in particular, is a genre especially suited to devoted amateurs with minimal musical experience and education.

A look at early rock culture in China shows us how the same social energies of the young unfolded in similar trajectories across different periods, classes, and cultural forms. Interpreted as an alternative political discourse online, the "Steamed Bun" video spoof provided a glimpse into a discernible amateur audiovisual culture rooted in preinternet piracy. But its development and, in particular, its distribution, as the founders of Tudou so clearly learned from firsthand experience, were technologically constrained. Instead of traveling by hyperlink, the "Steamed Bun" video spoof went viral as a downloadable file, a digital artifact that nevertheless assumed materiality. The birth of video-sharing websites such as Tudou made it much easier for young people like Hu to express themselves through online audio and videos. Beneficiaries of this technology also included many small institutions as well as professional or semiprofessional creatives, for example, students of fine arts whose works did not have the imprimatur of established cultural institutions, either state run or private. In fact, even before "Steamed Bun" appeared, Tudou was becoming popular among internet users. My informant Wai, a veteran Tudou staff member who joined the company in 2006, told me that she found very "innovative" and "original" content when she was first introduced to the website in 2005 by her friends.[42] From this, we can infer that video-sharing websites were quickly discovered and exploited by audiovisual communities. As Hu himself admitted, "Things became more convenient after Tudou appeared."[43]

As of this writing, it has been extremely difficult to determine the extent of user-created content such as video spoofs that surfaced with the rise of video-sharing websites.[44] Although there are no statistics, official or unofficial, on the actual number of parodies produced at the time, there is ample discursive evidence of their abundance. For example, a search of mainstream newspaper articles with *egao* (parody or spoof) in their titles in the *China Important Newspapers Full-Text Database* shows that the number of such articles increased from none in 2005 to some forty in 2006. Indeed, the terms these articles used to describe or denounce the phenomenon, such as "prevalent" (*chengfeng*), "overwhelming" (*fanlan*), and "rampageous" (*hengxing*), conjure up a picture of video spoofing as a sweeping cultural trend.

State media and official culture were frequent targets in these productions. A 2006 video spoof, "China Won the World Cup" (*Zhongguo ying le shijiebei*), for example, through its ridicule of both Chinese Central Television's flagship news program *Xinwen Lianbo* (literally, "News Simulcast") and the inept Chinese Football Association then affiliated with the Chinese State General Administration of Sports, mocked the long-standing Maoist principle that literature and the arts must serve politics. In another example, an amateur videographer from Shandong Province derided Chinese Central Television's propaganda-infused program *Spring Festival Gala* in his spoof of the 2006 blockbuster *The Banquet,* originally published on the video-sharing website 56.com. In the mid-2000s, websites such as Tudou and 56.com made this flourishing video spoof culture possible and visible. Much like YouTube, these websites were sites of participatory culture.[45] However, Tudou and its many imitators would certainly not have grown to the extent that they have without the energies of the video-making community. Here we see a mutually constitutive relationship between the ever-growing social demands for audiovisual expression and the development of video-sharing sites like Tudou. To some extent, the flocking of venture capitalists to Web 2.0 sites was simply investors exploiting the sudden awakening of popular consciousness shaped by earlier generations of distributive and productive media technologies (VCDs, DVDs, webcams, digital video recorders), which gave rise to commercial platforms like Tudou.

Fansubbing

Another example of alternative media production that shows us how intimately the development of online video was associated with piracy-informed internet culture from the very beginning, fansubbing was organized around P2P file-sharing networks and was itself a kind of digital piracy. As described earlier, P2P networks emerged around 2003, and because they enabled faster distribution of large-size files, the networks appealed to those who were dissatisfied with the slow distribution rate of physical piracy, especially piracy of the latest television programs, animes, and movies. Unlike the production of Chinese dramas, where the entire series is completed before airing, many foreign dramas are produced on a live-shoot system and aired weekly. Large-scale physical piracy operations are less likely to copy each weekly episode immediately after the broadcast;

instead, they go into production after the entire series or season has been aired, likely due to the necessary compromises between economies of scale, time, and space in the commercial piracy of physical formats. But, as GB explained: "Fans like to chase the drama [*zhuiju*]. They cannot wait for new releases. ... The [physical] piracy really could not catch up."[46] In this sense, the time-space compression brought about by globalization is actually a relative process. Global cultural flows are less immediate than imagined, even with technological advances. The local desire to overcome the temporal and spatial barriers in global cultural flows became the major force in generating the practice of fansubbing, a practice made possible by technological developments like P2P file-sharing networks, especially BitTorrent networks.

Using online forums and instant messenger (IM) programs, early fans began to connect throughout China and across the globe, forming a network of volunteers. Fansubbing communities were highly organized, with distinct internal roles. Taking Japanese animes as an example, Chinese fansubbers based in Japan would live-record an anime episode when it was first shown and upload the copy to a group-owned hosting server, either in China or overseas. Fansubbers in China could then download and subtitle it. The subtitling would be managed by a leading fansubber and a few others, using QQ, one of the most popular instant messenger programs in China, to connect with one another. Translating a 25-minute anime episode normally took four to five hours. Once the subtitles were completed, other fansubbers would proofread and synchronize them with the video and embed them there, creating special effects for them, after which they would compress and upload the fansubbed video to the server. The torrent descriptor file would then be created and published in the fansubbing group's forum and distributed widely across the internet. Highly organized fansubbing groups were dedicated to different types of drama and genres (e.g., Japanese drama, Japanese anime, Korean drama, U.S. drama), and fansubbed videos proliferated.

In 2004, GB joined the group KTXP (Jiying she), which specialized in introducing Japanese animes. He was open and accommodating, generously sharing his knowledge and reflecting the cooperative culture of fansubbing communities in his openness. He had studied Japanese in college, and his initial motivation to become a fansubber came from GB's desire to improve his proficiency, especially his listening skills, in Japanese.

English-language-oriented fansubbing communities had a larger social basis
than Japanese-language-oriented ones did because the hegemony of English in China in the previous few decades had produced a larger community
learning English. Yi Chen was another veteran fansubber, who worked for
YDY (Yidian yuan), one of the most influential fansubbing groups dedicated to American television series, movies, and reality shows. "We had
many subgroups within YDY," Chen recalled. "The group I belonged to
could easily summon seventy to eighty fansubbers in its heyday."[47]

Although mainly responsible for the translation part of subtitling in
KTXP, as someone who liked to delve into any matter he found interesting, GB also taught himself the more technical parts of fansubbing, such
as postproduction. Very few fansubbers had professional backgrounds in
fields such as the media, the fine arts, design, or computer science. Most
were amateurs like GB and had started from scratch. To learn video postproduction, GB studied instructional and sharing posts he found in the online
forums of KTXP and other fansubbing groups (see figure 5.1, for example),
some of which were written by more experienced amateur members. Thus,
fansubbing was not only a community of piracy, but also a community of
learning.

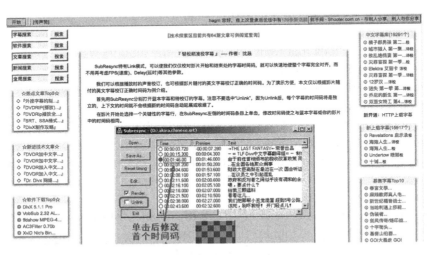

Figure 5.1. Instruction post saved by GB in 2004 that taught him how to proofread
subtitles.

Like video-making communities, fansubbing groups initially lacked a means of distribution. Early fansubbers relied on online forums and the P2P networks, especially BitTorrent networks, for distribution. On major BitTorrent seed resource websites, numerous new torrent files were released each day. The torrent files' titles often began with a bracket containing names of different fansubbing groups such as KTXP, which indicated the immediate source of those productions. GB put the relationship between fansubbing and BitTorrent downloading/sharing in this way:

> Fansubbing relied heavily on BT downloading to emerge because online streaming and direct downloading were impossible back then. It was a purely voluntary practice, and we were unwilling to invest much money in buying [high-capacity] servers. ... Our server was unable to handle thousands of simultaneous downloads. ... BT downloading was all about sharing, and didn't consume many [network] resources. ... It reduced [bandwidth] pressure on the server. ... Without BT downloading, it would be very difficult for fansubbing groups to operate.[48]

The dominance of P2P networks in distributing pirated digital content ended with the emergence of video-sharing websites in the mid-2000s. Since these websites allowed online streaming and thus freed users from searching for "seeds" and configuring download-managing applications, they soon became another digital platform where ordinary internet users could share online both physical and digital copyrighted materials they had collected and where fansubbers could publish their reproductions of foreign content. GB could not recall exactly how this change took place: "There might be a gap there. One day, you suddenly found that there were a lot of online streaming sites, and then you could [upload and] watch stuff online." By October 2007, more than half of the content delivered through Tudou consisted of cultural products shared by users, which meant piracy.[49]

To some extent, fansubbing can also be seen as a form of parody production because adding subtitles transforms so-called fixed texts into fluid and dynamic ones that are open to parodic creativity. In reality, fansubbers often refuse to use the lexicons, styles, and tone appearing in dubbed foreign content provided by state media such as Chinese Central Television. Instead, they incorporate popular internet slang into their translations. They also use subtitling to comment on or satirize social phenomena.[50] For example, in the 2008 movie *Hancock*, when the character Ray Embrey attempts to persuade a businessman to give his company's products away for free, the businessman responds: "As a concept, free is kind of up there with, you know, lethal side effects." In subtitling, Chinese fansubbers translated "lethal side effects" into "Sanlu milk." Sanlu was a state-owned dairy producer in China whose infant formula was reported in 2008 to be contaminated with a chemical called "melamine." The tainted milk killed at least six infants and sickened nearly 300,000 others, raising wide concerns about food safety, regulatory oversight, and corrupt collusion between the dairy business and government officials. Thus, in this and other ways, the cultural politics of fansubbing go well beyond simply challenging the cultural import regime in China with which the state maintains its ideological grip and protects its domestic cultural industries.

When we turn from ideological to economic outcomes of fansubbing, it is important to note that the practice has not affected global cultural industries to the extent that transnational corporations claim. The economics of fansubbing are complex, but it is doubtful that fansubbing harms the interests of global media giants, which profit nicely from the legal regime of intellectual property rights because most of fansubbers' productions cannot legally enter the Chinese market due to the country's strict import quotas. In contrast, fansubber communities have significantly facilitated transnational cultural flows, which has cultivated a large audience base for Hollywood content in China, laying a solid social foundation for Hollywood blockbusters' healthy box office revenues in recent years. In this sense, Gary Hall may be right in arguing that "there is nothing inherently emancipatory, oppositional, leftist or even politically or culturally progressive about digital piracy [fansubbing]."[51]

Online Video in the Mid-2000s

Audiovisual user content propelled the development of video-sharing websites. Thus, having been quickly discovered by internet users, Tudou experienced a rapid growth in 2006 and 2007. Whereas, in early 2005, the website received only about five audio clips per day, that number climbed to more than 200 per day by August 2005.[52] By August 2006, daily audiovisual clips received by the website had increased to more than 3,000, and the number of registered users had surpassed 500,000.[53] Weekly video views of Tudou totaled about 350,000 in August 2005, but this number exploded to 360 million two years later. Tudou's impressive performance in developing user bases quickly brought it a second round of venture capital investment of

$8.5 million, jointly made by Granite Global Ventures, JAFCO, and its initial investor, IDG Ventures China, in mid-2006.[54]

At the time, the concept of Web 2.0 was still popular among venture capitalists. In early 2006, Oak Pacific Interactive, a leading Web 2.0 internet company owning a wide array of online assets including the forum mop.com, received its second round of financing and the largest investment in Web 2.0 in the Chinese internet—$48 million—from General Atlantic, Doll Capital Management, Technology Crossover Ventures, Accel Partners, and Legend Capital.[55] The rapid growth of YouTube also made it possible to envision the lucrative potential of a global video user-generated content network. In 2006, a number of local imitator sites emerged after Tudou's debut, including Youku.com, 6.cn, ku6.com, pomoho.com, TVix.cn, and 56.com, companies that benefited greatly from the Chinese government's selective bans on both YouTube and the companies' other foreign competitors. Although, by now, most of the imitators have disappeared, a casualty of market consolidation, at the time, hundreds of them absorbed some $100 million in venture capital investment.[56] Among the imitator companies, only Youku, which merged with Tudou in 2012, survived, to become one of the major players in today's monopolistic video market, and it is also the only video giant currently in the industry with a history of video sharing. Launched in beta in June 2006,[57] Youku soon maximized its visibility by exploiting several sensational news stories of that year, including actress Yu Zhang's sex tape, the deadly snowstorm in Shenyang, and the holdout house (whose owners held out against developers for two years) in Chongqing. Youku received its second round of financing, $12 million, from Sutter Hill Ventures, Silicon Valley's oldest venture capital firm, Farallon Capital, and local investor Chengwei Ventures in December 2006.[58]

When another online video service, P2P live streaming, appeared slightly before video-sharing websites did, the extraordinary success of its service providers, such as PPLive, PPStream, UUSee, and QQLive, in attracting users garnered considerable attention from venture capitalists. Service providers in this model delivered video services to users through a P2P network. In practice, users needed to download a P2P software program designed to distribute and redistribute real-time video streams on a P2P network. Essentially, these provider appropriated the P2P network commonly employed by internet users in sharing files to provide proprietary live streaming services. By exploiting the P2P network, live streaming service companies substantially alleviated traffic pressure on the bandwidth of their streaming server, a problem that was also affecting video-sharing websites around the same time.[59]

Because it is not participatory, P2P live streaming is closer to the VOD model than video sharing is. Although some companies such as UUMe allowed users to create personal channels amid the Web 2.0 surge, P2P live streaming service providers largely remained aggregators and transmitters of professionally produced content. They acquired—both legally and illegally—movies, sporting events, and live streaming television programs from domestic television channels and from overseas subscription channels such as HBO and ESPN. Most of the time, however, they searched, migrated, and categorized content from P2P file-sharing and fansubbing communities. As my informant Peng, a veteran staff member from PPStream, admitted, "our job was basically to sort out the vast [pirated/fansubbed] content for users."[60] Thus, even though it was not a platform known for user participation, P2P live streaming services were still sustained by user practices.

Unlike the service providers for VOD, which are generally not considered part of online video's early history, live streaming service providers, along with video-sharing websites, quickly made their way into industry discourses on online video in trade newspapers. The private nature of China's online video industry means that the industry version of its history begins, not with the VOD services developed by the sluggish state-dominated telecom sector in the early 2000s, but, rather, with the venture capital–supported online video services developed in the mid-2000s.

Although they are two different types of online video services, P2P live streaming was often conflated with video sharing in trade newspapers. Video-sharing platforms, in particular, were interchangeably referred to as "video blogging" and "video podcasting" websites at the very beginning. Podcasting platforms allowed internet users to make audio recordings and distribute them online. Websites like Tudou did the same thing, but used different technologies and focused on video recordings. Still, terms like "video podcasting," by which users named and imagined online video websites, gave online video its earliest identity as a medium of free expression and made it a cultural zone of exception to state socialist norms—a developing zone of unofficial culture constituted by user energies and practices.

Conclusion

The rapid growth of the online video industry starting from 2005 was enabled and spurred on by a vast amount of user content mainly produced by video-spoofing and fansubbing communities, who helped video companies develop user bases and retain high visibility in public life. The level of activity in video spoofing and fansubbing, particularly between 2003 and 2005, reflected a less commercial internet and a more "authentic" representation of the people—a Chinese internet culture we no longer see. This culture served as a solid foundation for the conspicuous rise of the online video industry, especially video-sharing platforms that aimed to capitalize on user energies. Although video spoofs and clips of social events and everyday life were certainly the most genuine instances of internet user content, my informant Wai recalled that "user-generated content" was not a distinct idea guiding industry practices at the very beginning.[61] It was instead a construction of the media industry, which attempted to typify different types of content through the lens of commercial value. User-generated content only began to assume a definite presence in both industry and public relations discourses in a much more commercial context later on. In retrospect, early industry professionals had only a loose sense of such content, as encompassing everything uploaded by users. This included not only original content created by users, but also a vast amount of content that users imported (pirated) from elsewhere, although, as a reproduction of copyrighted content, fansubbing blurred the distinction between "pure creation" and "pure migration."

Video-sharing sites like Tudou were not originally intended for distributing pirated (fansubbed) content. Rather, identifying with the concept of Web 2.0, these websites' ready tolerance of piracy was a response to the cultural milieu at the time. After all, early Chinese internet culture, from which the online video industry developed, was entirely built upon and intimately associated with piracy. Media scholars Elaine Zhao and Michael Keane argue that internet-based companies in China came into existence largely by exploiting the informal media economy.[62] Indeed, given China's relatively isolated and state-dominated system of cultural provision at the time, it is clear that internet culture and new media industries, including the online video sector, would not have survived, let alone thrived, without piracy.

The temporary alliance between capital and popular demand in China in the mid-2000s made visible a distinct online video culture, one that disavowed the cultural legacies of state socialism. Major party organs published a series of editorials in 2006 condemning the destructive potential of the video spoof as a new cultural form, especially after a number of video parodies of revolutionary classics went viral. In August of that year, *Guangming Daily*, in particular, convened a group of experts who collectively argued that "we must firmly oppose online spoofing of red classics, and national, traditional culture."[63] It returned to this theme in a November editorial:

> "Spoofing" overthrows mainstream ideologies, confuses the right and wrong, the honorable and shameful, and disregards the traditional culture of the Chinese nation. ... In every way, online "spoofing" counters a harmonious ideal. ... We must build a harmonious culture ... using socialist ideology as a guide. ... Under all circumstances, revolutionary canons cannot be "parodied" in any form.[64]

The editorial's pronouncements were echoed in a number of state media outlets including *People's Daily* Online.

Although fansubbing was not as ideologically vexing to state and cultural authorities as video spoofs were, and their objection to it not as strong, it was still a matter of concern to them, not only because fansubbers often acted as video spoofsters during the process of subtitling, but also because video spoofsters increasingly turned to fansubbing groups for source material. Thus, early online video culture was part of what Guobin Yang calls a "culture of contention" in Chinese cyberspace from the very start of the new century.[65] Such content as fansubbed videos and video spoofs satisfied popular domestic demands for unofficial culture, but, ironically, what stood behind this content was online video companies backed by venture capital, much of it foreign. The convergence of culture and capital at that particular moment teaches us that the ethos of piracy-informed early video culture fit in with nascent capital's disinclination to submit to the state in a newly emerging market.

Eventually, the online video industry, as we will see in the next chapters, broke away from piracy and embraced the intellectual property rights regime under pressure from advertisers and copyright holders. Video companies' aggressive move toward that regime drove them to participate in the production of original content instead of wholly relying on users' creations. Meanwhile, early video makers also began to go through a process of commercialization that was at once independent of and intricately involved with video companies. Amateur video makers who succeeded in building their fame online such as Hu, for example, were soon approached by advertisers who sought to exploit vernacular creativity to promote their products. But, in either case, as I will show in the next chapters, the ethos of early video culture was retained within the commercial environment, presumably for its workability, which was already being tested socially in the mid-2000s. Thus, seen in terms of its relationship with an increasingly commercialized video industry, the popularity of video culture at that time functioned as a kind of market test for the industry.[66] In a commercially-driven context, the legacy of China's culture of piracy has increasingly been used to make profits rather than to provide individual and communal enjoyment, and genuine identification with that legacy has gradually faded away, leaving it as an empty signifier, a commercial principle, and a commodity.

6 Bidding on the Rights to Stream: The Industry, Copyright, and New Cultural Flows

The video industry's initial dependence on piracy and its later disarticulation from it are integral parts of its formation and transformation. Early online video culture described in chapter 5 had a short-lived existence in the mid-2000s. Contrary to venture capitalists' expectations, video-sharing websites soon found it difficult to monetize the vast traffic brought about by user-generated content, traffic Tudou founder Gary Wang would scornfully dismiss as "industrial waste" in September 2008.[1] Under growing pressure to make profits, the industry adopted an aggressive content strategy based largely on buying the rights to popular intellectual properties, first from domestic companies and later from foreign content providers including the Hollywood majors. Meanwhile, both domestic and foreign piracy, which once contributed to the strong user base for early online video websites, were now considered to impact the development of the industry negatively, not only because advertisers were reluctant to place ads alongside pirated content, but also because of the backlash against streaming websites from intellectual property rights owners. Initial antipiracy efforts made by a few entrepreneurial companies that owned intellectual property rights escalated into an industry-wide campaign against piracy, which forced online video companies to provide only legal content and helped to advance the copyright regime on the Chinese internet.

This chapter focuses on copyright as an aspect of the online video industry's transformation. It first describes how the dual pressure of advertisers and intellectual property rights owners led video companies to abandon piracy and how this process contributed to the consolidation of the industry. It then examines how these video companies negotiated with producers and copyright owners (especially the Hollywood majors) as they actively began to acquire digital rights. Internally, video companies were also in constant negotiation with piracy/fansubbing communities with whom they previously had close ties, but they became estranged from pirated sources when the consequences of piracy grew worse and they found ways to use copyright as a source of income. Finally, this chapter describes how video companies' copyright-related activities operated within a lax content regulation regime that, in diverging from the strict regime imposed on television and film, made online video an alternative cultural zone.

The Rise of the Five Video Giants

Beginning in the second half of 2006, when the cash-strapped small blog service provider Minsi closed down in August and several video companies declared layoffs at the end of the year, a counterdiscourse emerged predicting the end of the Web 2.0 bubble.[2] Paradoxically, these events occurred around the same time that venture capital was still pouring into the video industry. In fact, trade newspapers at the time were home to conflicting discourses that exalted the upsurge of Web 2.0, especially video sharing, on the one hand, and deplored its decline, on the other. Mindful of both trends, we need to acknowledge the increasing consolidation in online video and in Web 2.0 in general. After initial rounds of investment, venture capitalists began to concentrate on market leaders. Tudou completed its third round of fundraising, an estimated $20 million, in April 2007 from General Catalyst (United States) and Capital Today (China), together with existing investors JAFCO, IDGVC, and Granite Global Ventures.[3] In November 2007, Youku raised a still larger third round, $25 million, from Bain Capital's subsidiary, Brookside Capital Partners, and from existing investors Sutter Hill Ventures, Farallon Capital, and Chengwei Ventures.[4] Meanwhile, promising new companies began to attract fresh investment. For example, 56.com received its first round of venture financing in June 2007 with approximately $10 million from Disney's investment arm Steamboat Ventures, Sequoia Capital, and SIG, quickly followed by a second round later that year.[5] But, behind the veil of apparent prosperity, the industry's capital and resources were being distributed unevenly, with most of Tudou's and Youku's imitators being abandoned.

How to make a profit before "angel investors" lost patience and left was a challenge for most video companies at the time, especially for the video-sharing websites, given the formidably high bandwidth costs of running streaming businesses. Sharing websites made various efforts to monetize their traffic from the outset, including advertising, paid subscriptions, and e-commerce. As diverse as those strategies were, most of them failed: sharing websites and P2P live streaming service providers alike still had to rely on advertising as their primary source of income. In addition to standard banner ads, Tudou began to place in-stream ads in March 2006. To avoid losing users, the company let user-generated content producers decide whether they wanted to have in-stream ads incorporated into their productions. If they agreed, producers would receive the equivalent of one penny for each view/download and could cash out when they earned ¥100 (about $12).[6] In addition to traditional advertising, some smaller sites such as Mofile created specialized "sponsor channels" for advertisers to display their products visually.[7] Unlike the ones tried before, these strategies, which marked the initial commercialization of the online video industry, did in fact work. The reported advertising revenue of ku6.com in 2006 was ¥6 million (about $750,000), increasing to ¥10 million (about $1.25 million) in 2007. Around the same time, the CEO of 56.com revealed that the monthly advertising revenue of her company was about ¥1 million (about $125,000).[8]

But these revenues could not offset the online video companies' high operational costs. Chinese online advertising revenues (excluding those from search engines and online advertising agencies) were considerably smaller than those of traditional media, accounting for only ¥4.66 billion (about $582 million) in 2006, whereas the total advertising revenue of the broadcasting sector was ¥40.4 billion (about $5 billion) in the same year, and that of newspapers was around ¥31.3 billion (about $4 billion).[9] Traditional web portals accounted for 28 percent of online advertising revenue, search engine sites for 26.4 percent, and vertical industry portals, a new favorite outlet for advertisers, for another 22.2 percent, with the remaining 23.4 percent divided up among miscellaneous internet services such as blogging, wireless application protocol (WAP) ads, and online video.[10] The total advertising revenue of the online video sector in 2006 was estimated to be ¥170 million (about $21 million), or only 3.6 percent of all online advertising revenue,[11] and it had to be divided up among more than one set of market players, including P2P live streaming service providers.

Limited support from advertisers was at least partly due to their reluctance to place ads on online video sites, especially sharing websites backed
by user content. As ku6.com's vice president admitted, "The biggest challenge is to persuade more advertisers to place ads on our website."[12] To
Youku's CEO Victor Koo this difficulty was an inevitable part of the commercial history of any new medium;[13] however, as communication scholars Dan Schiller and Christian Sandvig point out, advertisers are simply
not inclined to reach out to poor people, no matter how sophisticated the
technologies involved may be.[14] One consulting agency even described the
mainly young people with less income who used video-sharing websites as
being "of low quality,"[15] a comment chillingly reminiscent of the new U.S.
advertising jargon that divides people into "targets" and "wastes."[16] Advertisers were perhaps more understandably reluctant to place ads alongside
pirated content, which was a problem for P2P live streaming service providers as well. Even though their bandwidth costs were much lower than those
of sharing websites owing to their use of P2P technology, the advertising
revenue they lost because of piracy still put them in financial jeopardy.

Industry professionals began to realize the challenge of monetizing the
vast streams of amateur and pirated content. In September 2007, Yan Liu,
CEO of 6.cn, publicly declared that *egao*/user-generated content would not
be the future for video websites: "As a service provider, I would not like
people to associate us with 'grassroots media.' While grassroots content is
desired [by the masses], it is not appreciated by advertisers. For example,
the "Steamed Bun" video got huge traffic, but it cannot attract advertisers. I hope that 6.cn can give expression to mainstream culture ... which
can generate more value."[17] By "mainstream culture," Liu presumably
meant content from traditional media organizations. It is no coincidence
that right before this talk, 6.cn partnered with Phoenix TV, a Hong Kong–
based satellite television network that offers Mandarin- and Cantonese-
language programming, to deliver professionally produced, copyrighted
content to users. Liu considered this collaboration to be the beginning of
his organization's transformation from the grassroots low ground to the
commercial high ground as legitimized by advertisers: "Programs from
Phoenix TV could attract more high-end users. ... They are worth more to
advertisers. For example, our web banner pricing originally ran at ¥30,000
[about $3,750]. With programs from Phoenix TV, it could go up to ¥50,000
[about $6,250]."

In addition to pressure from advertisers, the piracy/copyright issue also troubled both domestic and foreign intellectual property rights owners in the context of a tightening intellectual property rights regime. They exerted considerable pressure, which forced online video companies to start acquiring legitimate rights to their content. Exploiting that tightening regime, intellectual property rights owners managed to obtain redress for their piracy grievances and even turn copyright violations to their benefit, thereby becoming important actors in advancing a tighter copyright regime for the Chinese internet. Intellectual property rights owners' antipiracy activities had been growing with online music, and online video followed, becoming a new area of contention.

In August 2007, the producer of the television series *The Return of the Condor Heroes* (*Shendiao xialu*), for example, sued Sina for streaming the series without permission. The Beijing court ordered Sina to remove the content from its server, publish an acknowledgment of wrongdoing, and pay ¥300,000 (about $37,500) in damages for the illegal distribution.[18] According to an industry anecdote, one production company hired more than ten lawyers in 2006 to scour their computers in order to obtain evidence of copyright infringement. This enabled them to send a "cease and desist" order and to sue infringers if the order was not obeyed in 15 days.[19] Indeed, as Zhongjun Wang, founder of the film production company Huayi Brothers, publicly revealed, Huayi's income from the internet sector mainly came from damages for copyright infringement, not from transferring or granting rights.[20]

The most prominent actors in the antipiracy process were a few intermediary companies that had acquired exclusive digital and associated rights from producers and could act on those rights to grant licenses and combat piracy.[21] By late 2010, these companies owned nearly 80 percent of the digital rights to films and television series produced in China.[22] They included companies that specialized solely in rights acquisition and distribution, such as Shengshi Jiaoyang, and other companies, mostly former service/content providers to telecom operators, that had set up shop in the intellectual property business under particular circumstances, like the LeTV.

Founded by Yueting Jia, a businessman from the coal-rich northern province of Shaanxi, and previously affiliated with Jia-owned Sinotel Technologies, a wireless telecom infrastructure provider, LeTV was spun off in 2004 to capitalize on the emerging lucrative 3G market as a service/content provider for telecom companies' wireless value-added service portals.[23] As part of this strategic move, LeTV recruited Hong Liu, whose background as a television journalist was rumored to have provided the company with easy access to a huge amount of quality content from the broadcasting system.[24] In other, unofficial accounts, LeTV founder Jia was said to have a mysterious yet substantial government background, which allowed him to acquire exclusive digital rights to a vast amount of copyrighted content at relatively low prices from state-owned media enterprises such as the China Film Group (CFG).[25] Also, according to my informant Hao, one of LeTV's copyright directors, who participated in its early rights acquisition, the internet market in the mid-2000s was far less developed than it is today, and since traditional production companies were not familiar with or even interested in the new media market, LeTV was able to acquire rights to their content at fairly low prices. As he recalled, the company could get exclusive digital rights to domestic television dramas for just a few thousand yuan per episode, which amounted to a mere 1 percent of their selling price to state-owned television stations.[26]

When the wireless service/content provider bubble burst after 2005, LeTV caught the rising tide of online video, operating as a service/content provider for telecom companies' video on demand (VOD) services.[27] This expedient path enabled LeTV to capitalize on its history in telecom businesses and on its networks in the telecom sector. Meanwhile, the company was also operating its own subscription VOD service website, which did not succeed, however, because Chinese users were unaccustomed and unwilling to pay for content.[28] Indeed, beginning in 2006, with the rise of video-sharing websites and P2P live streaming, which, by providing a vast amount of free content, threatened their businesses even more seriously than P2P sharing did, major VOD service providers were all looking for alternatives. Thus bbvod.net and jeboo.com, for example, entered the internet café VOD business.[29] In response, LeTV began to capitalize on the large collection of exclusive digital rights it had squirreled away in its early years. In sync with the tightening intellectual property rights regime, it first sought financial redress for piracy and copyright infringement and later profited from granting licenses to potential licensees.

To combat piracy, LeTV started filing lawsuits against online video websites and other information service providers, like internet cafés, which were illegally streaming content. Claiming rights soon turned into a lucrative business. According to Hao, for a movie whose digital rights it had acquired for less than ¥100,000, LeTV could request compensation of ¥200,000 from each infringer. It could file simultaneous suits against several copyright infringers and still make money from the fines even after paying court costs and attorneys' fees. Profiting from its antipiracy initiatives, it began to acquire rights to more content and to file more lawsuits. The specific rights it claimed covered not only the internet, but also a wide range of digital platforms including mobile phones and Internet Protocol television (IPTV).[30] Though one of the very early players in the growing online copyright business, LeTV was soon joined by joy.cn, another former service/content provider, and by others as well.

Online video websites, especially video-sharing platforms, became an immediate target for copyright enforcers. In 2009, for example, the People's Court of the Haidian District in Beijing, having most Chinese internet companies, including online video companies, within its jurisdiction, handled 712 cases of copyright infringement by online video companies, most of which involved video-sharing websites.[31] In 2010, each of the court's six judges had to handle a dozen such cases every day.[32] Between 2007 and 2011, the court handled 2,263 cases of online video copyright infringement. Of these, 89 percent implicated online video websites, including video-sharing websites such as Youku and 6.cn.[33]

Although an estimated 90 percent of online video companies that were sued lost in court, litigation was neither an easy nor an uncontested process for plaintiffs. In general, despite a top-down tightening of the copyright regime, in the view of my informant Long, a former legal advisor to LeTV, there were still some outdated ideas about intellectual property rights lingering in the judiciary, where providing legal protection was seen as specifically advantageous to the plaintiffs instead of something to which they were inherently entitled. For Long, protecting intellectual property rights was supposed to establish order and promote commercial development in the media sector, and he saw the residual backwardness of the judiciary as a hindrance to achieving that.[34]

In addition, China's online copyright regulations were largely modeled after the 1998 U.S. Digital Millennium Copyright Act (DMCA) and, in Hao's view, lagged behind the current reality of the industry.[35] The Act on the Protection of Information Network Transmission Rights passed by the State Council in 2006 included a rule similar to the "safe harbor" provision in the DMCA, which protects internet companies from the consequences of content uploaded by users.[36] According to articles 22 and 23 of the 2006 act, when service providers simply provide storage, search, and linking services to users, when they do not know or have no reason to know about the alleged infringement by those users, and when they remove the infringing content upon receipt of notification from copyright owners, the providers are not liable to the owners for monetary compensation. Sharing websites invoked this "safe harbor"–like rule to shield themselves from legal liabilities for user-related piracy. As part of its response in dealing with the increasing demands from the copyright regime, Tudou, for example, set up a copyright management system that allowed organizations such as the Motion Picture Association of America (MPAA) to detect infringing content on Tudou's website and send it takedown notices. The system presumably resembled the Content ID tool introduced by YouTube, which allows copyright owners to identify and manage their content on the website. Using this system, Tudou received nearly 30,000 notices and deleted 24,000 instances of offending content each month in early 2009.[37]

The main thrust of infringement lawsuits was to determine whether sharing websites knew or should have known of the existence of infringing content before they were notified and told to delete it by the copyright owners. It was difficult for owner plaintiffs to prove the subjective fault of sharing websites and for judges to decide against the website defendants, even though it was an open secret that, in actuality, many websites bribed users or pretended to be users themselves to upload infringing content.[38] In the case of NuCom Online, a sports media company, which sued Tudou in 2008 for illegally streaming its movie *Crazy Stone* (*Fengkuang de shitou*), the Shanghai First Intermediate People's Court found Tudou to be a willful violator because its prescreening mechanism should have identified one of the most popular movies of the time. There were also suits, though not many, in which sharing websites prevailed and were found not liable for infringement. Thus, in November 2008, 56.com won the lawsuit filed against it by the production company Ciwen Media.[39] It could be difficult for the judges to determine not only whether websites willfully violated copyright, but also the economic amounts both of damages caused the copyright owner and of compensation owed by the violator; since there were no predetermined rules or precedents to follow, these matters were largely left up to the discretion of the judges. At first, copyright owners were able to win high compensation. In 2007, for example, the compensation for infringing the copyright of the movie *Seven Swords* (*Qi jian*) was ¥200,000 (about $25,000).[40] Copyright lawsuits were welcomed by notaries, lawyers, and judges alike for the fees and bonuses these suits incurred.[41] High payouts motivated many copyright owners to take legal action, and many brought lawsuits as another source of income, not simply to defend their intellectual property rights. Some copyright owners reportedly entrapped sharing websites by intentionally uploading content to those websites and taking screenshots of the "evidence" before the website was able to block them. Those attempts at entrapment became abundantly clear when the uploaded content had not yet been officially released.[42] Online video companies complained bitterly about these underhanded tactics, and judges were obliged to be more careful in deciding the amounts of compensation, if any, they awarded. Payouts should not be so high that copyright owners would view antipiracy actions as a profitable part of their business, leading them to favor filing lawsuits over granting licenses to users; nor should they be so low that online video companies would simply endure the lawsuits and consider the penalties to be part of the cost of doing business, cheaper than paying for official permission to use content. After these concerns were weighed and resolved, average compensation amounts for successful infringement lawsuits fell to about ¥50,000 (about $6,250) in late 2009.[43] And, around the same time, the cancellation of court opening fees (*kaiting fei*) also acted as a disincentive for judges to hear copyright lawsuits.[44]

With declining compensation for infringement, copyright owners began to form antipiracy leagues to share their costs and empower themselves.[45] These groups were also a means to generate media attention and exert pressure on violators, even though some league members' claims to own so-called exclusive rights were unsubstantiated.[46] In early 2009, joy. cn led more than eighty copyright owners, including both intermediaries and production companies, in forming an antipiracy league, with the aim of collectively suing Tudou.[47] One important goal of such campaigns was to force video companies to buy licenses from copyright owners since buying licenses was replacing compensation from lawsuits as the major way of settling disputes between plaintiffs and video companies. Among all the closed cases the Haidian District People's Court dealt with between 2007 and 2011, only 15 percent were actually adjudicated, whereas 82 percent were subject to mediation and withdrawn before a formal judgment was made.[48] LeTV became one of the biggest winners in this process. In 2011, the company earned ¥356 million (about $45 million) from granting licenses, accounting for 60 percent of its total revenue.[49] In this way, copyright owners, by taking an entrepreneurial approach to acting on the rights they owned, effectively established a copyright regime in the online video industry.

When a more effective intellectual property rights regime forced online video companies not only to obtain licenses from copyright owners but also to directly acquire rights from producers, before they embarked fully on their own content production, the value of rights began to inflate, especially after 2009. As we have seen, the needs of advertisers also drove online video companies to acquire legal rights to content. Ultimately, the companies, especially those backed by venture capital, needed to provide legal content in order to launch successful IPOs and enter the stock market. By the end of 2008, it had become obvious that sharing websites were giving up their user-oriented model. Although users could still upload content, these websites increasingly began to introduce professionally produced, copyrighted content. For example, Youku reportedly began to acquire content/rights from 268 television stations and production companies in late 2008.[50] Gradually, online video companies that acquired rights also joined the ongoing war against piracy. Because no single company could monopolize all the rights in the market, it happened that some companies were plaintiffs in some cases and defendants in others.

During that period, copyright replaced bandwidth as the new industry bottleneck that online video companies had to find their way through, and a consensus emerged that free, ad-supported streaming-video services would be the future of the industry since the monetizing potential of different forms of online video (VOD, video sharing, and P2P live streaming) had become evident. In a reshuffling of the industry, some players withdrew, some transformed themselves, new players joined, and five video giants emerged to dominate the market. In large part because of their unattractive subscription model, VOD services were already experiencing a decline since the mid-2000s, and former service providers were seeking a transformation. Leveraging its control over the industry bottleneck of copyright, former VOD service provider LeTV became a streaming-video portal and a major player in the field. In 2010, upon launching its IPO on the Shenzhen Stock Exchange, LeTV became the first publicly listed online video company in China.[51] The P2P live streaming services that required users to download a P2P software program were outmaneuvered by portal operations with direct, easy access.[52] Although top performing service providers such as PPLive (renamed "PPTV" in 2010) were still operating, no new entrants into the market opted for the P2P live streaming model. Free portals from the outset, sharing websites retained their portal operations, but transformed themselves from providers of user-generated, pirated content to providers of professionally produced, copyrighted content, and Youku and Tudou were among the very few that survived the competition. After further rounds of fundraising in 2009 and 2010, the two companies successfully listed themselves on NASDAQ and merged in March 2012 to become the unquestionable leader of the industry.[53] The once-promising ku6.com was acquired by Shanda in an all-stock deal in late 2009; 6.cn transformed itself into an online performance service provider (*xiuchang*) in late 2010. And 56.cn, once a leader in the industry, experienced a steady decline after the failure of its self-censorship process in 2008 and was sold to the social networking site Renren for $80 million in September 2011.[54]

New market entrants unanimously adopted the free, ad-supported streaming model, and received the backing of the internet giants. Web portal Sohu was one of the most aggressive internet companies setting up shop in online video; its history in online video could be traced back to 2006, when it was selected as the online portal partner for the 2006 World Cup.[55] But it only began to provide a concentrated streaming service in 2009, actively riding the tide of antipiracy campaigns. As it began to acquire new media rights, Sohu joined joy.cn and another intermediary, voole.com, to convene 110 copyright owners in September 2009 to form the China Online Video Anti-Piracy League,[56] which mounted a furious attack on Youku that brought Sohu a great deal of attention. Indeed, Sohu's high-profile presence in the antipiracy movement was widely believed to be a tactic to boost publicity for its new business in online video.[57] Following Sohu, the search giant Baidu established its online video venture qiyi.com (later renamed "iQiyi") in early 2010. Tencent, which at the time already provided video services through the P2P live streaming software QQLive, used that software to launch an online video-streaming website.[58] The enthusiasm of large internet companies for online video seemed unaffected by the fact that the industry was not yet able to turn a profit. Acquiring a share of the online video market was for them more about following a long-term strategy than about making short-term profits.

There were hundreds of video companies in 2006, but fewer than twenty by the end of 2011. It became clear that the industry was increasingly dominated by Youku/Tudou, iQiyi, Tencent Video, Sohu Video, and LeTV. At this stage of their competition, having concentrated on high value-added content and advertising, these companies now turned to focus on bidding for the rights to external content.

Bidding on the Rights to Stream

In response to the antipiracy campaign, online video companies immediately invested in domestic television dramas and films. Their pursuit of licensed content quickly pushed up the price of rights, with an unexpected and significant increase in 2009. Whereas, early in that year, the exclusive digital rights to most television series were still priced well under ¥10,000 (under $1,250) per episode, by late 2009, the price had soared to four or five times that much.[59] And, in the next two years, it would soar even higher. In June 2011, for example, Sohu Video secured the exclusive rights to the 96-episode *The New My Fair Princess* (*Xin huanzhu gege*) for ¥30 million (about $3.75 million), or about ¥300,000 (about $37,500) per episode.[60] Concurrently, LeTV bought the 46-episode *Empresses in the Palace* (*Zhenhuan zhuan*) for ¥20 million (about $2.5 million), and Youku landed the digital rights to the 33-episode production *Allure Snow* (*Qingcheng xue*) for ¥25 million (about $3 million). The price war came to a climax later that year with iQiyi's acquisition of the exclusive rights to *The Secret History of Princess Taiping* (*Taiping gongzhu mishi*) for ¥50 million (about $6.25 million).[61]

Initially, as weaker buyers, video companies purchased any available series that were shown by television stations/channels. As they gained more leverage, however, they focused on prime-time series shown by top-performing satellite television channels such as Hunan TV, Anhui TV, Jiangsu TV, Shanghai Dragon TV, and Zhejiang TV. Buying only series that were to be aired on television stations/channels—rather than also (overproduced) series that would not be—allowed video companies to maximize their traffic by riding on the coattails of the stations/channels' preshow publicity.[62]

The price war would subside in 2012, when competitors colluded to form a monopoly over rights to popular television series.[63] By the time it did, however, it had served to raise online video's ranking from last place in the distribution chain for television dramas—behind satellite television, broadcast television, and audiovisual publishers—to second place, behind only satellite television. Although broadcast (ground-based) television had prospered for a time, with the accelerated commercialization of the television sector, advertisers' appetite for a national market fueled the rapid development of satellite television, which quickly overtook broadcast television in acquiring quality content. The rise of online video seems to tell the same story of the commercial triumph of the transterritoriality embedded in other newer media technologies.

As it had with television series, video companies' pursuit of content also led to a price increase in digital rights to domestic movies and transformed the release window sequence for Chinese-made films, which traditionally went from movie theaters (theater window), to DVDs (audiovisual publishers window), then pay TV services, and, finally, free-to-air services.[64] The pay TV market had historically developed very slowly in China.[65] When online video emerged as a game changer and video companies hoped to advance their ranking on the release window sequence, their most immediate rivals were audiovisual publishers, although, in reality, both were actually victims of piracy. The release window strategy is designed to maximize profits for distributors, but that works only to the extent that there is no "leakage" or piracy from those in the earlier (higher-ranking) windows or that it would not impact revenues for those in the subsequent (lower-ranking) windows.[66] In fact, it could be argued that, for pay TV and DVDs in China, the release windows never functioned as intended because of piracy. Being at the bottom of the release window sequence, video companies could make only meager profits from the content they acquired. When a movie is released through theaters, a low-image-quality version recorded by an audience member during the movie's theater screening (*qiangban*) often becomes available online. After the DVD release, which is normally four weeks after the theater release, a high-definition pirated copy typically becomes available online, which makes releasing the high-definition legitimate digital copy two weeks later largely unprofitable. To defend their interests, video companies first persuaded copyright owners to give them the rights to combat piracy immediately following the DVD release. Later, as video companies increased their buying power, they succeeded in advancing the ranking of their release window to roughly coincide with that of DVDs.[67] Today, the digital release window has been advanced to just two weeks after the theater release window, and some digital titles are released at the same time as the theater release.[68] A similar pattern of change is found in the sequence of release dates for Hollywood movies released in China, to which I will soon turn.

While Chinese video companies continued to invest in domestic television series and movies, they also turned to foreign content providers. But when, for example, LeTV sought to build initial contacts with sales representatives from the Hollywood majors even before 2008, according to my informant Hao, its attempts to do so met with little success, largely owing to the problem of piracy in China. Though eager to collaborate with Hollywood because that could exponentially increase their brand value, the Chinese companies were discouraged from buying rights to the Hollywood movies by the majors' rigid system of release windows and pricing and their reluctance to adjust to the circumstances of the Chinese market (especially the new media environment).[69] After shifting according to the development of new media technologies in previous decades, Hollywood's release window sequence had become relatively stable before the rise of streaming technology.[70] But, following their established rules, the Hollywood majors now required that the release date for pay-per-view (PPV) and VOD services, for example, come a full six months after their movies' theater release date.

Moreover, most of the Hollywood majors' movies could not be streamed for free but instead had to be streamed by pay-per-view or subscription only, which made them less appealing to Chinese audiences, who were used to free content, enabled by piracy.[71] Together with the majors' prohibitively high prices and overly complicated differential pricing, these restrictive requirements kept Chinese video companies from pursuing collaboration with them.

For their part, the Hollywood majors were cautious about licensing their content to a digital market like China's, notorious for its piracy.[72] Indeed, as communication professor Michael Curtin rightly points out, protecting the integrity of its system of release windows is at the core of Hollywood's global antipiracy campaigns, and likely more important than eradicating piracy itself, given the system's key role in Hollywood's ability to maximize its profits.[73]

To end the impasse, Chinese video companies offered the Hollywood majors the use of local antipiracy legal services. And, given the ineffectiveness of Hollywood's own attempts to combat piracy in China, the video companies even teamed up with the Hollywood majors' local representatives to persuade higher levels of studio management to negotiate antipiracy rights. But, Hao told me, those efforts quickly came to nothing when confronted with the multilayered bureaucratic operations of Hollywood's colossal transnational media conglomerates. As Hao put it: "It is very difficult to deal with the 'Big Six.' The Chinese film market develops very quickly, and we want changes to be made as soon as possible. But the Hollywood majors are very bureaucratic and systematic ... slow in change, long in procedure, very rigid and inflexible."[74] Hao's description of Hollywood suggests an inflexible managerial control of global Hollywood that stood in stark contrast to its flexible mundane operations.[75] Meanwhile, Hollywood's more enterprising and responsive Chinese counterparts, at their "junior" stage of capitalist development, did not seem to share the market ethos of U.S./transnational monopoly capital.

As competition in the online video industry intensified, the acquisition of Hollywood content, considered part of the high-end cultural experience of well-educated, well-paid audiences in China, became essential if video companies wanted to attract advertisers. Thus, according to an industry anecdote, Sohu Video's acquisition of American television series in late 2009 was triggered by advertisers' clear preference to place their ads during shows like Warner's *The Big Bang Theory*.[76] And Sohu's purchase of *Lost* around the same time was clearly supported by Mercedes-Benz and other high-end advertisers.[77] These series attracted viewers with significant amounts of money to spend. The monthly household income of the *Lost* audience, for example, was nearly six times higher than the average for urban and twenty times higher than the average for rural households.[78] Like Hollywood movies, American television series represented a relatively higher ground of commercial legitimacy in the view of advertisers, and this drove Chinese video companies to acquire them. "Buying American television series," Hao explained, "was a strategy to target high-end audiences in first-tier cities ... attract high-end advertisers ... and optimize advertising sales."[79] The journey of Hollywood content in China lends considerable support to communication professor Herbert Schiller's observation that the spreading of U.S. commercial culture is largely driven by transnational corporations' dependence on advertising.[80]

In this context, Chinese video companies became willing partners with Hollywood; their increased visibility also made them a force to be reckoned with if Hollywood studios wanted to break into the China market.[81] And China's slowly improving intellectual property rights regime may also have reassured Hollywood, at least to some extent. Thus changing circumstances on both sides facilitated partnering between Chinese companies and Hollywood studios. LeTV, for example, signed a five-year contract with Sony in 2010; on the heels of that deal, it partnered with other majors, including Paramount and Universal, under multiyear contracts according to which LeTV would buy a stipulated number of hours of both old and new movies from a studio each year. Specifically, it would buy all new releases—from several to as many as twenty—produced by the studio in a year. It would then select old movies from the studio's collection, significantly increasing the amount of content it acquired. In total, LeTV acquired streaming rights to as many as 100 movies from a single studio each year. On average, it cost the company several thousand dollars to purchase a movie; in addition to the one-time fixed purchase price, it divided its revenues from pay-per-view/subscriptions with the Hollywood studios. Expanding beyond the "Big Six," LeTV also partnered with MGM, Lionsgate, and Miramax.[82]

Other video companies in the race to acquire rights to Hollywood movies made arrangements similar to LeTV's. In 2009, Sohu Video signed contracts first with Warner and then with Disney. In 2011, it entered into partnerships with 20th Century Fox and Lionsgate. And, in 2012, Sohu signed a contract with Sony, under which it would be licensed the streaming rights to nearly 600 new and old titles over the following three years; later in 2012, it announced its partnership with Miramax.[83]

Alongside their investment in Hollywood movies, Chinese video companies also invested in American television series (*meiju*), a move that was more than expedient given that piracy in China had already cultivated a stable viewership for *meiju*, and that most of those viewers were the urban professionals favored by advertisers. And, in light of the accelerated pace at which cultural industries were developing, to strengthen protection of intellectual property against piracy, the SARFT issued its Opinions on

Implementing Intellectual Property Strategies for Radio, Television, and Film in late 2010—to the immediate benefit of video companies seeking to acquire rights to American television series.[84]

But, as with Hollywood movies, the video companies' efforts to acquire American television series did not go smoothly at first. Indeed, Sohu Video's senior director of acquisitions recalled that, because of the disparity between the Disney studio's established foreign distribution policy in the United States and local circumstances in China, Sohu's negotiations for the purchase of *Lost* took nearly a year and, in the end, required that alternative arrangements be made (as discussed in detail in the next section).[85] And Youku reportedly took two years to achieve a breakthrough with NBC.[86] Despite these difficulties, however, negotiations between Chinese video companies and U.S. distributors would soon give rise to an established protocol, so that, in 2013, for example, it only took Sohu Video a few weeks to finalize acquisition of *House of Cards*.[87]

Each May, buyers from the Chinese video companies traveled to the international television market in Los Angeles to attend screenings of the pilot episodes of the television series that would debut that fall in the United States.[88] They would then choose series based on a variety of considerations, from cast and crew, on-air scheduling (prime time or not), and foreign media reviews, to discussions on social media sites such as Facebook and Twitter. Social media posts were thought to reliably reflect young people's response, not only abroad but also in China, an important consideration when deciding whether to import a television series. Video companies tended to avoid sitcoms because they were mainly sustained by dialogue, which often did not translate well. When a contract was finally signed, it normally specified how many hours of content the companies would purchase.[89] Compared to the soaring prices for domestic television dramas at the time, prices for American television series were far more reasonable—and much more stable as well. Before synchronous streaming, series were sold for $20,000–$30,000 per episode, which increased to $80,000–$120,000 per episode when synchronous streaming became available.[90] As they had with pay-per-view/subscription revenues for Hollywood movies, after paying the acquisition fees for the television series, Chinese video companies would also share advertising revenues with the American studios.[91]

Since Sohu Video's acquisition of *Lost* in 2009, China's major video companies have invested heavily in American television series. LeTV has been an all-time pioneer in content acquisition from the United States (see figure 6.1). Youku followed suit, creating its "*meiju* channel" in 2010 and introducing seventy titles by 2013.[92] Tencent Video and iQiyi started to acquire American television series slightly later, but soon gained momentum. Over the years, the series that Chinese video companies bought shifted from U.S. network shows, which appealed to the widest audiences, to spicier cable shows. The gradual growth in diversity of content from different sectors of the American television industry was a result of video companies' exploitation of a relaxed regulatory regime (which I will discuss later). As the competition between them intensified, video companies also sought to acquire exclusive streaming rights to hit shows, even though the price of exclusive rights was some five times higher than for nonexclusive ones.[93] Well-heeled pioneers in this field, such as Sohu Video and Youku, had an advantage in that regard, with both acquiring exclusive rights to ten titles in 2013. Youku, for example, purchased exclusive rights to *Under the Dome* from CBS and *Orange Is the New Black* from Netflix.[94]

In addition to Hollywood movies and American television series, video companies also acquired content from other countries, such as Britain, India, Japan, and South Korea. Tencent Video, for example, built a niche for itself with British television dramas, in 2013, forming partnerships with

Figure 6.1. LeTV webpage showing its American television series in July 2014.

six production companies in Britain, including the BBC Worldwide and ITV Studios—in the largest acquisition deal for British television dramas at the time.[95] Owing to a relatively lax regulatory regime, video companies have become an important gateway for American and other foreign cultural productions to legally enter China.

"They Were Never Able to Beat Us."[96]

In the first decade of the twenty-first century, as the antipiracy campaigns and demands from advertisers exerted more influence over them, video companies no longer served as distributors of pirated content. Video-sharing websites, in particular, were moving away from their user-oriented strategies. In response to this change, digital pirates reverted to P2P sharing, their predominant mode of distribution prior to the emergence of video-sharing websites. Although, with the virtually unlimited scope of its content provision, digital piracy persisted alongside video companies' foreign content strategy, this position in China's internet culture was now much weaker than in the previous decade. There were continual state crackdowns on BitTorrent communities, especially after late 2009, which made it harder for users to consume pirated content. But P2P sharing, together with fan-subbing groups, was still a force video companies and Hollywood had to contend with.

Ever since their first contact with the Hollywood majors, video companies had tried to persuade them to advance the release window for online video so the companies could compete with the pirated content that sprang up almost immediately after a movie's theater release. Given the significance of their new market in China, the majors now had to seriously consider doing just that. Over the years, the delay for the online video release in China after a movie's theater release in the United States had been reduced first from six to four months, roughly the same delay as for the DVD release, and then to three months, or one month less than for DVDs (the source of high-definition pirated copies). In 2014, if a Hollywood blockbuster was imported into China to be shown in theaters, it was not streamed online until three months after the theater release in order to keep people going to theaters and to protect its box office revenues. If the movie would *not* be shown in China's theaters, however, it could be released online there just two weeks after its theater release in North

America.[97] In 2013, Warner and Universal began to experiment with an advanced release window for Chinese video companies. Thus the Warner-distributed 2013 American comedy *We're the Millers*, which failed to make its way onto the big screen in China, was released online there by Tencent Video two weeks after its release to North American theaters.[98] Hao considered a delay of only two weeks for the online release of a movie to be quite attractive, and he attributed the continual advance of the digital release window to Chinese video companies' persistent lobbying of the Hollywood majors and to the growing leverage of the Chinese digital market.[99] What he failed to see, however, was that this phenomenon was global. Far from being solely the result of pressure from the Chinese market, the change in Hollywood's release windows occurred worldwide. Overall, the years from 2012 to 2014 were marked by a drastic shortening of the time between the theater and the digital release.[100]

Pricing was also a strategy available to video companies and Hollywood majors competing for Chinese audiences. In 2014, users could pay a monthly subscription fee of ¥24 (about $4) to become a VIP member for unlimited viewing of nonnew releases at LeTV. Alternatively, pay-per-view cost about ¥5, about the same as a pirated DVD, and was expected to divert users from piracy to streaming websites. Not expected to bring short-term high returns to Hollywood and Chinese video companies, this nearly free pricing was instead a long-term strategy, intended to cultivate the habit of paid viewing among Chinese audiences and to keep the digital market growing.[101]

Chinese video companies used the same antipiracy strategies they had deployed for Hollywood movies to acquire American television series as well. U.S. network television shows followed a release sequence similar to the one for Hollywood movies, only shorter, starting with the broadcast network release.[102] Although technically difficult to make pirated high-definition digital copies of movies immediately following their theater release in the United States, Chinese fansubbing groups managed to do so with American television series. To combat their piracy would require that the digital release of series episodes in China be synchronous or nearly synchronous with their network broadcast release in the United States. But such a quick release was against U.S. broadcast networks' established practice in television distribution, both domestically and internationally (as it had been for Hollywood studios).[103] Another point of contention concerned how the television series were to be streamed. Before the emergence of Chinese online video companies, most of the overseas buyers of American television series were pay television channels, which required viewers to pay a subscription fee. But, given Chinese audiences' viewing habits and preference for free content, it was anticipated that this way of streaming would fail in China.[104] The early long and laborious negotiations between the parties mainly focused on these two issues. But, as Hao recalled, the painstaking efforts by Chinese video companies to educate and persuade American broadcast network companies about local circumstances in China eventually succeeded,[105] with the American companies sending a digital copy of each series episode to Chinese video companies one hour before its U.S. airing.[106]

Even in this nearly synchronous arrangement, video companies still had to compete with fansubbing groups—in subtitling and, ultimately, in delivering content to audiences. Although the companies could get the legal digital copies slightly earlier than fansubbing groups could, they were generally unable to complete the subtitling as fast (let alone as accurately) as fansubbers could. Indeed, according to my informant Nan, a fansubber from YYeTs, fansubbing groups were even able to achieve a "zero-day" delay for hit series episodes. They also provided subtitled pirated episodes with one-day or longer delays depending on the popularity of the series. A zero-day-delay episode such as one from *The Big Bang Theory* required seven to eight fansubbers to complete the whole process of subtitling within four to five hours, with each fansubber responsible for about five minutes of dialogue. If they wanted to get their content out first, video companies had to beat the fansubbers' zero-day-delay operation. But, describing how persistently she was urged by her project leader to have an episode out before Sohu Video did when she was subtitling the fourth season of *Gossip Girl*, Nan proudly recalled that the video companies "were never able to beat us ... and their subtitles had lots of errors."[107]

Unable on their own to subtitle series episodes as quickly and accurately as fansubber groups could, the video companies began to collaborate with them. Fansubbers would continue to subtitle American television series for in-house use, but they agreed to give their work and their first rights to publish it to the video companies in return for a share in the companies' preroll advertising revenues.[108] The fansubbers would then release their in-house files only after the companies' copies had been on video websites for a certain period of time.[109] In that way, the video companies were able to contain the damage caused by piracy to their properties. To attract the largest possible audiences, the companies usually published a copy without subtitles—called the "raw meat version" (*shengrou ban*) in industry jargon— after they received it from the copyright owners. Then, as soon as the fansubbers had completed their work, usually within no more than a few hours, the companies would replace the "raw meat version" with the subtitled version.[110] The copy that video companies published online was, in actuality, a pirated copy, but, unlike the fansubbers, they had a license from the copyright owners to publish it, thus revealing the paradoxical nature of intellectual property as a constructed value conferred by the market system.

In their collaboration with fansubbers, video companies did not intervene to change the ways in which fansubbers subtitled a series, nor did they analyze the fansubbers' translations for any ideological manipulations, however likely these might be. Nan received neither requirements nor preferences from video companies concerning her translations, which she did not consciously censor. In fact, fansubbers at the lower end of their group's hierarchy often did not know whether their work would be used for in-house purposes or turned over to the video companies. They simply did the subtitling in the way they were accustomed to. Once the subtitling was completed and sent to Sohu Video, in Nan's case, it was not edited further by the company.[111] What video companies needed most of all was to reach their audiences as fast as possible, and fansubbers were able to satisfy that need. Besides, having unmediated contact with internet culture, fansubbers produced subtitles that strongly appealed to audiences, engaging them in ways that professionally prepared subtitles could not.[112] In this way, early video culture managed to leave its imprint on the newly formed commercial regime, at least for a time.

The payment fansubbers received from video companies was meager. Nan, for example, only received ¥300–¥400 (about $40–$50) for subtitling the entire fourth season of *Gossip Girl*. But she did not complain because the work she did for her group, YYeTs, was in any case unpaid.[113] This casual ad hoc alliance formed between video companies and fansubbers shows how video companies and American broadcast networks incorporated fansubbers into the process of "decentralized accumulation"—a post-Fordist labor strategy by which a few vast organizations are able to reinforce their power through a globalized network of subcontracted firms and individuals.[114]

The phenomenon of fansubbing also raises the question of the contradictory nature of affective labor in the media industries. On the one hand, as media studies professor Mark Andrejevic suggests, media corporations can easily exploit fan labor to serve their ends;[115] but on the other, financial troubles, illegal status, and pressure from the global intellectual property rights regime have in recent years led many fansubbing groups to seek work with media companies.[116] Indeed, the willingness of fansubbers to collaborate with video companies stemmed in no small part from their struggles to survive within the increasingly powerful global copyright regime. Piracy has been considerably weakened, especially since late 2009, as a result of a series of state-led crackdowns on BitTorrent communities and P2P sharing, both of which were all but essential for fansubbers to distribute their works. Working with video companies was one of the few options fansubbers had to continue their operations. Relying mainly on members' donations at the beginning, fansubbing groups struggled to make a living.[117] To improve their financial status, some set up their own websites to serve fans and also to earn income through advertising and by selling DVDs. Others collaborated with BitTorrent websites in return for a share of the websites' VIP membership fees and advertising revenues.[118] Collaborating with video companies was thus another way for them to secure an additional small source of income.

Ironically, this collaboration seemed only to enrich video companies and to accelerate the fansubbing groups' decline. In particular, giving their first rights to publish to the video companies drove viewers to the video companies' websites. In 2014, hit series reportedly could attract tens of millions of viewers online at peak times, compared to the hundreds of thousands of downloads fansubbers could attract.[119] As veteran fansubber Yi Chen (quoted in chapter 5) recalled:

> In the old days, people relied on us to watch [movies and series]. Now ... people can watch what they like to watch everywhere. Fewer and fewer people join the group for original sources [*pianyuan*]. The number of active members drops drastically. Fewer and fewer people are willing to do the job. ... All [these things] are related to the rise of video websites.[120]

Video companies collaborated with—and, indeed, co-opted—fansubbers in a move to contain them and combat piracy. Because the companies would have been happy if the fansubbing groups disappeared altogether, as they successfully poached the fansubbers' audiences and stabilized their own viewership, they began to break away from the fansubbers and turn to professional translation companies. LeTV, for example, had already begun to use outsourced translation services in 2014.[121] Meanwhile, fansubbing groups and their close associates, BitTorrent communities, had come under constant attack by the video companies' Hollywood allies. In October 2014, for example, the Motion Picture Association (MPA; the MPAA's international wing) announced a global survey of audiovisual piracy, and YYeTs was on its blacklist.[122] In September that year, the MPA had filed a complaint against the fansubbing website shooter.com with the Shanghai Administrative Law Enforcement Corps of the Culture Market.[123] Fansubbing groups were dying out, and the Chinese internet was entering a more commercialized stage.

"The Local Government Might Be Unhappy ... But Who Cares?"[124]

Video companies' legal acquisition of foreign content broadened the scope of legitimate cultural provision in China. Although China traditionally imported foreign films through theaters, television stations, and audiovisual publishers, these traditional means were mostly state dominated and subject to certain quotas and state planning.[125] Theaters, for example, were allowed to import a total of thirty-four revenue-sharing foreign movies per year, most of them newly released Hollywood blockbusters, and fourteen of the thirty-four had to be enhanced-format films.[126] By contrast, the movie channel of Chinese Central Television (CCTV6), owned and operated by the state-owned China Film Group (CFG), enjoyed many more privileges than provincial and local television stations/channels and regional movie channels, which allowed it to import hundreds of foreign films each year, but the scheduling and actual broadcasting of those films were constrained in many ways.[127] In contrast, video companies were allowed to import all the foreign content they could afford.

Adding to the divide between television (together with movie theaters and audiovisual publishers) and online video, foreign films imported through traditional means had to follow established licensing and permitting procedures. For example, revenue-sharing foreign movies to be shown in theaters were each required to go through an initial vetting by the China Film Group or Huaxia, the second largest state-owned film distributor in China, and a second vetting by the Film Bureau of the SARFT to obtain an import license and a screening permit before they could be shown to audiences (i.e., a "film public screening permit").[128] Imports of foreign television programs were also handled by the SARFT. According to the agency's Rules on Importing and Scheduling Overseas Television Programs implemented in 2004, in their application to import foreign films or television series, television stations and channels were required to submit, for each film or series episode, the contract, proof of copyright, a half-inch tape with the full image, voice, and time code, a content synopsis of no fewer than 300 words, and Chinese and foreign-language subtitles for both opening and closing credits.[129] The application was processed first by a provincial SARFT bureau and then by the central SARFT. It was through these procedures, updated in 2012, that the SARFT regulated the number, topic, and origin of foreign films and television series.

In contrast, no such procedures were put in place for online video before 2014, though the SARFT's attitude toward the importation of foreign content by online video appeared capricious at times. Its rule 39, passed in 2004, required foreign television dramas and films streamed online to each obtain a "television drama distribution permit" or "film public screening permit", but this requirement was removed in 2007 by the agency's rule 56, governing online video and issued with the highest authority, which instead called for those dramas and films and other media works to comply with related rules governing radio, film and television programs, but did not specify which ones. Yet, the day before announcing its rule 56 in December 2007, the SARFT had issued its Notice Concerning Strengthening Regulations of Films and Television Dramas Transmitted via Internet to its provincial and local bureaus.[130] And, like the agency's rule 39, this notice required foreign films, television dramas, and cartoons streamed online to each obtain the appropriate permit from the SARFT in addition to authorization from copyright owners. This notice might have limited foreign online content to what had been officially imported through traditional means, unless the SARFT could set forth separate procedures for video companies to apply for those permits. But it had not, and the notice seemed to get buried among the numerous regulatory actions following the implementation of rule 56.

A similar rule attracting more attention was the SARFT's Notice to Strengthen the Content Regulation of Online Audiovisual Programs, issued two years later, in April 2009.[131] In it, the SARFT reiterated both the permit requirement for imported foreign programs and its position on intellectual property protection. But, since most foreign online content not officially imported through traditional means (i.e., without permits) at the time was pirated, this notice was largely interpreted by the online video industry as an attempt to combat piracy.[132] In fact, the new notice appeared just as the government launched what would be its year-long campaign against online piracy. Some considered the notice to be the SARFT's response to the interministerial antivulgarity campaign aimed at "sanitizing" the Chinese internet launched earlier in 2009, and thought that it was unlikely to be implemented in any meaningful way.[133] They may also have seen this new rule as the SARFT flexing its regulatory muscles. In either case, implementation of the 2009 notice seemed weak in terms of content regulation. In fact, later, as video companies began to acquire a massive amount of copyrighted foreign content not officially imported through traditional means, the SARFT did not stop that practice (as required by the notice), nor did it establish a permitting procedure specifically for online video. But its inaction does not appear to have resulted from the agency's incapability to intervene, for when the latitude granted to online video at this and earlier periods was gradually withdrawn after 2014, the SARFT showed itself to be fully capable of developing various creative methods to manage foreign content introduced by video companies (as I will show in chapter 8). Rather, it was more of an active choice by the state not to intervene excessively in the emerging online video business.

In this context, the only regulatory mechanism to which video companies deferred was that of self-censorship as stipulated in the SARFT's rule 56, which allowed online video companies to regulate their content by themselves, and which, in allowing online video a considerably greater degree of autonomy than any other medium, subsequently enabled its companies' aggressive acquisition of foreign content. As a general rule, video companies and their transnational allies self-censored only to avoid or excise content that was so politically extreme or sexually explicit that publishing it would inevitably trigger a severe response from the SARFT. For example, Sony consciously avoided titles such as *Seven Years in Tibet* on the list it provided to LeTV. More often than not, transnational companies were even more circumspect than their Chinese counterparts in their efforts to avoid negative attention from the SARFT. Thus, in an episode of *Agents of S.H.I.E.L.D.* that LeTV acquired, there was a scene in which a secret agent is killed on a

Shanghai street. Sony was concerned that this scene would make China's public security appear weak and held the episode back to avoid potential political controversy and to protect its other businesses in China.[134]

Apart from self-censoring unacceptable political or sexual material, video companies' criteria for selecting content were much more flexible than those of the traditional media, especially television. Having previously worked for a privately owned local distribution company that introduced foreign independent (non-Hollywood) films to CCTV 6, Hao saw obvious differences between television and online video in terms of the regulation of ideological material. When choosing movies for LeTV from the list provided by the Hollywood majors, Hao consciously acquired movies that contrasted with those shown on state television stations, but, at least at first, he was cautious. When LeTV began to buy movies from Sony, it used movies imported by CCTV6 as a benchmark for acceptable content. But soon, however, it set aside such considerations. Now, according to Hao, the foreign content LeTV was looking for had to "have celebrities and be interesting and spicy."[135]

Hao relied on his personal history of media consumption, especially his consumption of pirated Hollywood movies in selecting foreign content for LeTV. He identified with the generation growing up with pirated movies, particularly Hollywood movies, which, to Hao, represented universal human values and had a profound influence on him: "For example, I have been longing for freedom. I want to go abroad for further education, and I want to go to the U.S."[136]

The lax regulatory regime over online video enabled alternative cultural flows online, where Chinese viewers were allowed to see political and sexual content that would normally be forbidden. For example, when the R-rated Hollywood comedy *Ted* (2012) was banned from China's theaters and state television channels (but allowed to be shown on online video's websites), an internet user satirized the ban on the Chinese social media site douban.com in a parody news article, reporting that the SARFT had in fact approved import of the American comedy, but would be deleting 105 minutes of problematic scenes from the 106-minute-long movie.[137] Though unavailable in theaters, *Ted* had been acquired from Universal by LeTV and Tencent Video and released online on their websites.[138] Similar examples included *The Conjuring* (2013), *Escape from Tehran* (2012), *Kick-Ass 2* (2013), *The Purge* (2013), and *R.I.P.D* (2013).

The importation of American television series also contributed to China's online video becoming a significant alternative cultural zone to Chinese television since state television stations rarely imported such series. According to a staff member of Shanghai Media Group's Center for Films and Television Dramas, before they could be imported and aired, these series each had to go through a long process of vetting and approval at state television stations, which meant at least a one-year delay following the series' debut in the United States. Moreover, in another blow to the stations' viewership, the series also had to be dubbed into Mandarin. Facing strict regulation by the SARFT, state television stations often preferred less risky content such as that found in Hong Kong, Japanese, and Korean dramas.[139] Online video companies therefore became almost the only path for American television series to officially enter the Chinese market. When acquiring foreign series, Chinese video companies considered television as "the other." "We mainly buy what television stations don't have," Hao told me. "Usually, what television stations cannot broadcast is spicy [*zhong kouwei*]."[140]

Before a series was put online, video companies would make the cuts they considered necessary, though this practice varied from company to company. Sohu's importation of the second season of *House of Cards* in 2014 sparked curiosity in its audience regarding whether and to what extent the company had censored the series, given the high proportion of Chinese elements in the show. Sohu's CEO, Charles Zhang, publicly announced that the series was not censored.[141] Meanwhile at Zhihu.com, China's biggest Quora-like Q&A community, some avid fans compared the Sohu with the Netflix version and, after analyzing various technical characteristics such as running speed and frame rate, concluded that Sohu had indeed not censored the series.[142] Whereas Sohu appeared to keep self-censorship to a bare minimum, LeTV seemed slightly more cautious. According to Hao, in double-checking the subtitled version, LeTV would routinely remove nude scenes or add mosaic strips over the offending body parts. But other content that might have been censored by television stations would appear online. For example, in one episode of the *Agents of S.H.I.E.L.D*, the line "Are you from Shaanxi, China?" which alludes to illegal coal mining in Shaanxi Province, was kept. Hao joked: "The local government might be unhappy about this. But who cares?"[143]

Although acting boldly within the wider latitude given to online video, Hao, like others I spoke with, had always felt that this latitude would not last forever. They all anticipated that what they were now allowed to do would someday be brought to a halt, but none of them could predict when. They lived on this borrowed leniency from the SARFT, exploiting its lax regulatory regime to the fullest extent, while at the same time preparing both for significant and sudden restrictions overall and for the outright cancellation of specific shows.

Conclusion

In exploring the transformation of the online video industry since 2008, this chapter has focused on intellectual property/copyright—to show how the industry that was built upon piracy broke away from it and embraced the copyright regime in response to pressure from both advertisers and copyright owners. Part of the larger commercialization of the Chinese internet around the same time, this transformation was marked by a noticeable decline in early internet practices such as fansubbing, though fansubbers were able to maintain a presence in the rising commercial video culture at least until 2014. The emerging commercial regime of online video was, in some respects, a legitimized version of the piracy regime that had operated alongside state media for decades. In contrast to television and other media, online video developed under the tolerance of the Chinese state.

No longer satisfied with acquiring content from others, China's online video companies soon began to produce their own content, which took off right around the time their investment in content acquisition did. Indeed, as some media industry scholars have observed in the case of television, the proliferation of new satellite and cable channels reduced the importance of controlling distribution outlets and induced an upstream value shift, from control of distribution to control of intellectual property/content.[144] Chinese online video matured commercially at the same time that its U.S. counterpart, Netflix, started to resemble a Hollywood studio. Years of struggling to make a profit impressed upon Chinese video companies the importance of exclusive rights to content. But they also came to realize that, however good it was to acquire content, it would be even better if they could create it. This catalyzed their in-house content production strategies, which I will discuss in chapter 7.

7 Online Video as an Emerging Network of Cultural Production

While they were acquiring foreign content, China's online video companies turned to producing their own content, transforming online video there from a technology of distribution into a technology of production. Their in-house content production strategies were strongly informed by the earlier video-spoofing culture. Inspired by the great popularity of video spoofs among internet users, online video companies partnered with advertisers to produce video ads that would go viral, ads that eventually morphed into online cultural forms called "micro movies" and "web soaps." Early online video makers also went through a commercial transformation, becoming what the industry called "professionally generated content" (PGC) producers; they relied on online video websites to distribute their work and, in return, enriched the content provided on those websites.

In both cases, early video-spoofing culture and its popularity among internet users were especially important for producers catering to content needs unmet by a heavily politicized television culture. In the new commercial context, online productions thus reflected the aesthetics and ideological orientations of early, piracy-informed internet culture. This was particularly evident in the case of professionally generated content. As former amateur video makers entered into commercial media production, they were able to exploit the antiestablishment stance that helped build their reputation online in order to pursue economic gain. And, in both cases, online productions appeared to be driven not by any unifying political ideologies but, rather, by the pursuit of profit. Nevertheless, these two sources of content provision still established an alternative network of production and distribution, one distinct from that of state television, and produced a digital cultural sphere with distinct ideological features. Just as their acquisition of foreign content had been, video companies' production of their own content was subject to much more relaxed regulation than television's was, as I will show in this chapter.

Video Companies' In-House Initiatives

Evolving from viral video ads, micro movies and web soaps are distinct products of a commercializing Chinese internet.[1] When Hu Ge's "Steamed Bun" went viral in 2006, the economic potential of the video spoof became evident, and this new and powerful cultural form was soon appropriated by advertisers both to promote their products online and to serve their other business needs. Incorporating subversive elements from online parody culture in an attempt to produce short, comic video commercials that would appeal to their audiences but could not be shown on television, advertisers and ad agencies partnered with video companies to make the online commercials go viral. The video companies and their advertising partners began to experiment with longer commercials, which eventually turned into micro movies and multiepisode web soaps in concert with the companies' emerging content production strategies, nearly always supported by product placements.[2]

Video companies began to make their own programs around 2008, even as the industry moved toward acquiring professionally produced, copyrighted content. In 2008, for example, Youku developed and released an eight-episode web soap called *Hip Hop Office Quartet (Xiha sichongzou)*,[3] which reportedly received more than 3.6 million views per episode.[4] As external content like domestic television series became more and more unaffordable, these early efforts, however small and random at first, became increasingly important for the companies' balance sheet.[5] In fact, even as video companies rushed to acquire content from private film/television production companies, some of them had already begun to seek out new projects and, through preproduction investments, to secure new media rights. This practice, called "investment as acquisition" (*yitou daigou*) in the industry,[6] was much like a form of presale and represented video companies' very first step in moving upstream into the domain of content production.

The companies soon began to expand their content production. In 2010, Tudou announced its "Orange Box" original production initiative and released its first romance soap, *That Love Comes (Huanying ai guanglin)*, sponsored by the beer brand AB InBev.[7] Youku partnered with the China Film Group to produce a series of online movies sponsored by Chevrolet.[8] Youku and Tudou's ventures were quickly followed, in 2011, by a wave of in-house initiatives by other market players. LeTV announced "LeTV Productions" and planned to invest ¥120 million (about $15 million) in developing web soaps and other online shows.[9] Sohu Video kicked off its long-term content production strategy that year by releasing two web soaps, *Qian Duoduo Wants to Get Married* (*Qian Duoduo jiaren ji*) and *Crazy Office* (*Fengkuang bangongshi*). *Crazy Office* was sponsored by the joint-venture car manufacturer Dongfeng Peugeot-Citroën and the local job recruitment website Zhaopin.[10] Over the following years, video companies fostered numerous new media production companies, to which they outsourced their projects.

Meanwhile, as an unintended consequence, the SARFT's heavy-handed management of television throughout the 2000s cleared the way for the development of online video productions, including web soaps. In October 2011, the agency issued its Opinions on Further Strengthening the Regulation of Television Programs on General Interest Satellite Channels to limit what it considered to be the excessive commercial development of the country's thirty-four satellite channels.[11] Informally known as the "restraining entertainment order" (*xianyu ling*), the policy allowed no more than nine entertainment programs a day, including dating shows, talent shows, confessional/therapeutic shows, game shows, and variety shows, between 7:30 p.m. and 10:00 p.m. on those channels and limited the number of such shows to two per week on each channel. Moreover, any show airing between 7:30 p.m. and 10:00 p.m. could not exceed 90 minutes. In lieu of entertainment programs, each channel was asked to provide at least two hours of news programs between 6:00 a.m. and midnight and at least two in-house news programs between 6:00 p.m. and 11:00 p.m., each running for at least 30 minutes. In addition, each channel was required to broadcast a program designated as "morality building" to promote Chinese traditional virtues and socialist core values. On the heels of the "restraining entertainment order," the SARFT issued its Supplementary Rules on "The Measures for the Administration of Radio and Television Commercials" in the same month, which presented a new set of restrictions on television commercials.[12] Industry observers considered these interventions by the SARFT to be a lucky break for video companies.[13] The restrictions imposed on televised entertainment programs and commercials alike were expected to cause audiences, professionals, and ultimately advertisers to desert television for a medium with fewer constraints. It was estimated that television stations would lose at least ¥20 billion (about $2.5 billion) of annual advertising revenue, most likely to online video.[14] Thus, by this time, online video had emerged as a significant alternative to television, not only according to the industry's self-positioning rhetoric, but also as evidenced in the changing attitudes of both the wider industry community and the public itself.

With few exceptions, at least before 2014, video companies embarked on web soap and other online productions only when they had firmly secured sponsors for them. According to my informant Hua, the script developer and web soap project manager at LeTV, this was particularly true if the production was based on an original script. Productions adapted from popular online novels that already had a solid audience base and could ensure good viewership and advertising revenues were a different story altogether.[15] The origins of web soaps in viral ads accounted for their strong commercial characteristics, and their status as a fledgling cultural form, lacking sufficient recognition among advertisers, also resulted in their heavy reliance on sponsors. Because video companies were not yet able to make a profit and thus unable to invest heavily in web soaps, it followed that their early attempts at them were tentative and exploratory. Unlike television dramas, web soaps would generally remain low-budget productions until after 2014, when they became a more accepted cultural form, and video companies could more aggressively invest in them. Based on Hua's calculations, the production costs for early web soaps amounted to only about 10 to 20 percent of those for television dramas. LeTV's hit online series *Good Man from the Tang Dynasty* (*Tangchao hao nanren*) should have been set in the Tang dynasty, but, because of a limited budget, it was set in the less opulent Qing dynasty instead.[16] Mindful of their budgetary constraints, video companies drew upon internet culture and consciously made their web soap productions different from televised dramas and other entertainment programs in both form and content. In this way, they turned constraints into advantages, making the web soap a new genre with distinct features.

Whereas television dramas ran from 45 to 60 minutes per episode, web soaps were only 10 to 20 minutes in length. They were intended to be watched in the small pockets of free time in their viewers' everyday lives—on their lunch breaks or during their commutes, for example. The growing popularity of web soaps was both enabled and promoted by improved mobile connectivity and the prevalence of mobile digital devices. Thus web soaps and other online shows filled parts of Chinese social life that television dramas and other products of popular culture failed to reach. Also, in keeping with their intended mobile viewership, web soaps were quirky enough to immediately catch their viewers' attention and light enough not to demand too much from them. Most important, however, web soaps set themselves clearly apart from television dramas both in their aesthetics and in their ideologies. Exploiting a lax regulatory regime as they had in acquiring foreign content, video companies now provided content state television stations were not allowed to broadcast. As Hua put it:

> We are disadvantaged in terms of budget, but we do have one advantage, which is we are not subject to censorship. Thus we can have more elements and longer yardsticks [chidu; i.e., looser guidelines] than television dramas. Basically, what we shoot is what is not allowed in television dramas. ... We must make our productions more interesting and challenging than television dramas to attract audiences.[17]

This comment was echoed by my informant Fan, another producer who worked for television stations before entering the online video industry (and whose observations I will turn to soon).

Video companies exploited all possible forms of content catering to popular needs unsatisfied by the heavily politicized state television. To attract as many viewers as they could, violence, crime, ghost stories, horror, conflict, absurdity, sex, privacy, hedonism, and extravagant lifestyles—or what cultural regulators had called "vulgarity"—were all on view. They also aimed to represent the transformation of social and cultural practices during marketization by portraying sex-related bribery and corruption, extramarital affairs, and "cooperative" marriages.[18] Their treatment of socially and morally challenging topics, mostly not allowed on television, attracted a multitude of viewers online. And, to that end, their productions also capitalized on social discontent at the abuse of power, at fraud, corruption, collusion between businessmen and officials, at hypocrisy, and even (somewhat ironically) at excessive commercialism. The liberal values such productions touted or at least hinted at were well received among young college-educated urbanites.

Web soaps and online shows carried the imprint of online parody culture into a commercial context. Both demonstrated a liberal perspective and a disapproval of state-supported values. Early internet culture was certainly far from static. Video spoofing, for example, was shaped by forces of popular participation and commerce right alongside video companies' transformation (as I will discuss later). And the connection between commercial video culture and early internet culture was no accident: video companies had been emulating the ethos of video spoofing since the online ads went viral and had attempted to incorporate popular spoofsters and their works in their production of original content. The annual Tudou Video Festival, started by the company in 2008, served as a way for the company to discover talented new creators of user-generated content, whom Tudou then provided with multifaceted support in education, finance, technology, marketing, and distribution so that it might eventually capitalize on their labor and creativity.[19] That connection was further strengthened as video companies began to invest in adaptation rights to popular internet novels. According to Hua, the established fan base of online novels meant that web soaps adapted from them could attract more viewers and thus become less dependent on sponsors and product placements, with a greater potential for monetization. Before 2014, LeTV acquired adaptation rights to around twenty-four popular online novels each year; adaptations of online novels accounted for some 70 to 80 percent of LeTV's content reservoir. Full-fledged literary portals like qidian.com (*qidian zhongwen wang*) and jjwxc.net (*jinjiang wenxue cheng*) were all, according to Hua, "huge resource centers" that LeTV exploited.[20]

Along with watching online videos and listening to music online, reading online novels was a major form of online cultural consumption for Chinese internet users.[21] As a technologically less sophisticated form of internet culture, writing and publishing online novels became popular when online forums and literary portals emerged (and before blogs and online video websites did) to fulfill social needs for cultural expression in the late 1990s. Like user-generated content in the domain of online video, over the years, internet literature has become an institution in its own right, leading to a fairly exclusive commercial model in online literary production.[22] Shanda Literature, a subsidiary of the online game giant Shanda, has consolidated major literary portals in China and managed popular works for publishing and associated business activities such as rights sales and online game adaptations.

The burgeoning internet literature sector serves as an alternative to the traditional, state-regulated publishing system. According to the CEO of Shanda Literature, Xiaoqiang Hou, Shanda's subsidiaries were subjected to far fewer interventions from censors than traditional publishing houses were.[23] This relatively unmonitored environment, as Chinese literature professor Michel Hockx suggests, has created considerable space for a wide variety of literary genres, such as fantasy, urban, and romance, whose works were frequently transgressive and politically edgy.[24] Among the most prominent examples were Murong Xuecun's novels, which told tales of official corruption. When video companies reached out to adapt and exploit these novels, they brought them to even wider audiences in the form of online video productions.

The potential of online video in organizing alternative cultural production was soon noticed and recognized by professionals in the entertainment and cultural industries of greater China. Media personalities, celebrities, former television producers/hosts who had resigned to gain more personal and artistic freedom in the pluralist liberal cultural environment, and even incumbent television producers/hosts came to work for video companies on a project-by-project basis. This gave rise to an ad hoc, fluid network of cultural production that enlisted resources, labor, and knowledge unappreciated by the state sector. Fan told me of a well-known Chinese Central Television host she invited to manage one of her video company's daily news talk shows on a part-time basis. As Fan recalled, "he always came into the studio saying that he was unable to address a topic to the full on television and wanted to finish it here."[25] Online video had clearly become an alternative to television for industry professionals from television. Those straddling the two spheres of television and online video worked with a sense of being in a dual reality, switching between two sets of discourses and practices.

The Commercial Life of User-Generated Content

Starting around 2008, video companies, especially video-sharing websites, began to acknowledge the unprofitability of user-generated content and to downplay the importance of such content, which had fueled the earlier development of the industry. Although video-sharing websites like Youku and Tudou were still open to users uploading content, user-generated content was no longer their strategic focus. This shift in corporate strategy, however, still did not bring an end to users' practices. Over the years, early online video makers, especially spoofsters who remained in the field, constantly adapted to changes in the ever-shifting online landscape, and newer enthusiasts kept joining them. Today, prominent user-generated content providers have become producers of what the industry calls "professionally generated content," constituting another pillar of video companies' content provision. Although some scholars have discussed the commercialization and professionalization of amateur content production, both in China and in the West, given its sparse treatment in the literature overall, the subject merits further investigation.[26]

User-generated content's commercial turn in China probably began even earlier than the video companies' strategic transformation and took various forms. As soon as Hu Ge built up his reputation through the hit "Steamed Bun" spoof, advertisers sponsored and placed products in his subsequent productions (2006–2008), and they also hired him to produce viral video ads for their products. He shot his first viral video ad for the e-commerce company Alibaba in 2009 and, since then, has produced viral ads for various other companies, mainly to make a living, though he also enjoys the job and considers it a means to realize his dream of eventually making films.[27] Spoofsters like Hu He were also sought by various intermediaries as informal labor for outsourced projects. These economic opportunities became the impetus for them to carry on with their creations, believing that sensational or at least good spoofs would bring them fame and eventually be monetized in some way or other. In the course of pursuing these opportunities, however, video makers' genuine aspirations to create became mixed with economic interests and other pragmatic considerations.

My informant Siwen came from the agricultural province of Henan in northern China.[28] His immersion in internet culture began with a year spent writing online novels during college. After graduating in 2008, he went to work for a Chinese electronic home appliance manufacturing company in Guangdong Province in southern China for a period of time. With a lingering aspiration to write, Siwen quit his job and went to work for a few writing-related companies and then for a private film/television production company in Zhengzhou, the capital city of his home province, before he quit working for others altogether. During this period, he became attracted to the vernacular video culture online and participated in it in his spare time, first as a songwriter for music video spoofs.

One of Siwen's early music videos, "My Dad Is Li Gang," satirized the notorious "Li Gang" incident, which occurred in the city of Baoding in Hebei Province in 2010. After causing a fatal accident, a drunk driver attempted to speed away from the scene. But when stopped by security guards, he warned them off by shouting, "My dad is Li Gang!"—the deputy director of the Baoding Public Security Bureau. The catchphrase "My dad is Li Gang" quickly became popular on the internet, especially among those satirizing the corrupt and manipulative privileged classes in China. Siwen produced his music video when the "My dad is Li Gang" meme was ascendant. Appropriating the melody of a popular song, "I am Xiao Shenyang," Siwen replaced the original lyrics with his own, which his collaborator then edited and sang on the video. Siwen recalled that his production was motivated by the extreme anger he and many others felt, as reflected in a comment he left in an online forum in 2010:

> Yesterday, I read the news about a second-generation government official running over people and causing one death. I was very angry. ... He did not care about the girls he crashed into but blamed them for damaging his car. I am so angry. A living being is nothing compared to his vehicle. The indifference of this second-generation official is inhumane. What's more, after he crashed into the two girls, he continued to drive to the dormitory to pick up his girlfriend without any sense of guilt. When he was stopped by the school security, the moron yelled out, "My father is Li Gang!"[29]

Today, it is difficult to know whether that first production was motivated by Siwen's "extreme anger" or by a desire to leverage this incident for overnight fame online. In any case, economic and pragmatic considerations soon loomed large as the hit "Li Gang" music spoof's immediate popularity attracted small advertisers, who approached Siwen's collaborator about product placements and future viral video productions. Although the song was written by Siwen, the public seemed to be more impressed by his collaborator, the singer. These placements brought the collaborator an income of several thousand yuan, but, as the contractor, he paid Siwen only a tiny fee for his labor. This unequal distribution of fame and money made Siwen grumble—and then act.

He taught himself basic video editing skills using a textbook on Adobe Premiere Pro and went on to produce numerous spoofs, most of them without sponsors, either by himself or collaborating with others on various social and cultural topics. His enthusiasm during that period was presumably sustained by creative aspirations and a deferred fantasy of fame.[30] At the time, smaller companies like Ku6 would pay ¥300 apiece (about $38) for spoofs they released exclusively, but Siwen preferred to publish his works on more influential websites for free, seeking, in his words, "accumulation of fame," which he knew had value.

In late 2012, working solo, Siwen took some twenty days to complete a parody video called "2012 Micro Spring Festival Gala" (2012 Wei chunwan). Satirizing the annual variety show produced by Chinese Central Television in celebration of the Chinese New Year, the spoof became a hit online and established his fame. Not long after that, he quit his job in the production company and began to live entirely on the proceeds of his spoofs. He came up with a new, modern, and more professional way of organizing production, including the expansion of his team, division of labor, and serialization. The series *Tianjin Girl Joking Around* (*Tianjin niu'er tucao xilie*) and *Dongbei Girl Joking Around* (*Dongbei niu'er tucao xilie*) were both signature productions, sustained mainly by product placements.

Although producers of professionally generated content have now reached an agreement with video companies on product placements, video companies had earlier disapproved of these because they thought the placements might taint their user-generated content or negatively affect the monetization of their own content through preroll ads, for example. In response to video companies' objections, Siwen turned to a softer form of placement—the placement of cultural products, promoting new film releases and upcoming reality shows produced by a wide range of cultural institutions, including even Chinese Central Television. Ironically, the way Siwen promoted these shows was to incorporate them into a satirical narrative of the ad-supported cultural industry and its superficial outcomes, of which his own works were a part. From the "Spring Festival" spoof to his recent *Joking Around* series, Siwen's spoofs still retained at least some of the ethos of his earlier works when we spoke in July 2014, despite his increasingly commercial orientation. But the once-antiestablishment stance that had helped make his reputation as online spoofster had become a largely empty rhetorical legacy, to be exploited in pursuit of economic interests.

Sometimes, that legacy appeared to be a burden to Siwen because he had to constantly maintain the vernacular image expected by his fans, especially his long-time followers, in ways that constrained the economic value of his productions, by limiting his use of product placements, for example. In addition to the spoof series, he also had contracts for corporate identity video production, wedding videography, and other video-related businesses. Seizing opportunities opened up by the commercialization of online video in China, Siwen had successfully transformed himself from an amateur spoofster into a professional content producer through the development of professional skills and entrepreneurial initiatives.

But, unlike Siwen, who started as an amateur, my informant Tong, the founder of the professionally generated content brand UFO Talk (Feidie shuo), entered online video as a PGC entrepreneur from the start, aiming to exploit the huge potential at the intersection of culture, video technology, and entrepreneurship.[31] Born into an intellectual family in the traditionally affluent province of Jiangsu in eastern China, Tong completed his bachelor's degree in digital arts and design in 2006. His first job was in a state-owned animation film studio in Shanghai. After working there and in a few other private animation production companies, around 2010, Tong moved to a private education service provider, where he was responsible for its online product development, and where he conceived of an ambitious online video encyclopedia based on *South Park*–style two-dimensional (2D) graphics.

Whereas Siwen was ambivalent about his UGC past, Tong was frank in admitting that the creation of his show *UFO Talk* was guided by a specific business plan from the outset. Indeed, holding to a tenet of absolute professionalism, he refused to be associated with user-generated content in any way. As a professional trained from the start for the cultural and creative economy, he knew how to "manage" culture like a product. According to Tong, an audience was created by the regular provision of serialized and standardized content. An online show had to be operated like a brand, and when the parent brand matured, it should be followed by affiliated brands and other derivatives. UFO Talk as a brand worked exactly according to these rules. Even in the educational context, the plan for Tong's video encyclopedia was an evaluative decision along market-based principles. As an encyclopedia, the show could accommodate all kinds of product placements. Overall, Tong represented a more cultivated model of entrepreneurship than Siwen did. Whereas Siwen's business engagements were rudimentary, rough, and grassroots oriented, Tong's were more sophisticated, refined, and gentrified. In line with sociologist Pierre Bourdieu's theories, this difference may be attributed to their different class positions, which determined the extent to which they possessed cultural as well as financial capital and thus also their respective capabilities of navigating the cultural economy.

With Tong's well-thought-out plan, his shrewdness, and his resourcefulness, the success of the *UFO Talk* show came easily. After one year of development, in late 2012, Tong and his business partner began to roll out weekly short videos on Youku. By the third week, their productions had reached a daily webpage viewership of one million, and Youku had recommended the show on its homepage. In early 2013, the first product placement in *UFO Talk* went for the price of ¥30,000 (about $3,750), and they began to recruit people, standardize their processes, and scale up production. By July 2014, the price for a product placement in the show had reportedly reached ¥300,000 (about $37,500).

Tong's rule of thumb for content production was what he called "extraordinarily interesting stuff," which specifically included parodic and "anticommonsense" elements. He wanted to promote an attitude that challenged the mainstream but was based on facts and objectivity, as evidenced in the company motto—"Questioning is also a form of concern; science popularization is also a form of power." Certainly, Tong admitted, sensational topics like sex would always sell and was often promoted by his and other Chinese video companies to attract viewers, even though, in unintended irony, sexually suggestive content was flagged, separately categorized, and sometimes even removed by YouTube from its website.[32]

In general, Tong's content was characterized by an affinity with early video-spoofing culture. Although he himself was never a spoofster, he had engaged in online writing of film reviews, novels, and other pieces over a long period in various forums and Web 2.0 websites, both of which were part of the internet culture strongly shaped by piracy. Indeed, Tong attributed much of his creativity, now and then, to his early consumption of pirated content, which had also inspired the first spoofsters such as Hu Ge. Tong's high school years were filled with countless hours of watching pirated Hong Kong and Western films from VCD and DVD rental shops. As he enthusiastically recalled, "I spent a lot of time watching those films ...

including those very old and lousy productions that you could hardly name today."[33] He considered his preinternet exposure to piracy a main source of creativity for him and his business partner: "We shared the same love of films as teenagers. ... When we chatted and talked about creativity, many of our inspirations came from what we watched at the time."[34] To maintain the ethos of his content, which echoed early spoofing culture, Tong wanted to hire people with similar experiences to his own, specifically, people who had a deep engagement with online culture through forums and other Web 2.0 websites, people with what Tong called "internet sense" (*wanggan*). Tong's story further supports a central argument of this book: that a global informal cultural economy—above all, piracy—produced long-lasting though dispersed social energies in China that eventually converged to give rise to a distinct online video culture.

Like video companies' in-house projects, which brought together cultural professionals outside of the state sector, emerging professionally generated content companies like UFO Talk (named after its core brand) also led to a network made up of more widely and remotely dispersed members of the middle and lower classes of Chinese society, people it would have been difficult for state cultural institutions and larger companies to approach and mobilize otherwise. For example, UFO Talk's employees included former hotel receptionists and Foxconn workers who had published online. Their presence in UFO Talk brought working-class sensibilities into a nascent bourgeois-oriented cultural enterprise, with the possibility of reaching a cross-class consensus with their bourgeois colleagues on certain political and social issues, even as those sensibilities diverged and were repressed in other ways. Alternatively, working-class employees might be co-opted by their environment and come to identify themselves as members of the middle class. Either way, professionally generated content companies such as UFO Talk, which itself benefited from opportunities opened up by commercializing online video companies, now created spaces for young aspirants from the lower classes.

The stories of Siwen and Tong show two different paths to professionally generated content, one transforming from user-generated content provider and the other beginning as a "native" professionally generated content startup. Both men relied on video companies, mainly those with a history in video sharing such as Youku, to get started. Professionally generated content companies developed at a time when online video companies were busy with their own content production strategies. Since 2011, the copyright war had dragged video companies into an environment of homogeneous competition, which led them to burn through their cash reserves. As that happened, these companies came to realize the importance of user content—or, in the new context, professionally generated content—in setting them apart from competitors and in best displaying their unique charms to users.[35] Despite becoming a mostly empty signifier in the changing context, however, user-generated content continued to have a presence in industry discourse. Meanwhile, like their Western counterparts, online video companies continued to call themselves "platforms" (*pingtai*), a term internet companies strategically use to position themselves and suggest their "open, neutral, egalitarian, and progressive support" for online activities, even though, in reality, these companies have become less open and more selective, both in China and in the West.[36] Certainly, what used to be called "user-generated content" and "amateurs" were also changing in nature. Both Siwen and Tong called video companies "platforms" in our conversations, but, by "platforms," they meant distribution outlets. Indeed, the ways they used the term did not seem to suggest any of the nuances video companies intended to convey in their discourse, such as the suggestion of being open, supportive, and progressive in their attempts to attract third-party developers. But these developers had a rather pragmatic attitude toward the video companies, and professionally generated content assumed increasing importance. Indeed, the term "professionally generated content" epitomized the commercial transformation of early video makers, gave them a more definitive identity label in the new context and, most important, suggested a new relationship between them and video companies.

As online video companies began to renew their user-oriented strategy, those with a user-generated content history such as Youku surveyed their vast user uploads, selected premium content, and recommended it on their homepages. Others, without such advantages, surveyed websites like Youku's for reputable producers of professionally generated content and attempted to attract them to their own websites.[37] In early 2012, iQiyi created a space for professional production companies and individuals in the guise of "user-generated content," although "professionally generated content" would have been more accurate.[38] Like iQiyi, Tencent Video opened a "V+" page to attract what it called "high-end user-generated content providers," which in the new context, presumably meant professionally generated content producers.[39] In addition, policies such as advertising revenue sharing were developed to retain existing content providers and attract new ones.[40] The advertising revenue-sharing mechanism, however, was considered by professionally generated content providers to be an empty gesture because the income was insignificant compared to what they earned from product placements.[41] In 2013, Youku's Photosynthesis Initiative (Guanghe jihua) pioneered a more sophisticated effort in fostering professionally generated content. The company invested in and supported its PGC partners in sponsorship solicitation, publicity, brand building, and so on, provided that they chose Youku as the exclusive online platform on which to publish their work and agreed to divide their revenues from product placements with Youku.[42] At this time, video companies became patrons for professionally generated content producers, but advertisers had beaten them to it by a considerable amount of time. To video companies, supporting professionally generated content was a cost-effective strategy. By opening up their platforms, they could benefit from an increase in traffic and potentially also in advertising revenues generated by the extra, almost-free content provided by PGC producers. Beyond that, they could benefit through incubation projects such as the Photosynthesis Initiative.

Today, a growing professional production community has formed around online video companies, innovating various online video forms including short video spoofs, online talk shows, and web soaps. As a loosely coupled system of creatives, many professionally generated content producers across the country have become connected to one another through a QQ group maintained by content/page editors from video companies and other voluntarily formed social networking site groups, and more were joining every day.[43] Video companies communicated their preferences to PGC producers in these groups, thereby influencing their decisions about "content, availability, organization, and participation."[44] In the QQ group, for instance, Youku's editor would suggest topics to PGC producers, encouraging certain productions by promising to promote them on its homepage.[45]

The young artists who aspired to fame and fortune were mobilized by the creative possibilities, autonomy, and economic opportunities promised by new technology and by the corporations that stood behind it. Looking back, Siwen thought he was born in the right generation, which allowed him to benefit from the development of online video and, in his words, to have "both fame and economic gains" (mingli shuangshou). Tong was likewise filled with a naive optimism when we spoke in July 2014. Indeed, both men were among the fortunate few of the many content entrepreneurs who struggled to be noticed. What they would soon face, however, was a precarious, increasingly competitive and exploitative environment in which only the top creators would succeed. When I met Tong again in 2016, anxiety and uncertainty about his company's future hung over our conversation. In recent times, the term "multichannel network" (MCN), coined by YouTube to refer to companies that aggregated and managed YouTube channels, has been introduced into China to describe any group of small individual creators/channels that merge to survive the harsh commercial environment collectively. It is unclear at this point whether this new strategy will succeed. From UGC to MCN, individual creators' circumstances have been constantly changing, and whether or not they have benefited personally, they have been effectively employed to contribute to the profit-maximizing goals of video companies.

"No One Really Did the Censorship."[46]

Web soaps and other online shows, like online video companies' acquired content, had been developed under industry self-censorship, a general regulatory approach formally introduced by the SARFT in 2007, and one that subjected online video to much less state regulation than television. After a year's survey and research into the industry, in July 2012, the SARFT announced its Notice on Further Strengthening the Regulation of Web Soaps, Micro Movies, and Other Online Audiovisual Programs, which put in place a regulatory framework for formalized self-censorship by the makers of web soaps and similar productions.[47] Likely a response to earlier, ineffective and poorly performed self-censorship by the industry, the notice was jointly issued with the State Internet Information Office, an agency created in 2011 to direct and coordinate internet governance. Daring content like LeTV's web soap Once Upon a Time in Dongbei (Dongbei wangshi) in early 2012 had irritated regulators,[48] and voices in the industry, speculating about the SARFT's possible responses, had proposed possible self-regulatory methods to head off such responses. Pro-industry parties, arguing for modest regulation of online content as long as it did not cross the party-state's ideological "bottom line" (*dixian*), called for an age-based content rating system, like the one long used in the West and long expected in China.[49]

Unlike the proposed rating system, however, the SARFT's new self-censorship framework centered on training censors from video companies and required postproduction registration of their programs (*bei'an*). To implement its framework, the agency authorized and instructed the China Netcasting Services Association (Zhongguo wangluo shiting jiemu fuwu xiehui), a social organization mediating between regulators and the industry, to conduct training workshops, first organized in the summer of 2012 and since held twice a year. The workshops required that each video company send two to three staff members holding content-related positions. My informant Fan attended one such workshop, held at the training center of Chinese Central Television and lasting one week. "It was at CCTV," she said with a smile, "so you can roughly imagine the general background."[50] The workshop consisted of lectures given by SARFT officials, the agency's internal researchers, and professors of Marxism and Leninism from the People's University of China—known unofficially as the "Second Party School" in China (after the Central Party School) for its prestigious programs on Marxism-Leninism—as well as by senior video company managers. The lecturers, Fan recalled, instructed participants on what was allowed and, more important, what was *not* allowed online by giving attendees examples of content that endangered national interests or that harmed minors, for instance. Whereas regulation of television dramas was intended to ensure the promotion of certain values, self-regulation of online video was intended to ensure that its content did not challenge or cross the party-state's ideological bottom line. After attending all the lectures, trainees had to pass an exam, after which they were considered qualified censors.

And only qualified censors could operate the postproduction program registration system, specially designed by the SARFT for web soaps and other online shows. The system required online programs such as web soaps, micro movies, and documentaries to be screened by three censors after they were produced and to be registered before going online. To register a program, the censors logged into the system and provided basic information such as the program's title and length, a synopsis of its content, and sample screen shots. After filling in the online form, the censors printed it out and all three signed it. After the signed form was scanned and uploaded into the system as an attachment, the system generated a specific registration number, which had to be included in the program's credit titles.[51] Thus, unlike the preventive censorship and permitting regime established for television dramas, what was now in place for web soaps was a formalized industry self-censorship regime.

The now-formalized self-censorship nevertheless remained a more permissive form of censorship than the one the SARFT imposed on television because, as well designed as the system was, the uncertainties associated with each of its links made failure outside the purview of the SARFT a likely outcome. Indeed, anticipating such failures, video companies welcomed the new regulatory regime when it was announced.[52] However, an opinion article in the *Worker's Daily* expressed its disappointment with the so-called new method, which the article said was nothing new and predictably unreliable, and urged adoption of an external mechanism.[53] Grounds for both welcome and disappointment would soon become clear in what was taking place on the ground. For example, although all three censors were supposed to watch each video from beginning to end, "No one really did the censorship," Fan recalled. "We did not strictly apply those rules to censor stuff. We only did the gatekeeping as a matter of form."[54] The perfunctory screening was, in her words, "just a stage show" (*zou guochang*). And, according to my informant Tao, the government public relations person at Sohu Video, the new regulatory regime, though intended to track who was responsible for what, was also hindered by frequent job-hopping in the volatile internet economy.[55] Although likely aware of such regulatory failures, the SARFT was also likely willing to grant more latitude to online video.

We should also consider the possibility that the SARFT's lax regulation of online content might at least in part result from its inability to exert control, though, even if that were the case, the logic of cultural zoning would still hold. As I pointed out at the beginning of this book, cultural zoning can be an active choice (lack of will) or one compelled by special circumstances (lack of capability), or it can result from both lack of will and lack of capability, for the two are not mutually exclusive. A policy choice in a system as complex as China's internet governance is rarely driven by a single factor, though some factors certainly count more than others. Now that we have discussed the SARFT's regulation of online video as an active choice, we need to look at the special circumstances that influenced its regulation and consider it within the context of cultural zoning.

In 2013, major video companies produced fewer than 1,000 episodes of web soaps, compared to some 15,000 episodes of television dramas produced in the same year. In this context, it does not seem a daunting task for the SARFT to replicate its regulatory approach to television in the online environment, although there are certainly other types of professionally generated online content besides web soaps that would quickly add to the political costs if the SARFT were to decide to regulate online video in the same way it has television. But we should also note that online video today has moved away from its early user orientation. An increasing reliance on professional content and a trend toward increasing monopolization in the industry have together worked to limit the quantity of online content, instead of allowing it to grow unchecked. Presumably, this would also have a moderating effect on regulatory costs, though it would be difficult to prove such an effect. Indeed, it is hard to speculate about the capability of the Chinese state in general. This is clearly one of those matters where facts are elusive and we must rely on inferences to make our best judgment. And, in any event, speculation would be of little use given that the Chinese state has shown it will muster all possible resources to achieve any goal that arises from a serious concern. Numerous historical examples attest to this, as does what happened after 2014, when the state decided to impose harsher constraints on the internet. Indeed, my point is that lax regulation of content in the case of online video was ultimately a matter of lack of will.

This can be readily observed in the SARFT's regulatory behavior in another instance. It is worth noting once more that one of the more interesting features of the industry self-censorship regime designed by the agency for online video has been post hoc, punitive censorship implemented by the regime's designer. As I have described in chapter 4, the SARFT put in place an audiovisual program monitoring system in 2006, through which it reviewed online video content and decided when and to what extent to intervene. If the power to censor content delegated to video companies was mainly compelled by the SARFT's inability to manage such content, then the industry should expect harsh and comprehensive post hoc censorship. At least, as my SARFT informant Lin said of web soaps, "it is very easy for us to close them down."[56] If this was not simply saber-rattling rhetoric, and most likely it was not, then it had to be taken seriously. Short of closing a series down, there were other punishment mechanisms such as warnings, fines, and the revocation of licenses clearly stated in the SARFT's policy documents. But, judging by what industry professionals actually experienced on the ground—at least before 2014—post hoc censorship was not actively attempted.

When the subject of the SARFT's attitude toward web soaps came up with Fan, she laughed and said: "By its standards, all the content online is disqualified. ... But, actually, we are still fine after showing all those."[57] The implied laxity with which the agency enforced its policy was likely an exaggeration. Video companies would not be able to show anything they liked and remain safe. A less regulated internet, as I have emphasized earlier, does not mean a free-for-all. Indeed, video companies still invested in self-censorship, in both labor and technology, and the SARFT was still watching what the companies showed online. But it appears that the established censorship regime mainly targeted those who clearly crossed the ideological bottom line, and a vast amount of ambiguous ideological content between what was shown on television and that bottom line was allowed. Indeed, anyone who closely followed internet culture in China at the time would have seen a wide range of online content that could be considered daring. If the general public could see such content, it is likely that the SARFT was also aware of it and, most likely, let it pass. As Lin explained, to my surprise, content produced using a longer ideological yardstick (*chidu da*) does not necessarily mean it is unacceptable. What she and her SARFT colleagues considered unacceptable was anything that was morally decadent, pornographic, or concerned with gambling and drug abuse, collectively known as *huangdudu* in China, and certainly also anything politically sensitive. She bragged about the effectiveness of the SARFT's online regulation compared to regulation by other ministries or agencies, pointing out, for example, that a massive amount of pornography and violence found in animation, online games, and internet publishing had escaped the attention of the Ministry of Culture and the General Administration of Press and Publication, despite their shared responsibility for censoring such content.[58] Again, if this was not simply public relations rhetoric, then the SARFT seemed perfectly content with a cultural duality in which one sphere of popular culture was more tightly controlled and the other sphere given the latitude to experiment.

In fact, from the SARFT's point of view, in a market-led environment, self-censorship by the online video industry followed by post hoc intervention as needed seemed the best option to at once encourage innovation in the industry, get rid of unacceptable content, and minimize the political cost of doing so. Indeed, the SARFT boasted about this option in its 2013 yearbook, describing it as a "creative approach" (*chuangxin silu*) to content regulation and showing more of a sense of pride than of helplessness in having no policy alternatives.[59] It is also a flexible arrangement because part of its regulatory regime, post hoc censorship, allows the SARFT room to tighten regulation when necessary by increasing the frequency and intensity of state interventions; this will almost certainly produce stronger self-censorship in the online video industry as professionals become aware that if they do not restrict content themselves, it will be restricted by external censors, most likely in ways far less to their liking. This flexible arrangement, like the variable interest entity structure in financial regulation, reflects a guerrilla approach to policy that freely allows for policy revision, improvisation, and adjustment.

In an industry marked by lax regulation of content, the presence of state regulators was only weakly felt among producers, and industry practices were much less informed by the logic of politics than were those of television. In Hua's words, "We don't have contacts with the SARFT. We create the scripts by ourselves, shoot them by ourselves, and air them on our own platforms."[60] In this context, online production was more freewheeling than television production, where ideological correctness was first and foremost. In contrast, professionals in the online video industry did not give such considerations much thought—and even seemed to stand in opposition to the notion that state politics should be embodied in video content. More than one professional told me that television was "the other" for online video, which aspired to produce what was not allowed on television. As Fan put it,

> Internet is always a supplement to ... television. ... When you develop a program, you rarely think about these [political things]. You only think about if it is interesting [*haokan*]. ... When we brainstorm for topics, we always ask what is not allowed on television. ... We want to fill in all the blanks, in terms of both subjects and forms. All the content that the SARFT does not allow television stations to broadcast becomes online video programs.[61]

The news talk shows Fan produced aimed to reach the angry young generation (*fenqing*), college students and other young people from the lower middle classes who are in uneasy circumstances and discontented with society, and who have their own distinct attitudes and opinions. She also directed documentaries that addressed political and historical topics, and which were another attempt to challenge the ideological bottom line. She and her colleagues were often prepared to be warned before they put a program online. To Fan, online video in China, though not as free as media in liberal democracies, was undoubtedly freer than television. As a former television producer, she knew well from personal experience that television and online video were subject to distinctly different regulatory regimes, and she was aware of the implications of this difference to production:

> I could not do talk shows for television as I have done for online video. ... I would first check what the Xinhua News Agency has to say on a topic. I censored what otherwise could not be broadcast. ... When I began the talk show, I initially copied the set of standards from television stations and I thought those scripts [written by her colleagues] must be problematic. But they told me it was the internet and it would be fine. After several times, you just learned the rules.[62]

Fan only avoided content and topics that were particularly sensitive politically or morally, which she knew might easily provoke regulators, and also any daring content at particularly sensitive times of the year, such as June 4 (the anniversary of the Tiananmen Square protests) and the period in March when the National People's Congress and the Chinese People's Political Consultative Conference (collectively known as *lianghui* in China) held their annual meetings in Beijing. Those were times when no exceptions were permitted in the media, when online video as a zone of exception ceased to exist—and when Fan replaced daring content with more anodyne fare.

There were certainly occasions when the SARFT intervened, and the politically edgy documentary series Fan directed experienced such interventions more often than other entertainment-oriented programs did. Depending on the situation, the identified episode would either be entirely removed or hidden from public view until the political attention it aroused died away. In the most severe case, her series was on the verge of being canceled altogether because an episode had "improperly" depicted a former Communist leader. Generally, however, the SARFT's interventions did not have a consistent chilling effect either on the industry's own productions or on those they acquired abroad, such as the movies they bought from Hollywood. According to Hao, LeTV's senior managers were sometimes "invited to drink tea" (summoned to meet) with state regulators, but those meetings did not constrain video companies as much as might have been expected. "Things remained the same after they came back," Hao told me. "After a few times, [the meetings] became wearisome for both sides."[63] This points to the ineffectiveness of post hoc censorship, which, occurring sporadically, did not generate lasting effects among industry professionals. In addition, the SARFT may have lacked a strong enough will to intervene effectively.

The producers of professionally generated content were subject to similar regulation. Like online video companies, they felt the presence of state regulators only weakly, and as a production community external to those companies, their connection with the state was remote. The social networking site groups that video companies used to connect with the PGC community were also the main communication means they used to deliver political messages to their outlying content providers. For instance, during both the North Korean nuclear crisis and the Bo Xilai scandal in 2013, PGC producers received notices from video companies' editors discouraging them from making productions on these topics.[64] Producers such as Tong quickly came to realize that the degree of autonomy he and his colleagues enjoyed in cultural production was much higher than they had imagined it would be. As Tong put it, "It is not that open, but also not as closed as we would have thought."[65] In this context, Tong said he would address sensitive, controversial topics because there was a demand from users for him to do so.

For instance, during the Ya'an earthquake in 2013, UFO Talk produced an episode titled "What Does the China Earthquake Administration Do?" which compared China's policies on earthquakes with those of Japan and the United States and questioned the administration for underspending on earthquake prediction and disaster relief and overspending on bureaucratic functioning.[66] In common with UFO Talk's other productions, the earthquake episode cited statistics, considered scientific evidence, and touted Western experience, thought to exemplify modernity and rationality.

In addition to the earthquake administration, UFO Talk also targeted the State General Administration of Sports, the SARFT, and other state agencies. The key to those challenging attempts, according to Tong, was to "grasp the yardstick" (*bawo chidu*). Like Fan, Tong avoided topics that would challenge the core interests of the Communist Party. As he confidently recalled, among the several hundreds of episodes the company had produced, there were only two that were kept from the public: one on North Korea's nuclear test and the other on sex.

Conclusion

In this chapter, we have seen how online video companies, exploiting a lax regulatory regime, developed and organized a distinct, alternative, yet commercial online video culture that incorporated many elements of early internet culture, including video spoofing and online writing. This alternative video culture was most evident in the content it produced and the ideologies and industry practices that sustained the production of that content. Always regarding television as "the other," online video became a new, clear component of popular cultural life in contemporary China and a promising discursive sphere that was otherwise unavailable.

But commercial online video culture has its own ideological contradictions: the logic of capital cannot genuinely appreciate the internet culture that it exploits. Commercial interests, which endorsed and capitalized on the ethos of early spoofing culture, may well abandon it when it is no longer needed to retain an audience. The maintenance and expansion of capitalist logic, Nicholas Garnham tells us, may not require any dominant ideology. Rather, commercial media and cultural enterprises will produce anything that can make a profit, including mocking themselves or the capitalist logic of which they are a part.[67] Youku's hit web soap *Absolutely Unexpected* (*Wanwan meixiangdao*), which features the unlucky tale of a young man with a wooden face but a rich interior life, contained such a paradox.

In one episode, the protagonist joins a group of gangs to extort money—"a protection fee"—from a film crew shooting in a local abandoned warehouse. Absurdly, members from different gangs have to line up and apply to collect the fee from the crew, and a staff member from the crew interviews them, situating the extortion within the context of venture capitalism. Mocking the excesses of capitalist logic, of which the company itself was a product, he asks: "Have you brought a business proposal? ... We need a business proposal from you concerning how your gang is going to protect us; PowerPoint would also work. ... If you have nothing, why should we give you the protection fee? ... Why should I give the fee to you instead of others? ... The industry nowadays is so competitive. You should think about what your selling point is, what special advantages do you have."[68] Moreover, later, when the protagonist decides to seize the film director as a hostage, the film producer casually says: "All right, let's use another director," satirizing the standardization of commercial cultural productions, with all their interchangeable elements, and again the web soap itself as just such a production. Clearly, online productions as such were not sustained by any fixed ideology. Ultimately, the only unchanging ideology was to attract viewers and make profits—the logic of capitalism. Understanding the economic base of online video companies' content helps us to recognize the limits of their representational politics—and to avoid naively romanticizing their radical potential.

8   Epilogue: The Operation of a Dual Cultural Sphere ... And?

After interviewing many industry professionals in television and online video, on a week in July 2014, I sat at home watching television on the set in front of me. At the same time, I turned on my computer and intermittently visited online video websites. In my week of observing these two spheres of Chinese popular culture, I attempted to experience and compare television and online video's cultural productions. I was, of course, not able to watch all the television programs on all the channels, given their conflicting schedules, nor was I able to watch all the available online shows, given their sheer number. But this small sociocultural experiment was not intended to capture every detail of the two cultural spheres. Rather, it was designed to reconstruct the cultural experience an ordinary Chinese viewer might have in the course of a normal day.

Still, to conduct the experiment in as systematic a way as possible, I selected three provincial satellite television channels to represent the national television market: Zhejiang Satellite TV from the first tier, Sichuan Satellite TV from the second tier, and Gansu Satellite TV from the remaining, lower tiers. I downloaded the day-to-day schedule of the three channels for that particular week from the online TV guide tvmao.com, switched from one channel to another to watch various, mainly popular programs such as television series and entertainment shows, from 7:00 a.m. to midnight, and jotted down my impressions, noting any changes to the announced schedule. When I missed programs because of conflicts in their scheduling and could find copies online, I would watch them later. Meanwhile, during news programs, commercials, and between series episodes, I would visit the five major online video websites, browse their content, and pay particular attention to those programs newly appearing online during that week. It was an interesting experiment. The small room I was in became packed with sounds and images from the two different sources, which, in colliding with and running into each other, conjured up the duality of popular culture in contemporary China.

Consistent with the different regulatory and industry practices described in previous chapters, programs from the television and online video spheres diverged in ideologies, aesthetics, and values. There were also divergences within the television sphere among the three television channels. For instance, the more marketized Zhejiang Satellite TV channel incorporated a greater number of market elements than the Gansu Satellite TV channel and was thus closer to and sometimes overlapped with the online sphere. But, in general, the television sphere remained more conducive to political stability and social harmony. The strongest ideological presence running through the programs on all three channels was that of patriotic songs extolling the "Chinese dream," the ideological call of the new leadership under President Xi Jinping. Songs I heard included "The Glory and the Dream" (Guangrong yu mengxiang), produced by the Opera Troupe of the General Political Department of the People's Liberation Army, "March of the Beautiful China" (Meili zhongguo jinxingqu), and "Building a Chinese Dream Together" (Gongzhu zhongguomeng). Interestingly, the Zhejiang TV channel aired songs like these more frequently than either the Gansu TV or the Sichuan TV channel during my week, likely as a way to counterbalance its more overt market orientation.

Like the music series, television dramas aired on the Chinese television channels were ideologically conservative, and, as expected, the less marketized the channel, the more ideology laden the drama. Gansu TV's prime-time television dramas in that week were *My Three Mothers* (*Wo de sange muqin*), a 2010 production, and *The Poor and Rich Life* (*Pinfu rensheng*), a 2009 production. As a channel with few financial resources, Gansu TV was unable to compete with its richer counterparts in acquiring hit dramas and could only air "subrun" series. *My Three Mothers* tells the story of how a child, after being forcibly separated from his mother and successively adopted by two different women, eventually reunites with his biological mother after many years of struggling. In telling of the lives and personal struggles of these three women who are deeply connected to one another through their child, the series praises the greatness of mothers' love and sisterhood. In another family melodrama, *The Poor and Rich Life*, a repentant couple have accumulated considerable personal wealth during the reforms yet failed to maintain their family relationships. Diagnosed with cancer, the wife sells the companies she has built in a desperate attempt to curb her family's obsession with money and uses the little time left her to turn her rebellious son into a promising youth. Both series highlight characters embedded in strong social and moral relationships and promote historically legitimized values such as caring for others. They are meant to persuade the viewing public of the value of familial harmony and social stability and to represent the moral authority of the party-state in the face of the politically problematic challenges of individual self-realization, competition, and social disintegration brought about by a market economy.

Sichuan TV's prime-time show was the urban light romance *Trial Marriage* (*Jiehun qian guize*), which tells how young couples learn to live and manage married life. Although it incorporates numerous popular elements to appeal to young audiences, *Trial Marriage* promotes social and family values no less strongly than the family melodramas just discussed do. Sichuan TV also aired daytime anti-Japanese dramas such as *The Perpetual Electric Wave* (*Yong bu xiaoshi de dianbo*) and *Fake Heroes* (*Maopai yingxiong*), both featuring Communist heroes during the war against Japan. Drama series aired on the more marketized Zhejiang TV channel were less overtly political, although none were politically challenging either, and included a domestic urban romance in prime time and a Korean romantic comedy in the daytime.

Entertainment and reality shows aired on these channels were also politically and morally motivated. Gansu TV's *A Good Man* (*Haoren zai shenbian*) shows the admirable deeds of ordinary people aiming to convey warmth and empathy in society. Sichuan TV's talent show *China Positive Energy* (*Zhongguo zheng nengliang*) features ordinary talented people who have overcome difficulties such as disabilities, not only to survive in life but also, through their positive energies, to inspire the community. The talent shows of the more affluent Zhejiang TV channel were much more professionally made, displaying expert knowledge of television formats, featuring celebrity judges, and having financially strong sponsors. But the channel was careful to tone down its commercial appeal to keep its business pursuits within prescribed political bounds. For instance, Zhejiang TV's premier talent show, *Voice of China* (*Zhongguo hao shengyin*), despite its many market elements in terms of format, set construction, and a celebrity cast, still finds political and moral relevance by relating to the personal struggles and inspirations of each contestant.[1]

Turning from the television sphere as represented by the more-marketized Zhejiang TV channel to the online sphere reveals differences between even their closely related cultural productions. Certainly, the two spheres sometimes overlapped since, as described in chapter 6, online video companies actively acquired prime-time series and entertainment shows aired on top-performing satellite television channels and streamed them on the companies' websites. But, apart from these, video websites streamed large amounts of much racier foreign content, web soaps, and profession-ally generated content that were mostly unavailable on television. Thus, in the week of my experiment, major video websites were streaming popular U.S. television series such as *Perception, Mistresses, Masters of Sex, Agents of S.H.I.E.L.D., Blacklist,* and *2 Broke Girls*, whose premises stood in immediate, direct opposition to the harmonious ideology of the television sphere. For example, the story of an unlikely friendship between a working-class girl and a demoted upper-class girl struggling to launch a business together, *2 Broke Girls* blithely displaces class conflict into the American dream, extol-ling the values of individual initiative, accumulation, and upward social mobility.[2] Although the show may have found a resonance among a rela-tively few urban Chinese striving for entrepreneurial success, it countered the efforts of the Chinese state to promote socialist collectivist ethics in state media programs. And, in another series, *Mistresses*, the depiction of scandals, ambiguity, betrayal, secrets, and deception in relationships and marriages starkly challenged the portrayal of social and moral relationships in Chinese family melodramas.

Video companies' in-house productions exhibited two tendencies, both appearing to be at odds with the party-state's mainstream standards. The first tendency was to show extravagant lifestyles, consumerism, and hedo-nism, pandering to tabloid tastes, in stark conflict with traditional Chi-nese virtues and socialist ethics. The second tendency, coming from online parody culture, was to satirize the establishment and mainstream values. Like *Absolutely Unexpected,* these in-house productions often centered on insignificant people in society, usually males, and portrayed social realities through the bizarre experiences of the protagonists. Taken together, such online content, not available on television, constituted a heterogeneous online sphere, which often stood in direct opposition to television.

This cultural duality, as I have shown throughout *Zoning China*, existed at the pleasure of the Chinese state, which, for the purposes of modernization and development, was willing to allow the greater marketization of online video, making concessions on the ideological as well as the economic front by allowing greater investment of foreign capital in the industry. The party-state's differential treatment of online video and television in relation to market principles represents what I have described as "cultural zoning" in the internet era. In addition to meeting economic imperatives, cultural zoning worked to accommodate different social needs, exposing different populations to different content. Internet culture was something the SARFT itself did not appreciate. Indeed, my SARFT informant Lin had complete contempt for live streaming, an online sector that became popular after 2014. In her view, online video catered to internet users whose tastes were "vulgar," whereas television, as a medium oriented to families, especially children and older family members, was and had to be "clean."[3] It happened that the SARFT, though generally content as long as the irritating and largely transgressive content stayed online, got upset if that same content entered into the living room on television.

The logic embedded in cultural zoning informs many other new developments in China in the reform era, notably, the formation of cultural and creative industry clusters in major cities and the creation of special economic zones (SEZs) nationally. Whether in the economy or culture, on a large or small scale, zoning logic has been invoked in many aspects of Chinese society, with different types of zones depending on place, time, or cultural activities. Yet all these zones are informed by a similar market-oriented logic, which inevitably makes them intersect with one another at time. The recent development of online video, for example, increasingly relies on big internet companies. Thus Tencent Video's backer Tencent established itself in China's earliest special economic zone, Shenzhen. This kind of connection between cultural and economic zones is not simply confined to the national system of regulation, and by no means could it be, given the global nature of capitalism. Domestic zones of exception are often connected to extraterritorial regulatory spaces characterized by reduced levels of regulation.[4] Online video in China, for example, is financially linked to offshore tax havens, as demonstrated in the case of the variable interest entity. Different zones seem able to connect with one another quite easily and in complex ways unknown or little known to outsiders—ways Sarah Nuttall and Achille Mbembe call "secrecy's softwares."[5]

The idea and practice of differentially regulating different media is not unique to China, as I noted at the beginning of this book. For example, legal scholar Lee Bollinger tells us there have been two traditions in the American experience of freedom of the press, a generally libertarian tradition for newspapers and a social responsibility one for the broadcast media (radio and television) involving both licensing and regulation of content.[6] But not all regulatory differences in these countries stem from the same consideration. Public regulation of broadcasting in the United States, Bollinger speculates, is designed to nurture journalistic values in the newer, ethically unformed media of radio and television and eventually absorb them into the First Amendment tradition of newspapers. Zoning in China, however, appears to be a development strategy more in line with the Singaporean experience. The internet in Singapore has historically been treated differently from broadcasting, with a more pragmatic and relaxed approach being applied to foster the country's becoming a media hub.[7] The difference between China and countries like Singapore may be that cultural zoning in China takes place in a less institutionalized policy environment, one more easily subject to changes, whereas cultural zoning in countries like Singapore takes place in a policy environment more likely constrained by a constitutional and legislative framework.

In a dual system, Bollinger suggests that there is a social psychology that recognizes a continuing link back to the original or the norm (in the dual press system he examines, it is print) and accepts a departure only if, after careful scrutiny, it is justified against that original or norm. A similar framework of reference is put in place in the Chinese regulatory experience. For example, people working in the online video industry believe that Chinese television is a living indicator of what lies ahead for online video in terms of regulation, namely, the end of cultural zoning, although nobody can predict when that will occur.

Noticeable changes in state regulation of online video began in 2014, but backstage planning presumably took place much earlier. In March 2013, China completed its ten-year-long leadership transition to President Xi Jinping, considered the country's most powerful leader since Mao, and a hardening management of public discourse ensued. In August 2013, in a speech at the National Propaganda and Ideology Work Conference, Xi called for strengthened regulation of online society to ensure that "the internet is manageable and controllable" and that "cyberspace becomes clear and crisp," adding that "doing this work is not easy, but however difficult it is, it must be done."[8] His remarks reveal the party's determination to strengthen internet governance and its capability to do so, and they came at a time when China was prepared to revisit the reform project and its ramifications. Half a decade has passed since Xi assumed power. Economically, it seems clear that, despite domestic troubles and deteriorating global conditions, notably, the escalating trade war with the United States since 2018, the new leadership is committed to renewing the reform and opening up. It is creating free-trade zones across the country to attract more foreign investments with fewer regulatory encumbrances. It has further liberalized some of the country's restricted industries such as financial services. In what it calls the "new economy," the leadership is committed to transform China's development from an export-led labor-intensive model to a service- and consumption-oriented one. Culturally, however, in contrast to previous decades, when relative economic freedom worked in tandem with partial liberalization in the cultural sphere, the leadership has now decided to revisit its experiment with cultural zoning and, specifically, to reconsider, if not revoke outright, the amount of market autonomy granted to certain media sectors or forms, from capital flows to content.

The variable interest entity (VIE) structure, commonly used by internet companies to attract foreign investments, is now under serious regulatory scrutiny, an intervention that began in early 2015, when the Ministry of Commerce released a draft law on foreign investment for public comment, and which has unfolded since with a series of supplements from relevant regulatory bodies as the legislative process has moved forward. The draft law defines Chinese domestic companies contractually controlled by foreign entities and individuals in a VIE structure as "foreign investments," thus subject to foreign investment restrictions. Since internet content provision such as online publishing and online audiovisual services remained then and have remained since on the list of industry sectors where foreign investments are prohibited, existing VIE structures in these areas could be deemed illegal and banned if the law is enacted. In light of this prospect, companies with VIE structures have immediately set about unwinding the structures, converting back to domestic companies in order to be listed on domestic exchanges or to raise funds from the domestic capital market, which appeared to be more mature than it was decades before. Unwinding the VIE structures meant introducing domestic investors into the market, buying back shares held by foreign investors, and, ultimately, terminating VIE contracts to ensure that companies were under actual, effective control of Chinese investors. The entire process, involving labor-intensive negotiations among the relevant parties and likely taking years, might appear to be less financially damaging than the sudden banning of the Chinese-Chinese-foreign (CCF) scheme in the telecom sector in the late 1990s, but foreign investors are still likely to suffer considerable financial loss.

As of this writing, the foreign investment law is not yet enacted, leaving uncertainties about the legality of the VIE structure. In early 2018, instead of declaring the VIE structure illegal and void, the government announced the introduction of what it called "Chinese depository receipts" (CDRs), a variation on American depository receipts, to lure overseas-listed internet companies to return to China. Using CDRs, foreign listed companies would transfer a portion of their shares to a custodian bank in China, which then would sell the depository shares on a local exchange. The Chinese depository receipts were essentially designed to enable Chinese internet companies to indirectly and quickly offer their stock in China without the need for restructuring to allow domestic institutions and investors to own it. Although these companies should be able to keep the VIE structure for the moment, I do not think the introduction of CDRs signals imminent state recognition of the VIE structure as legal in prohibited categories, as some professionals would like to believe. It is, at most, a means of preserving the status quo, leaving the VIE structure in legal limbo while providing an expedient way to lure back the country's wealthiest tech companies listed in the United States. Nevertheless, according to press accounts and to my informant Ming, a senior financial officer from a leading internet company, use of CDRs remains on hold because of a global stock market slump, the ongoing trade war with the United States, and deadlocked negotiations between the government and tech companies over key terms such as "share pricing," adding further uncertainty to the future of VIE structures.[9] However the Chinese government ultimately decides to deal with these, the general direction of the current leadership is to decrease the influence of foreign capital over sensitive sectors such as the internet.

While doing my research in Beijing in March and April of 2014—customarily sensitive times of the year for any cultural activities in China, with two national conferences in March and the annual campaign against pornography and illegal publications in April—I heard rumors of an imminent, stronger intervention in the regulation of online video content by the SAPPRFT (the SARFT's successor). Sohu Video had attracted the SAPPRFT's attention because American television series, in which the company had invested heavily, were the agency's focus at the time. And Sohu's hit web soap *Diors Man* (*Diaosi nanshi*) was also rumored to have irritated regulators for its fairly explicit sexual content. But it was not until September 2014 that the SAPPRFT acted in earnest, issuing its Notice to Further Implement Related Regulations on Online Foreign Films and Television Dramas, which laid out its new system for regulating online video's acquisition of foreign content.[10] First, the SAPPRFT imposed a quota system (something that had long existed in film and television) for online video, limiting the annual combined length of foreign films and television dramas acquired by a single video company to 30 percent of the total domestic content distributed in the previous year, and it imposed a further quota limiting the import of foreign content from a single country to 9 percent of the total import of foreign content, thereby effectively regulating American content in particular. Video companies and their Hollywood partners now had to add supplementary clauses to their previously signed contracts, adjusting the hours and prices of content.[11]

Second, the SAPPRFT introduced a permitting system, which had existed for years in film and television, to filter foreign content online. In the case of American television series, for example, the SAPPRFT declared that before issuing an online distribution permit, it would by itself review a subtitled copy of an entire season, the series' acquisition contract, and proof of copyright rather than leaving the review to the video companies. Instead of acquiring new or forthcoming shows, video companies now had to wait until the North American airing of a season was complete or nearly complete in order to determine whether a show's content was ideologically acceptable. This wait, coupled with the time the SAPPRFT needed for review, meant that acquiring American series was delayed by at least six months. The nearly synchronous streaming that video companies had been able to do in the previous decade was now impossible. My LeTV informant Hao described the new permitting process as "long, busy, and complicated."[12] The delay it entailed undoubtedly dulled users' appetite for American series and dampened video companies' eagerness to purchase them. Since this intervention by the SAPPRFT, the brisk market for American series in China has slowed down considerably. As of this writing, the SAPPRFT is drafting a comprehensive regulatory framework for the importation of overseas programs by both television and online video, not surprisingly, with even more restrictive regulations for online video.

The SAPPRFT has also tightened regulation of web soaps and other indigenous online content. First, it has persistently reminded the online video industry of its self-censorship obligations and engaged in more stringent post hoc censorship, which had been fairly lax in the previous decade. In February 2016, at a national industry conference, Jianhui Luo, head of the SAPPRFT's Online Audiovisual Program Regulation Department, specifically mentioned harsher measures such as 24-hour nonstop surveillance by the SAPPRFT and the potential for its post hoc censorship of controversial programs.[13] Second, the SAPPRFT began to experiment with precensorship of web soaps, as specified in its Notice to Further Strengthen the Planning, Construction, and Management of Online Original Audiovisual Programs, issued in late 2016, suggesting its long-term plan to incorporate online content into the regulatory framework already in place for television.[14] Video companies were asked to inform the SAPPRFT of their production plans for key programs by registering each program's name and production studio, its topic and length, a synopsis of its content in no fewer than 1,500 words, and a summary of the program's ideological significance in no fewer than 300 words. Key programs to be registered were those the video companies planned to promote on their websites or mobile applications; those intended for premium members; and web soaps costing more than ¥5 million (about $625,000) or online movies costing more than ¥1 million (about $125,000). Video companies were asked to first seek clearance from relevant government agencies for programs concerning important subjects or special topics such as politics, military or foreign affairs, religion, and public security, which would then be reviewed by censors convened by the SAPPRFT itself.

It is rather clear now that, if it decides to do so, the SAPPRFT is capable of regulating online video in largely the same way that it regulates television. The further monopolization of the industry, with resources being increasingly concentrated now in the hands of the Baidu-backed iQiyi and Tencent Video, makes it easier for the SAPPRFT to intervene. If the large amount of content on the web were ever to become a concern, it could creatively reduce that amount, just as the agency has the amount of foreign content imported with its quota system. Moreover, regulation could move forward at a relatively fast pace. To construct an online system for coordinating quota application and approval, the SAPPRFT invited bids from system designers in October 2014, and put the system into operation in early 2015. Judging from the rapid pace of these changes, if there had been anything that prevented the state from imposing stringent regulations on online video in the previous decade, it was clearly its lack of will.

The current decision to discourage marketization in the cultural sector may have resulted from President Xi's personal goals of ideological purity and integrity. In his talk at the Beijing Forum on Literature and Art in October 2014, which forcefully evoked Mao's 1942 talk at the Yan'an Conference on Literature and Art, Xi warned artists not to become slaves to the market, not to allow their works to be tainted by the stench of money. But here it is important to also recognize the pragmatism in the party-state's cultural policy. Reregulating marketization may have been a response both to the undesirable social and ideological consequence of a laissez-faire approach to online video in the previous decades and to a backlash from traditional media against the new media. Television professionals had long grumbled about the SARFT's leniency toward video companies and loathed their vulgar orientation. We should also note that, concurrent with the state's curtailment of market forces in the new media is its increasing presence online. Television broadcasters have begun to get a foothold online, and Hunan Satellite Television established its streaming service Mango TV in 2014.

The curtailment of market autonomy, however, does not mean that cultural zoning has come to an end. Even though the latitude online video once enjoyed has been significantly reduced, at this moment, it remains more marketized than television. And big companies like Tencent could leverage their clout to negotiate greater leeway from regulators. However diminished it may be by this new, more restrictive oversight, cultural zoning still carries on. Indeed, although it has mainly found its expression in the dynamic of television versus online video in the past two decades, historically, cultural zoning has never been limited to this dynamic, nor does it consistently operate on a scale comparable to that of online video.

Cultural zoning made possible the Mandarin Ducks and Butterflies fiction in the 1930s; hand-copied entertainment fiction during the Cultural Revolution; and audiovisual piracy in the 1980s and 1990s. Given that the party-state's cultural policy has always had a pragmatic and populist component, market forces will naturally remain a means to regulate cultural life in contemporary China, and zoning as a technique of cultural governance will not fade away entirely. As a dynamic governing technique, cultural zoning mobilizes market forces to different degrees in different historical circumstances, aiming for a balance in cultural life—and online video is a historical product of this technique.

Appendix

Announced Policies Relevant to the Development of the Online Video Industry in China, 1999–2017

Policy	Year	Agency/Ministry	Abbreviation
Notice Concerning Strengthening the Administration of Quasi- Radio, Film, and Television Programs Communicated to the Public via Information Networks (Guanyu jiaqiang tongguo xinxi wangluo xiang gongzhong chuanbo guangbo dianying dianshi lei jiemu guanli de tongzhi)	1999	SARFT	
Provisional Measures for the Supervision and Administration of Quasi- Radio, Film, and Television Programs Communicated via Information Networks (Xinxi wangluo chuanbo guangbo dianying dianshi lei jiemu jiandu guanli zanxing banfa)	2000	SARFT	
Measures on the Administration of Internet Information Services (Hulianwang xinxi fuwu guanli banfa)	2000	State Council	ICP rule
Provisions on the Administration of Foreign-Invested Telecommunications Enterprises (Waishang touzi dianxin qiye guanli guiding)	2001	State Council	

Policy	Year	Agency/Ministry	Abbreviation
Measures for the Administration of Audiovisual Programs Communicated via Information Networks Including Internet (Hulianwang deng xinxi wangluo chuanbo shiting jiemu guanli banfa)	2003	SARFT	rule 15
Measures for the Administration of Audiovisual Programs Communicated via Information Networks Including Internet (Hulianwang deng xinxi wangluo chuanbo shiting jiemu guanli banfa) *A more elaborated version of rule 15	2004	SARFT	rule 39
Notice on Strengthening the Management of the Distribution of DV Works in Theatres, Television, and on Information Networks Including the Internet (Guanyu jiaqiang yingshi bofang jigou he hulianwang deng xinxi wangluo bofang DV pian guanli de tongzhi)	2004	SARFT	
Notice on Strengthening the Administration of Foreign Investment in and Operation of Value-Added Telecommunications Businesses (Guanyu jiaqiang waishang touzi jingying zengzhi dianxin yewu guanli de tongzhi)	2006	Ministry of Information Industry	
Regulations on Internet Audiovisual Services (Hulianwang shiting jiemu fuwu guanli guiding)	2007	SARFT and Ministry of Information Industry (joint policy)	rule 56
Notice Concerning Strengthening Regulations of Films and Television Dramas Transmitted via Internet (Guanyu jiaqiang hulianwang chuanbo yingshiju guanli de tongzhi)	2007	SARFT	

Policy	Year	Agency/Ministry	Abbreviation
Notice to Strengthen the Content Regulation of Online Audiovisual Programs (Guanyu jiaqiang hulianwang shiting jiemu neirong guanli de tongzhi)	2009	SARFT	
Notice on Further Strengthening the Regulation of Web Soaps, Micro Movies, and Other Online Audiovisual Programs (Guanyu jinyibu jiaqiang wangluoju, weidianying deng wangluo shiting jiemu guanli de tongzhi)	2012	SARFT	
Notice to Further Implement Related Regulations on Online Foreign Films and Television Dramas (Guanyu jinyibu luoshi wangshang jingwai yingshiju guanli youguan guiding de tongzhi)	2014	SAPPRFT	
Notice to Further Strengthen the Planning, Construction, and Management of Online Original Audiovisual Programs (Guanyu jinyibu jiaqiang wangluo yuanchuang shiting jiemu guihua jianshe he guanli de tongzhi)	2016	SAPPRFT	

Notes

Chapter 1: Introduction

1. In 2013, the SARFT merged with the General Administration of Press and Publication (GAPP) to become a single regulatory body (i.e., the SAPPRFT). Because *Zoning China* deals mainly with the era before 2014, I will use SARFT for most of the discussion and SAPPRFT for the period from 2014 on.

2. "Luo Jianhui: chuantong meiti bu yunxu bochu de xin meiti yiyang buneng bo" (Luo Jianhui: What traditional media cannot show cannot be shown on new media either), *Sohu Media*, last modified December 4, 2014, http://media.sohu.com/20141204/n406655434.shtml; "Cai Fuchao: xianshang xianxia tongyi biaozhun xianshen houbo" (Cai Fuchao: To unify online and offline standards), *Caixin*, last modified December 16, 2014, http://companies.caixin.com/2014-12-16/100763622.html.

3. The phrase "reform and opening up" refers to the program of economic reform and marketization introduced by the Chinese leader Deng Xiaoping after the death of Mao Zedong and the conclusion of the Cultural Revolution. The program officially began in late 1978.

4. Orville Schell, *Mandate of Heaven: The Legacy of Tiananmen Square and the Next Generation of China's Leaders* (New York: Simon & Schuster, 1995), 293.

5. Aihwa Ong, *Neoliberalism as Exception: Mutations in Citizenship and Sovereignty* (Durham: Duke University Press, 2006).

6. Sandra Braman, *Change of State: Information, Policy, and Power* (Cambridge, MA: MIT Press, 2006).

7. Adrian Athique, "Piracy at the Frontier: Uneven Development and the Public Sphere," *Media International Australia* 152 (2014): 87–97.

8. Samuel S. Kim, "China and Globalization: Confronting Myriad Challenges and Opportunities," *Asian Perspectives* 33, 3 (2009): 75.

9. Roselyn Hsueh, "Nations or Sectors in the Age of Globalization: China's Policy toward Foreign Direct Investment in Telecommunications," *Review of Policy Research* 32, 6 (2015): 627–648; Yu Hong, *Networking China: The Digital Transformation of the Chinese Economy* (Champaign: University of Illinois Press, 2017); and Yu Hong, "Pivot to Internet Plus: Molding China's Digital Economy for Economic Restructuring?" *International Journal of Communication* 11 (2017): 1486–1506.

10. Andrew Calabrese and Colleen Mihal, "Liberal Fictions: The Public-Private Dichotomy in Media Policy," in Janet Wasko, Graham Murdock, and Helena Sousa, eds., *The Handbook of Political Economy of Communications* (Chichester, UK: Wiley-Blackwell, 2011), 226–263; Graham Murdock, "Political Economies as Moral Economies: Commodities, Gifts, and Public Goods," in Wasko, Murdock, and Sousa, *The Handbook of Political Economy of Communications*, 13–39; Dan Schiller, *How to Think about Information* (Urbana: University of Illinois Press, 2007).

11. Ong, *Neoliberalism as Exception*.

12. As the "2000s" is now widely understood to mean only the first decade of the new century, throughout *Zoning China*, I use "early 2000s" and "mid-2000s" to mean the first few years and the middle years of that first decade.

13. The usage of "vernacular" in this book is drawn from Henry Jenkins, who uses the term to describe culture that is generated by amateurs. Henry Jenkins, *Convergence Culture: Where Old and New Media Collide* (New York: New York University Press, 2008), 334.

14. For a discussion of bureaucratic politics and its consequences for policy making and implementation in China, see Kenneth Lieberthal and Michel Oksenberg, *Policy Making in China: Leaders, Structures, and Processes* (Princeton: Princeton University Press, 1988); Kenneth G. Lieberthal and David M. Lampton, eds., *Bureaucracy, Politics and Decision Making in Post-Mao China* (Berkeley: University of California Press, 1992); and David M. Lampton, ed., *Policy Implementation in Post-Mao China* (Berkeley: University of California Press, 1987).

15. Dan Breznitz and Michael Murphree, *Run of the Red Queen: Government, Innovation, Globalization, and Economic Growth in China* (New Haven: Yale University Press, 2011); Martin Dimitrov, *Piracy and the State: The Politics of Intellectual Property Rights in China* (Cambridge University Press, 2009); Eric Harwit, *China's Telecommunications Revolution* (Oxford: Oxford University Press, 2008); Y. Hong, *Networking China*; and Andrew Mertha, *The Politics of Piracy: Intellectual Property in Contemporary China* (Ithaca: Cornell University Press, 2005).

16. Braman, *Change of State*, 80.

17. Lin, interview with author, Shanghai, June 7, 2016. In this book, I use aliases (or initial only, in the case of "GB") instead of their real names to protect the anonymity of my informants.

18. See, for example, Georgy Egorov, Sergei Guriev, and Konstantin Sonin, "Why Resource-Poor Dictators Allow Freer Media: A Theory and Evidence from Panel Data," *American Political Science Review* 103, no. 4 (2009): 645–668; Gary King, Jennifer Pan, and Margaret E. Roberts, "How Censorship in China Allows Government Criticism but Silences Collective Expression," *American Political Science Review* 107, no. 2 (2013): 326–343; and Peter Lorentzen, "China's Strategic Censorship," *American Journal of Political Science* 58, no. 2 (2014): 402–414.

19. Lorentzen, "China's Strategic Censorship."

20. King, Pan, and Roberts, "How Censorship in China Allows."

21. Mertha, *Politics of Piracy*, 20.

22. Andrew Nathan, "Authoritarian Resilience," *Journal of Democracy* 14, no. 1 (2003): 6–17.

23. Nathan, "Authoritarian Resilience"; Martin Dimitrov, ed., *Why Communism Did Not Collapse: Understanding Authoritarian Regime Resilience in Asia and Europe* (New York: Cambridge University Press, 2013); Barry J. Naughton and Dali L. Yang, eds., *Holding China Together: Diversity and National Integration in the Post-Deng Era* (New York: Cambridge University Press, 2004); and David Shambaugh, *China's Communist Party: Atrophy and Adaptation* (Washington, D.C.: Woodrow Wilson Center Press; Berkeley: University of California Press, 2008).

24. Kellee S. Tsai, *Capitalism Without Democracy: The Private Sector in Contemporary China* (Ithaca: Cornell University Press, 2007).

25. Lily L. Tsai, *Accountability without Democracy: Solidary Groups and Public Goods Provision in Rural China* (New York: Cambridge University Press, 2007); Peter L. Lorentzen, "Regularizing Rioting: Permitting Public Protest in an Authoritarian Regime," *Quarterly Journal of Political Science*, 8, no. 2 (2013): 127–158; and Yanqi Tong and Shaohua Lei, *Social Protest in Contemporary China, 2003–2010: Transitional Pains and Regime Legitimacy* (New York: Routledge, 2014).

26. Sebastian Heilmann and Elizabeth Perry, "Embracing Uncertainty: Guerrilla Policy Style and Adaptive Governance in China," in Sebastian Heilmann and Elizabeth Perry, eds., *Mao's Invisible Hand: The Political Foundations of Adaptive Governance in China* (Cambridge, MA: Harvard University Press, 2011), 22.

27. Sebastian Heilmann, *Red Swan: How Unorthodox Policy-Making Facilitated China's Rise* (Columbia University Press, 2018).

28. Breznitz and Murphree, *Run of the Red Queen*, 11.

29. Heilmann and Perry, "Embracing Uncertainty," 12.

30. Lin, interview with author, Shanghai, June 7, 2016.

31. Heilmann and Perry, "Embracing Uncertainty," 12.

32. Breznitz and Murphree, *Run of the Red Queen*, 40.

33. King, Pan, and Roberts, "How Censorship in China Allows," 327.

34. Bingchun Meng, "Moving beyond Democratization: A Thought Piece on China Internet Research Agenda," *International Journal of Communication* 4 (2010): 501.

35. The literature on the democratization paradigm is enormous. For a brief introduction, see Ronald J. Deibert, "Dark Guests and Great Firewalls: The Internet and Chinese Security Policy," *Journal of Social Issues* 58, no. 1 (2002): 143–159; Shanthi Kalathil, *Open Networks, Closed Regimes: The Impact of the Internet on Authoritarian Rule* (Washington, D.C.: Carnegie Endowment for International Peace, 2003); Bin Liang and Hong Lu, "Internet Development, Censorship, and Cyber Crimes in China," *Journal of Contemporary Criminal Justice* 26, no. 1 (2010): 103–120; Geoffry Taubman, "A Not-So World Wide Web: The Internet, China, and the Challenges to Nondemocratic Rule," *Political Communication* 15, no. 2 (1998): 255–272; and Lokman Tsui, "The Panopticon as the Antithesis of a Space of Freedom Control and Regulation of the Internet in China," *China Information* 17, no. 2 (2003): 65–82.

36. Tsui, "Panopticon as the Antithesis."

37. See Fan Yang, "Rethinking China's Internet Censorship: The Practice of Recoding and the Politics of Visibility," *New Media & Society* 18, no. 7 (2016): 1364–1381.

38. Matthew Bunn, "Reimagining Repression: New Censorship Theory and After," *History and Theory* 54 (2015): 25–44.

39. Bunn, "Reimagining Repression."

40. Guobin Yang, "Killing Emotions Softly: The Civilizing Process of Online Emotional Mobilization" (in Chinese), *Chinese Journal of Communication and Society* 40 (2017): 75–104.

41. Rongbin Han, "Defending the Authoritarian Regime Online: China's 'Voluntary Fifty-Cent Army,'" *China Quarterly* 224 (2015): 1006–1025.

42. Han, "Defending the Authoritarian Regime Online."

43. Heilmann and Perry, "Embracing Uncertainty," 4.

44. Michael Curtin, Jennifer Holt, and Kevin Sanson, eds., *Distribution Revolution: Conversations about the Digital Future of Film and Television* (Berkeley: University of California Press, 2014), 13.

45. Curtin, Holt, and Sanson, *Distribution Revolution*; Michael Curtin, "Matrix Media," in Graeme Turner and Jinna Tay, eds., *Television Studies after TV* (Abingdon, UK: Routledge, 2009), 19–29; Stuart Cunningham and Jon Silver, *Screen Distribution and the New King Kongs of the Online World* (New York: Palgrave Macmillan, 2013);

Jennifer Holt and Kevin Sanson, eds., *Connected Viewing: Selling, Streaming, and Sharing Media in the Digital Era* (Routledge, 2013); Michael Keane, "Disconnecting, Connecting, and Reconnecting: How Chinese Television Found Its Way Out of the Box," *International Journal of Communication*, 10 (2016): 5426–5443; and Amanda Lotz, *Portals: A Treatise on Internet-Distributed Television* (Ann Arbor: Michigan Publishing, 2017).

46. See James Bennett and Niki Strange, eds., *Television as Digital Media* (Durham: Duke University Press, 2011); and William Uricchio, "The Future of a Medium Once Known as Television," in Pelle Snickars and Patrick Vonderau, eds., *The YouTube Reader* (Stockholm: National Library of Sweden, 2009), 24–39.

47. Michael Newman, *Video Revolutions: On the History of a Medium* (New York: Columbia University Press, 2014).

48. Newman, *Video Revolutions.*

49. Lisa Gitelman, *Always Already New: Media, History, and the Data of Culture* (Cambridge, MA: MIT Press, 2006), 5–7.

50. Newman, *Video Revolutions.*

51. Newman, *Video Revolutions.*

52. Uricchio, "Future of a Medium."

53. Raymond Williams, *Television: Technology and Cultural Form* (Middletown, Conn.: Wesleyan University Press, 1992).

54. Uricchio, "Future of a Medium," 32.

55. Shujen Wang, *Framing Piracy: Globalization and Film Distribution in Greater China* (Lanham, Md.: Rowman & Littlefield, 2003).

56. Qin, interview with author, Shanghai, June 27, 2014.

57. Lawrence Grossberg, *Bringing It All Back Home: Essays on Cultural Studies* (Durham: Duke University Press, 1997), 113.

58. Newman, *Video Revolutions.*

59. See Curtin, Holt, and Sanson, *Distribution Revolution.*

60. Tom O'Regan, "From Piracy to Sovereignty: International VCR Trends," *Continuum: Journal of Media and Cultural Studies* 4, no. 2 (1991): 112–135.

61. Newman, *Video Revolutions*, 42.

62. *Video Revolutions*, 62.

63. Peng, interview with author, Shanghai, June 1, 2016.

64. Tristan Mattelart, "Audiovisual Piracy: Toward a Study of the Underground Networks of Cultural Globalization," *Global Media and Communication* 5, no. 3 (2009): 308–326.

65. Adrian Athique, "The Global Dynamics of India Media Piracy: Export Markets, Playback Media and the Informal Economy," *Media, Culture & Society* 30, no. 5 (2008): 699-717; quotation on p.701.

66. See, for example, Brian Larkin, "Degraded Images, Distorted Sounds: Nigerian Video and the Infrastructure of Piracy," *Public Culture* 16, no. 2 (2004): 289–314.

67. For an extensive discussion of scholarship holding this view, see Mattelart, "Audiovisual Piracy."

68. Larkin, "Degraded Images, Distorted Sounds," 298.

69. Ravi Sundaram, *Pirate Modernity: Delhi's Media Urbanism* (London: Routledge, 2009), 13.

70. Jonathan Zhu and Shujen Wang, "Mapping Film Piracy in China," *Theory, Culture and Society* 20, no. 4 (2003): 97–125.

71. Athique, "Piracy at the Frontier."

72. Xiaobo Wu, *Jidang sanshinian: Zhongguo qiye 1978–2008 (Thirty years of Chinese business, 1978–2008), vol. 2* (Beijing: Zhongxin Press, 2008).

73. Larkin, "Degraded Images, Distorted Sounds."

74. Larkin, "Degraded Images, Distorted Sounds."

75. Brian Larkin, *Signal and Noise: Media, Infrastructure, and Urban Culture in Nigeria* (Durham: Duke University Press, 2008), 6.

76. See, for example, Stuart Cunningham, "Emergent Innovation through the Co-Evolution of Informal and Formal Media Economies," *Television and New Media* 13, no. 5 (2012): 415–430; Stuart Cunningham and Jon Silver, "Online Film Distribution: Its History and Global Complexion," in Dina Iordanova and Stuart Cunningham, eds., *Digital Disruption: Cinema Moves Online* (St. Andrews. UK: St. Andrews Film Studies, 2012), 53–95; and Julian Thomas and Ramon Lobato, *The Informal Media Economy* (Cambridge: Polity Press, 2015).

77. Elaine Zhao and Michael Keane, "Between Formal and Informal: The Shakeout in China's Online Video Industry," *Media, Culture & Society* 35 (2013): 724–741.

78. Larkin, "Degraded Images, Distorted Sounds."

79. See Ramon Lobato, Julian Thomas, and Dan Hunter, "Histories of User-Generated Content: Between Formal and Informal Media Economies," *International Journal of Communication* 5 (2011): 899–914.

80. On the importance of industry contacts in such circumstances, see, for example, Aswin Punathambekar, *From Bombay to Bollywood: The Making of a Global Media Industry* (New York: New York University Press, 2013).

81. Amanda Lotz, *The Television Will be Revolutionized* (New York: New York University Press, 2007).

82. See Vicki Mayer, Miranda Banks, and John Caldwell, *Production Studies: Cultural Studies of Media Industries* (London: Routledge, 2009).

83. See Punathambekar, *From Bombay to Bollywood*.

84. Mayer, Banks, and Caldwell, *Production Studies*, 5.

85. John Caldwell, *Production Culture: Industrial Reflexivity and Critical Practice in Film and Television* (Durham: Duke University Press, 2008), 4.

86. "Fansubbing" (short for "fan subtitling") refers to the practices of online communities of fans dedicated to introducing and subtitling films and television programs from foreign countries. Most of the foreign content brought in by fansubbers was not officially imported by the Chinese state.

Chapter 2: Culture before the Millennium

1. Hsiao-t'i Li, "Making a Name and a Culture for the Masses in Modern China," *Positions* 9, no. 1 (2001): 29–68.

2. Li, "Making a Name and a Culture," 31.

3. Perry Link, Richard Madsen, and Paul Pickowicz, eds., *Unofficial China: Popular Culture and Thought in the People's Republic* (Boulder, CO: Westview Press, 1990), 8.

4. Hsiao-t'i Li, "Making a Name and a Culture."

5. David Holm, *Art and Ideology in Revolutionary China* (Oxford: Clarendon Press, 1991).

6. Tetsuya Kataoka, *Resistance and Revolution in China: The Communists and the Second United Front* (Berkeley: University of California Press, 1974).

7. Holm, *Art and Ideology in Revolutionary China*.

8. Roderick MacFarquhar, "On 'Liberation'," *China Quarterly* 200 (2009): 891–894.

9. Zedong Mao, "On New Democracy" (January 1940), in *Selected Works of Mao Tse-tung, Volume II* (Oxford: Pergamon Press, 1965), 344.

10. Mao, "On New Democracy," 349.

11. Holm, *Art and Ideology in Revolutionary China*.

12. Zedong Mao,"*Talks at the Yan'an Conference on Literature and Art": A Translation of the 1943 Text with Commentary* (Ann Arbor: Center for Chinese Studies; University of Michigan, 1980), 75.

13. Philip Smith and Alexander Riley, *Cultural Theory: An Introduction* (Malden, MA: Blackwell, 2009).

14. John Cammett, *Antonio Gramsci and the Origins of Italian Communism* (Stanford: Stanford University Press, 1967).

15. Mao, "On New Democracy," 381.

16. Holm, *Art and Ideology in Revolutionary China*.

17. Mao, "On New Democracy," 381–382.

18. Nigel Todd, "Ideological Superstructure in Gramsci and Mao Tse-Tung," *Journal of the History of Ideas* 35, no. 1 (1974): 148–156.

19. Mao, "On New Democracy," 381.

20. Boda Chen, as quoted in Holm, *Art and Ideology in Revolutionary China*, 53.

21. Hsiao-t'i Li, "Making a Name and a Culture."

22. Yuezhi Zhao, *Communication in China: Political Economy, Power, and Conflict* (Lanham, Md.: Rowman & Littlefield, 2008).

23. Hsiao-t'i Li, "Making a Name and a Culture," 60–61.

24. "Making a Name and a Culture," 61.

25. Chang-tai Hung, *Mao's New World: Political Culture in the Early People's Republic* (Ithaca: Cornell University Press, 2011).

26. Holm, *Art and Ideology in Revolutionary China*.

27. Hung, *Mao's New World*.

28. See, for example, Julia Frances Andrews, *Painters and Politics in the People's Republic of China, 1949–1979* (Berkeley: University of California Press, 1994); Xiaomei Chen, *Acting the Right Part: Political Theater and Popular Drama in Contemporary China* (Honolulu: University of Hawai'i Press, 2002); Godwin C. Chu and Francis L. K. Hsu, eds., *Moving a Mountain: Cultural Change in China* (Honolulu: University of Hawai'i Press for East-West Center, 1979); Brian DeMare, *Mao's Cultural Army: Drama Troupes in China's Rural Revolution* (Cambridge: Cambridge University Press, 2015); Holm, *Art and Ideology in Revolutionary China*; Hung, *Mao's New World*.

29. Hung, *Mao's New World*.

30. Qiliang He, "Between Business and Bureaucrats: Pingtan Storytelling in Maoist and Post-Maoist China," *Modern China* 36, no. 3 (2010): 243–268; Qiliang He,

"Between Accommodation and Resistance: Pingtan Storytelling in 1960s Shanghai," *Modern Asian Studies* 48, no. 3 (2014): 524–549.

31. Perry Link, "Hand-Copied Entertainment Fiction from the Cultural Revolution," in Perry Link, Richard Madsen, and Paul Pickowicz, eds., *Unofficial China: Popular Culture and Thought in the People's Republic* (Boulder, CO: Westview Press, 1989): 17–36; quotation on p. 18.

32. Guobin Yang, *The Red Guard Generation and Political Activism in China* (New York: Columbia University Press, 2016).

33. Link, "Hand-Copied Entertainment Fiction."

34. He, "Between Business and Bureaucrats."

35. Hsiao-t'i Li, "Making a Name and a Culture," 37.

36. World Bank, "OKR: Deepening Public Service Unit Reform to Improve Service Delivery," accessed October 20, 2014, https://openknowledge.worldbank.org/handle/10986/8648.

37. Nimrod Baranovitch, *China's New Voices: Popular Music, Ethnicity, Gender, and Politics, 1978–1997* (Berkeley: University of California Press, 2003).

38. Yuezhi Zhao, *Media, Market, and Democracy in China: Between the Party Line and the Bottom Line* (Urbana: University of Illinois Press, 1998).

39. Zhao, *Communication in China.*

40. Yu Huang, "Peaceful Evolution: The Case of Television Reform in Post-Mao China," *Media, Culture & Society* 16, no. 2 (1994): 217–241.

41. Zhao, *Communication in China.*

42. Huang, "Peaceful Evolution."

43. Michael Keane, *The Chinese Television Industry* (London: British Film Institute, 2015).

44. Zhao, *Communication in China.*

45. Jason McGrath, *Postsocialist Modernity: Chinese Cinema, Literature, and Criticism in the Market Age* (Stanford: Stanford University Press, 2008).

46. Lansheng Jiang and Shengwu Xie, eds., *2001–2002 Zhongguo wenhua chanye fazhan baogao* (2001–2002 Report on the development of Chinese cultural industry) (Beijing: Social Science Literature Press, 2002), 46.

47. Huang, "Peaceful Evolution."

48. Zhao, *Communication in China.*

49. SARFT, *China Radio & TV Yearbook 1988*; SARFT, *China Radio & TV Yearbook 1989*.

50. SARFT, *China Radio & TV Yearbook 1990*.

51. SARFT, *China Radio & TV Yearbook 1992–1993*, 32.

52. SARFT, *China Radio & TV Yearbook 1991*.

53. SARFT, *China Radio & TV Yearbook 1999, 2000*.

54. Yu Huang and Andrew Green, "From Mao to the Millennium: 40 Years of Television in China," in David French and Michael Richards, eds., *Television in Contemporary China* (London: Sage, 2000), 267–291.

55. Zhengrong Hu and Hong Li, "China's Television in Transition," in David Ward, ed., *Television and Public Policy: Change and Continuity in an Era of Global Liberalization* (London: Routledge, 2008), 89–113.

56. SARFT, *China Radio & TV Yearbook 1986*.

57. SARFT, *China Radio & TV Yearbook 1992–1993*.

58. Joseph Man Chan, "Administrative Boundaries and Media Marketization: A Comparative Analysis of the Newspaper, TV and Internet Markets in China," in Chin-Chuan Lee, ed., *Chinese Media, Global Contexts* (London: Routledge, 2009): 156–172.

59. Chan, "Administrative Boundaries and Media Marketization"; Yong Zhong, "Hunan Satellite Television over China," *Journal of International Communication* 16, no. 1 (January 1, 2010): 41–57.

60. Ruoyun Bai, *Staging Corruption: Chinese Television and Politics* (Vancouver: University of British Columbia Press, 2014).

61. Chan, "Administrative Boundaries and Media Marketization"; Bai, *Staging Corruption*.

62. For a detailed discussion of makeshift troupes, see Bai, *Staging Corruption*.

63. Wanning Sun and Yuezhi Zhao, "Television Culture with 'Chinese Characteristics': The Politics of Compassion and Education," in Turner and Tay, *Television Studies after TV*, 96–104 (quotations on p. 97).

64. Jing Wang, "Culture as Leisure and Culture as Capital," *Positions: East Asia Cultures Critique* 9, no. 1 (March 1, 2001): 69–104.

65. Ying Zhu, *Television in Post-Reform China: Serial Dramas, Confucian Leadership and the Global Television Market* (London: Routledge, 2008).

66. Anthony Fung, "Globalizing Televised Culture: The Case of China," in Turner and Tay, *Television Studies after TV*, 178–188. Similar observations were found in the local adaptation of *Ugly Betty*; see Anthony Fung and Xiaoxiao Zhang, "The Chinese *Ugly Betty*: TV Cloning and Local Modernity," *International Journal of Cultural Studies* 14 (2011): 265–276; and Xiaoxiao Zhang and Anthony Fung, "TV Formatting of the Chinese *Ugly Betty*: An Ethnographic Observation of the Production Community," *Television & New Media* 15 (2014): 507–522.

67. Bai, *Staging Corruption*; Wanning Sun, *Maid in China: Media, Morality, and the Cultural Politics of Boundaries* (Routledge, 2010).

68. Michael Keane, "Television Drama in China: Engineering Souls for the Market," in Timothy J. Craig and Richard King, eds., *Global Goes Local: Popular Culture in Asia* (Vancouver: University of British Colombia, 2001), 120–137; Michael Keane, "Television Drama in China: Remaking the Market," *Media International Australia* 115 (2005): 82–93.

69. Zhao, *Communication in China*, 216.

70. Laikwan Pang, "Post-Socialism and Cultural Policy: China's Depoliticization of Culture in the Late 1970s and Early 1980s," in Nissim Otmazgin and Eyal Ben-Ari, eds., *Popular Culture and the State in East and Southeast Asia* (London: Routledge, 2012): 147–161.

71. Perry Link, "The Limits of Cultural Reform in Deng Xiaoping's China," *Modern China* 13, no. 2 (1987): 115–176. "Clapper tales" are kuaiban stories told with bamboo clapper accompaniment.

72. Baranovitch, *China's New Voices*; Andrew Jones, *Like a Knife: Ideology and Genre in Contemporary Chinese Popular Music* (Ithaca: East Asia Program, Cornell University, 1992).

73. Lobato, Thomas, and Hunter, "Histories of User-Generated Content," 900.

74. Zhao, *Communication in China*.

75. Lisa Movius, "Imitation Nation," accessed July 8, 2002, https://www.salon.com/2002/07/08/imitation_nation/.

76. Baranovitch, *China's New Voices*; Thomas Gold, "Go with Your Feelings: Hong Kong and Taiwan Popular Culture in Greater China," *China Quarterly* 136 (1993): 907–925.

77. Baranovitch, *China's New Voices*; Thomas Gold, "Go with Your Feelings."

78. Baranovitch, *China's New Voices*, 11.

79. Joseph Man Chan, "When Capitalist and Socialists Television Meet: The Impact of Hong Kong TV on Guangzhou Residents," in Chin-Chuan Lee, ed., *Media, Money,*

and Power: Communication Patterns in Chinese Societies (Evanston, IL: Northwestern University Press, 2000): 245–270.

80. Angela Xiao Wu, "Broadening the Scope of Cultural Preferences: Movie Talk and Chinese Pirate Film Consumption from the Mid-1980s to 2005," *International Journal of Communication* 6, no. 1 (2012): 501–529. Although *luxiang ting* is commonly translated as "video halls" in English, to be precise, *luxiang* actually refers to a specific form of video technology: videotape.

81. This conclusion was drawn from a wide reading of personal reminiscences circulating online, trade magazines, and representations of video halls in Chinese media and popular culture.

82. Jinhua Dai, *Wuzhong fengjing: Zhongguo dianying wenhua 1978–1998 (Scenery in the mist: Chinese cinema culture, 1978–1998)* (Beijing: Peking University Press, 2000).

83. These studies include Douglas A. Boyd, Joseph D. Straubhaar, and John A. Lent, *Videocassette Recorders in the Third World* (White Plains, N.Y.: Longman, 1989); Gladys D. Ganley and Oswald H. Ganley, *Global Political Fallout: The First Decade of the VCR, 1976–1985* (Cambridge, MA: Center for Information Policy Research, Harvard University, 1987); and Armand Mattelart and Hector Schmucler, *Communication and Information Technologies: Freedom of Choice for Latin America?* (Norwood, NJ: Ablex, 1985).

84. Mattelart, "Audiovisual Piracy."

85. Video halls had a continuing presence in Chinese society after the mid-1990s but slowly declined as cinematic spaces for local residents of cities or towns. Into the 2000s, video halls found a second life on the outskirts of cities or in urban neighborhoods where migrant workers gathered and lived. Wanning Sun describes the meaning of video halls in migrant workers' cultural life. See Wanning Sun, *Subaltern China: Rural Migrants, Media, and Cultural Practices* (Lanham, MD: Rowman & Littlefield, 2014).

86. China's walled work-unit compounds were public housing complexes, each built to house state employees from a given work unit in post-1949 socialist China. Work-unit compounds, especially large compounds for universities and government ministries in Beijing, constitute in the view of many critical urban scholars "gated communities," where class-specific cultural practices and place-making strategies are enacted, and status distinctions are cultivated. See, for example, Choon-Piew Pow, *Gated Communities in China: Class, Privilege and the Moral Politics of the Good Life* (London: Routledge, 2009). For my detailed history and discussion of LeTV, see "The Rise of the Five Video Giants" in chapter 6.

87. Hao, interview with author, Beijing, April 16, 2014.

88. Sh. Wang, *Framing Piracy.*

89. A. Wu, "Broadening the Scope."

90. GB, telephone interview with author, July 19, 2014.

91. Larkin, "Degraded Images, Distorted Sounds."

92. Gold, "Go with Your Feelings."

93. William P. Alford, *To Steal a Book Is an Elegant Offense: Intellectual Property Law in Chinese Civilization* (Stanford.: Stanford University Press, 1995).

94. Mertha, *Politics of Piracy*.

95. Geremie Barmé, "The Greying of Chinese Culture," *China Review* (1992): 13.1–13.52; quotations on pp. 13.27–13.30.

96. Gold, "Go with Your Feelings," 924.

97. Barmé, "Greying of Chinese Culture."

98. Gold, "Go with Your Feelings," 921.

99. Gold, "Go with Your Feelings," 921.

100. Junhao Hong, *The Internationalization of Television in China: The Evolution of Ideology, Society, and Media Since the Reform* (Westport, Conn.: Praeger, 1994).

101. In 1993, people could buy a satellite dish, typically about five feet in diameter and ostensibly meant for their own use, for about $500 from dozens of shops in Beijing. Nicholas Kristof, "Satellites Bring Information Revolution to China," *New York Times*, April 11, 1993, http://www.nytimes.com/1993/04/11/world/satellites -bring-information-revolution-to-china.html?pagewanted=all.

102. See Anthony Kuhn, "Company Town: Chinese Wiring the Countryside for Satellite TV: Television: Program Is the First Experimental Step in Building a Nation-wide Direct-to-Home System," *Los Angeles Times*, September 23, 1999, http://articles .latimes.com/1999/sep/23/business/fi-13335; and Alex Lightman and William Rojas, *Brave New Unwired World: The Digital Big Bang and the Infinite Internet* (New York: Wiley & Sons, 2002).

103. Barmé, "Greying of Chinese Culture," 13.36.

Chapter 3: Stay Left

1. Wei, television drama producer and screenwriter.

2. Yuezhi Zhao, *Communication in China*.

3. Zhao, *Communication in China*; Joseph Man Chan, "Television in Greater China," in John Sinclair and Graeme Turner, eds., *Contemporary World Television* (London:

British Film Institute, 2004): 104–107; Chin-Chuan Lee, "The Global and the National of Chinese Media: Discourses, Market, Technology and Identity," in Chin-Chuan Lee, ed., *Chinese Media, Global Contexts* (London: Routledge, 2003): 1–31.

4. SARFT, *China Radio & TV Yearbook 2002.*

5. Yuezhi Zhao, *Communication in China.*

6. Ch.-Ch. Lee, "Global and the National of Chinese Media," 10.

7. Yuezhi Zhao, *Communication in China.*

8. Michael Keane, *Creative Industries in China: Art, Design and Media* (Cambridge: Polity Press, 2013).

9. There are many translations of *"wenhua shiye"* in current scholarship. For example, Michael Keane translates it as "publicly funded cultural institutions." See Keane, *Creative Industries in China.* And Elizabeth Perry translates it as "cultural undertakings." See Perry, "Cultural Governance in Contemporary China: 'Re-Orienting' Party Propaganda," *Harvard-Yenching Institute Working Papers,* 2013, http://dash.harvard.edu/handle/1/11386987. The translation used here is borrowed from Yuezhi Zhao. See Zhao, *Communication in China.*

10. Yuezhi Zhao, *Communication in China.*

11. Keane, *Creative Industries in China;* Central Department of Propaganda, Ministry of Culture, SARFT, and GAPP, "Guanyu wenhua tizhi gaige shidian gongzuo de yijian" (Circular on the Pilot Program in the Cultural System Reform), 2003.

12. Yuezhi Zhao, *Communication in China;* State Council, "Guanyu feigongyouzhi ziben jinru wenhua chanye de ruogan jueding" (Decisions on the Entry of Non-Publicly Owned Capital into the Cultural Industry), 2005.

13. SARFT Development and Research Center, *2006 Zhongguo guangbo dianying dianshi fazhan baogao* (2006 report on the development of China's radio, film, and television) (Beijing: Xinhua Press, 2006), 166.

14. Yuezhi Zhao, *Communication in China.*

15. SARFT, "Guanyu cujin guangbo yingshi chanye fazhan de yijian" (Opinions on Promoting the Development of the Radio, Television and Film Industry), 2003.

16. SARFT and Ministry of Commerce, "Zhongwai hezi, hezuo guangbo dianshi jiemu zhizuo jingying qiye guanli zanxing guiding" (Provisional Regulations on Sino-Foreign Joint and Cooperative Ventures in Radio and Television Program Productions), 2004.

17. SARFT, "Guanyu shishi 'Zhongwai hezi, hezuo guangbo dianshi jiemu zhizuo jingying qiye guanli zanxing guiding' youguan shiyi de tongzhi" (Notice on

Implementing the Provisional Regulations on Sino-Foreign Joint and Cooperative Ventures in Radio and Television Program Productions), 2005.

18. SARFT, Ministry of Culture, GAPP, National Development and Reform Commission, and Ministry of Commerce, "Guanyu wenhua lingyu yinjin waizi de ruogan yijian" (Opinions on Introducing Foreign Capital to the Cultural Realm), 2005.

19. State Council, "Wenhua chanye zhenxing guihua" (Plan to Revitalize Cultural Industries), 2009.

20. Cultural industries, Chris Bilton points out, are characterized by high levels of risk. One way to deal with that risk, Nicholas Garnham suggests, is to offer a repertoire of cultural goods, across which the risk can be spread, so that even "a small proportion of hits pays for the larger number of flops." But such a strategy favors larger corporations who can exploit economies of scale. For the other cultural producers, guarantee agencies and insurance become increasingly necessary. Chris Bilton, "Risky Business: The Independent Production Sector in Britain's Creative Industries." *International Journal of Cultural Policy* 6, no. 1 (December 1, 1999): 17–39; Nicholas Garnham, "From Cultural to Creative Industries," *International Journal of Cultural Policy* 11, no. 1 (March 1, 2005): 15–29 (quotation on p. 19); and Nicholas Garnham, *Capitalism and Communication: Global Culture and the Economics of Information* (London: Sage, 1990).

21. Yik Chan Chin, "Policy Process, Policy Learning, and the Role of the Provincial Media in China," *Media, Culture & Society* 33, no. 2 (March 1, 2011): 193–210. For more on administrative delegation in radio, film, and television, see Bai, *Staging Corruption.*

22. Chin, "Policy Process, Policy Learning."

23. Wei, interview with author, Beijing, April 20, 2014. Film/television production in China lends itself to money laundering because investment in this field enjoys sizable tax breaks. Moreover, Chinese production companies are notorious for their unclear and confusing accounting and financial record-keeping practices, which makes it extremely hard to track the flow of money. One speculation is that practices such as listing accounts or shareholders under aliases exist to hide government involvement in the companies. In project-based television and film production, crews are often disbanded right after the completion of a project, which makes it even harder to conduct accurate audits.

24. Gang Zhang, "Xiang 92 pai zhijing" (Salute to the '92 school), *China Entrepreneur*, no. 6 (March, 2012).

25. Xinian Tao, "Huace Yingshi shenmi ren 'bei gudong' zhi mi" (Mysterious shareholders of Huace), *Time Weekly*, no. 121 (March 2011).

26. Wei, interview with author, Beijing, April 20, 2014.

27. SARFT, "Guangdian Zongju xinwen fayanren jiu Zhejiang guangdian gaige fazhan jingyan dawen" (SARFT spokesman answered questions regarding the broadcasting reform in Zhejiang Province), April 29, 2010, http://www.gov.cn/gzdt/2010 -04/29/content_1595568.htm.

28. Xiaomei Wang, "Huace mishi: Lou Zhongfu cuoshi de kongzhi quan (Hidden history of Huace: The fortunes Zhongfu Lou missed), *Money Weekly*, May 7, 2012.

29. Wei, interview with author, Beijing, April 20, 2014.

30. Yanyan Chen, "Yu bacheng wenhua chuanmei qiye zhongbao baoxi; binggou reqing bujian yijia gaoshao butui" (Cultural enterprises performing well on market; Enthusiasms in mergers continue), *Securities Daily*, August 29, 2013.

31. Shao, interview with author, Beijing, April 21, 2014; Keane, *Chinese Television Industry*.

32. Baoguo Cui, ed., *2011 Zhongguo chuanmei chanye fazhan baogao* (2011 Report on the development of Chinese media industry) (Beijing: Social Science Literature Press), 144–145.

33. Bai, *Staging Corruption*.

34. Han, interviews with author, Shanghai, June 10 and 11, 2014.

35. Wei, interview with author, Beijing, April 20, 2014.

36. This subheading is a quote from my informant Han, the veteran television industry professional mentioned briefly in the previous section. Han, interviews with author, Shanghai, June 10 and 11, 2014.

37. SARFT, "Guangdian Zongju guanyu 2008 nian 1 yue quanguo paishe zhizuo dianshiju beian gongshi de tongzhi" (SARFT notice on the national television drama production in January 2008), accessed October 22, 2014, http://dsj.sarft.gov.cn/ tims/site/views/applications/note/view.shanty?appName=note&id=011fd9e3fc5504 54402881f71fd9e2a5.

38. Wei, telephone interview with author, October 17, 2014; Xin, telephone interview with author, October 19, 2014.

39. Bai, *Staging Corruption*.

40. The new procedures were set out in *Dianshiju paishe zhizuo bei'an gongshi guanli zanxing banfa* (Provisional Measures on Intent Registration and Publicization of Television Drama Production), issued by the SARFT in 2006.

41. Bai, *Staging Corruption*.

42. SARFT, "Dianshiju neirong guanli guiding" (Rules on Television Drama Content Regulation), accessed June 10, 2014, http://www.gov.cn/flfg/2010-05/20/ content_1609751.htm.

43. This incomplete list of unwritten rules was summarized by an anonymous industry professional and forwarded to me by Wei. I double-checked it with Wei and Xin to confirm the accuracy of its information.

44. SARFT, *Dianshiju neirong guanli guiding*.

45. Wei, interview with author, Beijing, April 20, 2014.

46. Wei, interview with author, Beijing, April 20, 2014.

47. Bai, *Staging Corruption*.

48. Xin, telephone interview with author, October 19, 2014.

49. Xiaoling Zhang, *The Transformation of Political Communication in China: From Propaganda to Hegemony* (Singapore: World Scientific, 2011), 110.

50. Bai, *Staging Corruption*.

51. Wei, interview with author, Beijing, April 20, 2014.

52. Keane, *Chinese Television Industry*.

53. Han, interview with author, Beijing, March 31, 2014.

54. Garnham, *Capitalism and Communication*.

55. Wei, interview with author, Beijing, April 20, 2014.

56. Karla W. Simon, *Civil Society in China: The Legal Framework from Ancient Times to the New Reform Era* (Oxford: Oxford University Press, 2013).

57. Jude Howell, "Striking a New Balance: New Social Organisations in Post-Mao China," *Capital & Class* 18, no. 3 (1999): 89–111.

58. Xin, telephone interview with author, October 19, 2014.

59. Wei, interview with author, Beijing, April 20, 2014.

60. Wei, telephone interview with author, October 17, 2014.

61. The Beijing Television Program Market and Exhibition is one of the most vibrant trade fairs in China's radio, film, and television sector, co-organized by the SARFT's Beijing bureau and the Capital Radio & Television Program Producers Association (*Shoudu guangbo dianshi jiemu zhizuo xiehui*).

62. Xin, interview with author, Beijing, April 21, 2014.

63. Xin, telephone interview with author, October 19, 2014.

64. This subheading comes from my conversations with both my informants Han and Wei. Han, interviews with author, Shanghai, June 10 and 11, 2014. Wei, interview with author, Beijing, April 20, 2014.

65. Han, interview with author, Beijing, March 31, 2014; Shao, interview with author, Beijing, April 21, 2014.

66. Han, interview with author, Beijing, March 31, 2014; Xin, interview with author, Beijing, April 21, 2014.

67. Alexei Yurchak, *Everything Was Forever, Until It Was No More: The Last Soviet Generation* (Princeton: Princeton University Press, 2005).

68. Han, interview with author, Beijing, March 31, 2014; Xin, interview with author, Beijing, April 21, 2014; Bai, *Staging Corruption*.

69. Bai, *Staging Corruption*.

70. Han, interviews with author, Shanghai, June 10 and 11, 2014.

71. Keane, *Creative Industries in* China; Jane Zheng, "'Creative Industry Clusters' and the 'Entrepreneurial City' of Shanghai," *Urban Studies* 48, no. 16 (December, 2011): 3561–3582.

72. Yuchao Zhu and Dongyan Blachford, "'Old Bottle, New Wine'? Xinjiang Bingtuan and China's Ethnic Frontier Governance," *Journal of Contemporary China* 25, no. 97 (2016): 25–40.

73. Shao, interview with author, Beijing, April 21, 2014.

74. Yuezhi Zhao, *Communication in China,* 86.

75. Keane, *Creative Industries in China,* 27.

Chapter 4: Early Online Video

1. Y. Hong, *Networking China.*

2. Hong, *Networking China.*

3. Lena L. Zhang, "Behind the 'Great Firewall': Decoding China's Internet Media Policies from the Inside," *Convergence: The International Journal of Research into New Media Technologies* 12, no. 3 (2006): 271–291.

4. China Internet Network Information Center (CNNIC), *Report on Internet Development in China 2002.* The CNNIC is a state-run agency responsible for internet-related affairs such as the administration of the domain name system.

5. Harwit, *China's Telecommunications Revolution.*

6. Harwit, *China's Telecommunications Revolution.*

7. As Naughton suggests, the command economy before the reforms in China was bureaucratic. Economic decision making was based on information collected from

production/consumption units through bureaucratic channels, and commands were passed down through the same bureaucratic network. Barry Naughton, "Hierarchy and the Bargaining Economy: Government and Enterprise in the Reform Process," in Kenneth Lieberthal and David Lampton, eds., *Bureaucracy, Politics, and Decision Making in Post-Mao China* (Berkeley: University of California Press, 1992): 245–281.

8. Harwit, *China's Telecommunications Revolution*.

9. "Zhongguo Liantong chengli" (Founding of China Unicom), *Telecommunications World*, accessed April 10, 2017, http://tech.sina.com.cn/t/2007-07-06/20041603151 .shtml.

10. Harwit, *China's Telecommunications Revolution*.

11. Harwit, *China's Telecommunications Revolution*.

12. Xiudian Dai, "Digital Inclusion: A Case for Micro Perspectives," in Gillian Youngs, ed., *Digital World: Connectivity, Creativity and Rights* (Abingdon, UK: Routledge, 2013): 34–51.

13. Chung-min Tsai, "The Paradox of Regulatory Development in China: The Case of the Electricity Industry" (Ph.D. diss., University of California, Berkeley, 2010).

14. Harwit, *China's Telecommunications Revolution*.

15. Ch.-m. Tsai, *"Paradox of Regulatory Development in China."*

16. Harwit, *China's Telecommunications Revolution*.

17. Harwit, *China's Telecommunications Revolution*.

18. CNNIC, *Report on Internet Development in China 2002*, 169.

19. See Dan Schiller, *How to Think about Information* (Urbana: University of Illinois Press, 2007).

20. Y. Hong, *Networking China*.

21. Johan Lagerkvist, "The Techno-Cadre's Dream: Administrative Reform by Electronic Governance in China Today?" *China Information* 19, no. 2 (2005): 189–216.

22. Y. Hong, *Networking China*, 62.

23. Ming Tong et al., "IDC shichang jiujing you duoda?" (How large is the IDC market?), *China InfoWorld*, 2000.

24. VNET, "Toushi IDC" (Deep analysis of IDC industry), *Computer World*, 2000.

25. Genesis Capital, "Dui Zhongguo IDC shichang de yuce" (Predicting China's IDC market), Sohu Tech, accessed October 23, 2014, http://tech.sina.com.cn/r/m/53883 .shtml.

26. Guo Huang, "18 wei gaoren bamai Zhongguo IDC" (18 experts diagnose problems for Chinese IDC), *Computer World*, 2001.

27. Hongbin Gao, "The Present and Prospect of China Internet Data Center," accessed October 23, 2014, http://unpan1.un.org/intradoc/groups/public/documents/apcity/unpan001519.pdf; Zixiang Tan, William Foster, and Seymour Goodman, "China's Unique Internet Infrastructure," *Communications of the ACM* 42, no. 6 (June 1999): 44–52.

28. Lisa Parks and Nicole Starosielski, introduction to Lisa Parks and Nicole Starosielski, eds., *Signal Traffic* (Champaign: University of Illinois Press, 2015): 1–27.

29. Baochun Shi, "Shuju zhongxin de dianli baozhang" (Power supply to IDC), *China InfoWorld*, 2001.

30. Shi, "Shuju zhongxin de dianli baozhang."

31. Guo Huang, "IDC bubi cong jian jifang kaishi" (IDC does not need to start with self-built space), *Computer World*, 2001.

32. B. Shi, "Shuju zhongxin de dianli baozhang."

33. Harwit, *China's Telecommunications Revolution*.

34. Genesis Capital, "Dui Zhongguo IDC shichang de yuce."

35. G. Huang, "18 wei gaoren bamai Zhongguo IDC"; Chuan Liu, "Zuo dianxin shichang de linglei wanjia" (To be alternative telecom market player), *Network World*, 2001.

36. Rui Yao, "Gao Hongbing: 'guaiquan' zhong de IDC" (Hongbing Gao: IDC caught in loop), *Computer World*, 2001.

37. G. Huang, "18 wei gaoren bamai Zhongguo IDC."

38. As reported in Qingfeng Yang, "Shuju zhongxin anju zhinan" (Guide to IDC location), *Network World*, August 20, 2007.

39. Tong et al., "IDC shichang jiujing you duoda?"

40. Genesis Capital, "Dui Zhongguo IDC shichang de yuce"; Genesis Capital, "Gaiyao: Zhongguo IDC shichang de guimo yu zengzhang" (Scale and growth of IDC market in China), Sohu Tech, accessed October 25, 2014, http://tech.sina.com.cn/r/m/53860.shtml. In China, telecom resources are unevenly distributed across the country. Using China Telecom's ChinaNET as an example, its internet exchange points, the physical nodes through which major network providers exchange their traffic, exist in three levels. At the first level, core network nodes are located in the cities of Beijing, Shanghai, and Guangzhou and are connected to the global internet. The second level of exchange points includes five additional regional nodes, located in Shenyang, Nanjing, Wuhan, Chengdu, and Xi'an. These second-level

nodes connect the lower-level metropolitan exchange points in their administrative areas to the three hubs (i.e., Beijing, Shanghai, and Guangzhou). And those third-level nodes handle local/municipal internet traffic. See Lisa Hanson, "The Chinese Internet Gets A Stronger Backbone," *Forbes*, February 24, 2015, https://www.forbes.com/sites/lisachanson/2015/02/24/the-chinese-internet-gets-a-stronger-backbone/#77b7bd411ff4. IDC providers at the time chose to build data centers in or near "node" cities because of the larger amount of network resources such as bandwidth in these places.

41. Genesis Capital, "Dui Zhongguo IDC shichang de yuce." In early 2001, the transmission capacity of ChinaNET's backbone network was 17 Gbps.

42. Zixin Li and Fan Hu, "Huanan IDC qidai shengju" (IDCs in southern China expect profits), *China InfoWorld*, 2001.

43. Zhang Liang, "Hulianwang xin de paomo jiao IDC?" (New internet bubble called "IDC"?), *Yesky*, last modified May 11, 2001, http://www.yesky.com/20010511/124520.shtml.

44. Ying Wu, "Minying IDC zaoyu hanliu" (Private IDCs encountered cold spell), *China Enterprise News*, 2001.

45. Guang Yang, "Zhongguo IDC: wang mei zhi ke" (IDCs in China: Longing for success), *Computer World*, 2001; Yao, "Gao Hongbing: 'guaiquan' zhong de IDC."

46. Tom Evens, "The Political Economy of Retransmission Payments and Cable Rights: Implications for Private Television Companies," in Karen Donders, Caroline Pauwels, and Jan Loisen, eds., *Private Television in Western Europe: Content, Markets, Policies* (Houndmills, UK: Palgrave Macmillan, 2013): 182–196.

47. Wen Man, interview with author, Beijing, April 23, 2014.

48. In peer-to-peer (P2P) live streaming, a video file is broken into multiple pieces and sent to a number of peers, who then relay the file to others. The process repeats itself until every peer in the network receives the file from multiple peers instead of from the service provider's server. Whereas, in the client-server model, the requested server has to deliver the video file N times for N users, in the P2P-assisted streaming model, the primary server has to respond to only a few initial requests because the peers in the network have taken on most of the burden of storage and streaming and thus have reduced the traffic pressure on the server's bandwidth. In the early 2000s, Chinese internet users relied on P2P networks to exchange large-size files (as I will show in chapter 5). Commercial companies, however, exploited P2P technology to provide proprietary video-streaming services to their users. Wen Man, interview with author, Beijing, April 23, 2014.

49. Chengdong Zhang, "Daikuan taotie" (Gulosity of bandwidth), *Network World*, August 6, 2007.

50. Hai Lei, "Shipin fenxiang wangzhan; Matai Xiaoying tuxian" (Matthew effect among video-sharing sites), *China Computer Education*, July 23, 2007.

51. Ch. Zhang, "Daikuan taotie."

52. Ji Wang, "YouTube men de zhongguoshi shengcun: 'tou' lai de daikuan" (Chinese YouTube's survival: Living on "stolen" bandwidth), *Telecommunications Weekly*, June 11, 2007.

53. Wang, "YouTube men de zhongguoshi shengcun" (Chinese YouTube's survival).

54. Ch. Zhang, "Daikuan taotie."

55. Wen Man, interview with author, Beijing, April 23, 2014.

56. Yong Ye, "Youku Wang zaihuo fengtou 2500 wan meiyuan zhuzi" (Youku received another $25 million), *Shanghai Securities News*, November 22, 2007.

57. Ch. Zhang, "Daikuan taotie."

58. Y. Hong, *Networking China*.

59. Hao, interview with author, Beijing, April 16, 2014; Wen Man, interview with author, Beijing, April 23, 2014.

60. Zhongbin Hu, "Waizi PE 'lao yi'" (Foreign PE is outdated), *Economic Observer Online*, July 22, 2011, http://www.eeo.com.cn/2011/0722/206907.shtml.

61. Hu, "Waizi PE 'lao yi'" (Foreign PE is outdated).

62. Sina Corporation, Form 10-K for the fiscal year ending June 30, 2000 (filed September 28, 2000), from Sina Corporation website, http://phx.corporate-ir.net/phoenix .zhtml?c=121288&p=irol-sec&secCat01.1_rs=561&secCat01.1_rc=20.

63. Sina Corporation, "Walden International Investment Group Announces the Nasdaq Listing and Successful Initial Public Offering of Portfolio Company SINA. com," June 28, 2000, http://phx.corporate-ir.net/phoenix.zhtml?c=121288&p=irol -newsArticle&ID=101569.

64. Sina Corporation, Form 10-K for the fiscal year ending June 30, 2000.

65. Sina Corporation, "Largest Chinese Internet Portal, Sina.com, Completes $25 Million Round of Financing," May 10, 1999, http://phx.corporate-ir.net/phoenix .zhtml?c=121288&p=irol-newsArticle&ID=68766.

66. See Ministry of Posts and Telecommunications, "Congshi fangkai jingying dianxin yewu shenpi guanli zanxing banfa" (Provisional Measures on the Approval of Operating Opened Telecom Services), 1993; "Fangkai jingying de dianxin yewu shichang guanli zanxing guiding" (Provisional Rules on the Administration of Opened Telecom Services), 1995.

67. Harwit, *China's Telecommunications Revolution*; James McGregor, *One Billion Customers: Lessons from the Front Lines of Doing Business in China* (New York: Free Press, 2005).

68. Harwit, *China's Telecommunications Revolution*.

69. For an extended discussion of the cancellation of the Chinese-Chinese-foreign (CCF) scheme and its consequences, see Harwit, *China's Telecommunications Revolution*.

70. Peng Xie, "Shui zhizao le VIE konghuang?" (Who manufactured VIE panic?), *Southern Weekly*, October 13, 2011.

71. State Council, "Dianxin tiaoli" (Telecommunications Act), 2000.

72. Jichuan Wu, as quoted in "China Bans Internet Investment," *BBC News*, September 15, 1999, http://news.bbc.co.uk/2/hi/business/448305.stm.

73. William Foster, "The Diffusion of the Internet in China" (Ph.D. diss., University of Arizona, 2001).

74. State Council, "Hulianwang xinxi fuwu guanli banfa" (Measures on the Administration of Internet Information Services), 2000.

75. Xu Zhao, *Shao.com (Burning.com)* (Beijing: Guangming Daily, 2001).

76. For a detailed chronology of China's steps toward WTO accession, especially in the telecom sector, see Marc Laperrouza, "China's Telecommunication Policy-Making in the Context of Trade and Economic Reforms" (Ph.D. diss., London School of Economics and Political Science, 2006).

77. X. Zhao, *Shao.com*.

78. In the final agreement, China committed to first opening 25 percent of its basic telecom services in Beijing, Shanghai, and Guangzhou three years after its WTO accession, then 35 percent in sixteen major cities including Beijing, Shanghai, and Guangzhou five years after the WTO accession, and finally 49 percent nationwide six years after its WTO membership began. In value-added services, it committed to opening 30 percent upon accession in Beijing, Shanghai, and Guangzhou, 49 percent in sixteen major cities including Beijing, Shanghai, and Guangzhou one year after it joined WTO, and 50 percent nationwide two years later. In this gradual opening, called a "crazy patchwork approach" by the foreign community, the Chinese state followed an established tradition of experimental liberalization without binding itself to an excessive extent, just as it had in introducing the special economic zones (SEZs). See Laperrouza, "China's Telecommunication Policy-Making."

79. Yining Zhao, "Zhuanfang yuan Xinxi Chanye Bu Fagui Si sizhang Liu Cai" (Interview with former head of Regulation Department of MII Cai Liu), *21st Century Business Herald*, November 21, 2011.

80. Laperrouza, "China's Telecommunication Policy-Making in the Context of Trade and Economic Reforms."

81. For an extended discussion of the rift between these bureaucratic factions, see Harwit, *China's Telecommunications Revolution*; Laperrouza, "China's Telecommunication Policy-Making"; and McGregor, *One Billion Customers*.

82. Joseph Lovell, "Structures for International Private Equity Investment in the PRC," *International In-House Counsel Journal* 4, no. 13 (2010).

83. Ewan W. Rose, "Will China Allow Itself to Enter the New Economy?" *Duke Journal of Comparative & International Law* 11, no. 2 (2001): 451–466.

84. X. Zhao, *Shao.com*.

85. Sina Corporation, Form 10-Q for the quarterly period ending March 31, 2000 (filed May 30, 2000), from Sina Corporation website, http://phx.corporate-ir.net/phoenix.zhtml?c=121288&p=irol-sec&secCat01.1_rs=561&secCat01.1_rc=20.

86. Scott Cendrowski, "Local Investors Miss out on Sizzling Chinese Tech Stocks," *Fortune*, July 11, 2014, accessed Nov. 1, 2014, http://fortune.com/2014/07/11/local-investors-miss-out-on-sizzling-chinese-tech-stocks/.

87. Andrew McGinty, Adrian Emch, Sherry Y. Gong and James Zhang, "China VIE Structure for Foreign Investment under Attack from Multiple Directions: Will it Emerge (Relatively) Unscathed or Is Its Very Survival Threatened?" *Hogan Lovells*, January 20, 2012, https://www.lexology.com/library/detail.aspx?g=94767bad-0dc0-4f05-ab90-9bdffa49cbee.

88. Fan Bao, interview with Sina Tech, http://tech.sina.com.cn/z/baofan/, 2014.

89. Rose, "Will China Allow Itself to Enter the New Economy?"

90. Rocky Lee, "Understanding the VIE Structure: Necessary Elements for Success and the Legal Risks Involved," *Cadwalader Wickersham & Taft LLP*, August 10, 2011, https://www.lexology.com/library/detail.aspx?g=aa820b96-ff4a-4704-b457-243dce432a81.

91. P. Xie, "Shui zhizao le VIE konghuang."

92. David Roberts and Thomas Hall, "VIE Structures in China: What You Need to Know," *An O'Melveny & Myers LLP Research Report*, October 2011.

93. Roberts and Hall, "VIE Structures in China."

94. R. Lee, "Understanding the VIE Structure."

95. Sina Corporation, Form 10-Q for the quarterly period ending March 31, 2000.

96. Heilmann and Perry, "Embracing Uncertainty," 12.

97. Ministry of Information Industry, "Guanyu jiaqiang waishang touzi jingying zengzhi dianxin yewu guanli de tongzhi" (Notice on Strengthening the

Administration of Foreign Investment in and Operation of Value-Added Telecommunications Businesses), 2006.

98. Roberts and Hall, "VIE Structures in China."

99. Jia Liu and Jieyun Xu, "Ma Yun shiyi Zhifubao 'danfei'; xieyi kongzhi buke xing?" (Jack Ma internalized Alipay; VIE no longer works?), *Yicai*, June 15, 2011.

100. Liu and Xu, "Ma Yun shiyi Zhifubao 'danfei'" (Jack Ma internalized Alipay).

101. Kathrin Hille and Joseph Menn, "Alibaba Settles Alipay Dispute with Yahoo," July 30, 2011, https://www.ft.com/content/40a66dd2-b9ec-11e0-8171-00144feabdc0.

102. Cendrowski, "Local Investors Miss Out."

103. Donald Clark, "Who Owns the Chinese Internet?" *Chinese Law Prof Blog*, July 7, 2011, http://lawprofessors.typepad.com/china_law_prof_blog/2011/07/who-owns -the-chinese-internet.html.

104. P. Xie, "Shui zhizao le VIE konghuang."

105. Yanbing Geng, "Shangwubu: waizi binggou jin zhan liyong waizi 3.1%" (Ministry of Commerce: Foreign mergers only account for 3.1% of foreign investments), *21st Century Business Herald*, September 21, 2011.

106. Roberts and Hall, "VIE Structures in China."

107. Giorgio Agamben, *State of Exception* (Chicago: University of Chicago Press, 2003).

108. Dongfang Ping, "Hulianwang guanli, cong pojie 'jiulong zhishui' qibu" (Internet governance starts from breaking bureaucratic turf war), *East Day*, October 19, 2014, http://pinglun.eastday.com/p/20141019/u1ai8398239.html.

109. Newman, *Video Revolutions*.

110. Ministry of Culture, "Hulianwang wenhua guanli zanxing tiaoli" (Provisional Rules for the Administration of Internet Culture), 2003.

111. SARFT, "Guanyu jiaqiang tongguo xinxi wangluo xiang gongzhong chuanbo guangbo dianying dianshi lei jiemu guanli de tongzhi" (Notice Concerning Strengthening the Administration of Quasi–Radio, Film, and Television Programs Communicated to the Public via Information Networks), 1999.

112. SARFT, "Xinxi wangluo chuanbo guangbo dianying dianshi lei jiemu jiandu guanli zanxing banfa" (Provisional Measures for the Supervision and Administration of Quasi–Radio, Film, and Television Programs Communicated via Information Networks), 2000.

113. SARFT, "Hulianwang deng xinxi wangluo chuanbo shiting jiemu guanli banfa" (Measures for the Administration of Audiovisual Programs Communicated via Information Networks Including Internet), 2003.

114. The SARFT's update from "rule 15" to "rule 39" was also made in the light of the new Administrative Permission Law released in March 2004. All ministerial rules that contradicted the new law had to be revised accordingly. See Dahong Min, Binyan Yang, and Fei Jiang, "Yinshipin neirong zai hulianwang shang de chuanbo jiexi" (Analysis of online circulation of audiovisual content), *International Broadcasting, Film, and Television*, nos. 3–4, 2005.

115. X. Dai, "Digital Inclusion."

116. Anthony Fung and Luzhou Li, "TV Box on the Internet: The Interplay between Politics and Market in China," in D. Y. Jin ed., *Global Media Convergence and Cultural Transformation: Emerging Social Patterns and Characteristics* (Hershey, Pa.: IGI Global, 2010): 327–339.

117. Yue Ping, "Goujian youxiao cujin IPTV yewu fazhan de jianguan tixi" (Constructing regulatory system to effectively facilitate the development of IPTV), *People's Posts and Telecommunications*, August 22, 2006.

118. Ping, "Goujian youxiao cujin IPTV yewu fazhan de jianguan tixi" (Constructing regulatory system to effectively facilitate the development of IPTV).

119. Ping, "Goujian youxiao cujin IPTV yewu fazhan de jianguan tixi" (Constructing regulatory system to effectively facilitate the development of IPTV).

120. Wei Xiong, "Hulianwang xin guiding yinchu wenhua huati" (Internet new rules bring about cultural topics), *Computer World*, 2003.

121. Da Hai, "Wangluo dianshi taidong" (Emerging online television), *Computer World*, June 7, 2004.

122. "Beifang Wang kaiban wangshang chuanbo guangbo dianying dianshi lei jiemu yi huode Guojia Guangdian Zongju pizhun" (Enorth's quasi–radio, film, and television programs services approved by SARFT), enorth, February 20, 2003, http://news.enorth.com.cn/system/2003/02/19/000510568.shtml.

123. SARFT, *China Radio & TV Yearbook 2003*, 48–49; SARFT, *China Radio & TV Yearbook 2004*, 59.

124. Hai, "Wangluo dianshi taidong."

125. SARFT, *China Radio & TV Yearbook 2005*.

126. Jiansen Zhou, "Wangtong shouhuo wangshang chuanbo shiting jiemu xukezheng" (Netcom becomes first receiver of online audiovisual program transmission permit), Sina News, May 27, 2004, http://news.sina.com.cn/c/2004-05-27/12362643791s.shtml; Hai, "Wangluo dianshi taidong."

127. SARFT, *China Radio & TV Yearbook 2005*.

128. Yan Shi, "Shanghai Wenguang shouhuo IPTV paizhao beihou" (Behind SMG's IPTV granted permit), Sina Tech, May 21, 2005, http://tech.sina.com.cn/t/2005-05-21/1454613793.shtml.

129. Liang Xie, "'Zuoxiu' de Tudou; qianwei de 'boke'" (Tudou is staging show), *CPPCC Daily*, December 23, 2005.

130. Peng, interview with author, Shanghai, June 1, 2016.

131. Robert Post, *Censorship and Silencing: Practices of Cultural Regulation* (Los Angeles: Getty Research Institute, 1998), 2.

132. Yue Lu, "Shipin wangzhan tante miandui guangdian xingui; xiao wangzhan jiangshou gengda chongji" (Video websites perturbed about new SARFT rules), *Yicai*, August 16, 2006.

133. Guohua Li, "Guangdian shenru 'jinqu'; wangluo jianguan xinhao jianqiang" (SARFT strengthens online regulation), *China Business Journal*, August 21, 2006.

134. Hongzhang Ni, "Shuzi dianshi 'xiaoao' IPTV" (Digital television outmaneuvered IPTV), Sina Tech, March 6, 2006, http://tech.sina.com.cn/t/2006-03-06/1126858615.shtml?from=wap.

135. Zeyun Wang, "Liumeiti zhandian tashang 'leiqu'" (Streaming sites stepped on minefield), *China InfoWorld*, March 26, 2007; CNNIC, *Report on Internet Development in China 2007*, 465–466; SARFT, *China Radio & TV Yearbook 2007*.

136. Hongzhang Ni, "Wangluo dianshi weihe zaojin" (Why online television was banned), *Computer World*, March 26, 2007.

137. Peng, interview with author, Shanghai, June 1, 2016.

138. Dingling Sun, "Wangluo egao jiang taoshang 'jinguzhou'" (Regulation strengthened on online spoofing), *China Press Journal*, September 6, 2006.

139. Xiaqing Yang, "Wangluo shipin jianguan nanti" (Thorny issue in online video regulation), *Computer World*, August 21, 2006.

140. Yang, "Wangluo shipin jianguan nanti"; Guohua Li, "Guangdian shenru 'jinqu.'"

141. X. Yang, "Wangluo shipin jianguan nanti."

142. Xuemei Zhai, "Zouzai jishu zhiqian de jianguan moshi tantao" (Exploration of regulatory model ahead of technologies), *Telecommunications Weekly*, September 5, 2005.

143. *Hulianwang shiting jiemu fuwu guanli guiding*, 2007.

144. L. Zhang, "Behind the 'Great Firewall.'"

145. SARFT, *China Radio & TV Yearbook 2008*.

146. SARFT, *China Radio & TV Yearbook 2009*.

147. Sina Corporation, "Tudou Wang bashe jiuge yue zhong huo shipin paizhao" (Tudou finally received video permit after nine months), Sina Tech, September 10, 2008, http://tech.sina.com.cn/i/2008-09-10/15032448867.shtml.

148. Pearl Research, "Chinese Authorities Punish Tudou and 61 Other Online Video Sites for Violating Regulations," *Forbes*, March 20, 2008, http://www.forbes.com/2008/03/20/china-video-tudou-tech-cx_pco_0320paidcontent.html.

149. SARFT, *China Radio & TV Yearbook 2000–2007*.

150. Tao, interview with author, Beijing, April 24, 2014.

151. SARFT, *China Radio & TV Yearbook 2009*.

152. As reported in Guohua Li, "Guangdian shenru 'jinqu.'"

Chapter 5: Piracy, Internet Culture, and the Early Online Video Industry

1. The "last mile" refers to the final stage of telecom network development, which delivers telecom services (including broadband internet service) to end users.

2. CNNIC, *Report on Internet Development in China 2006*, 14.

3. Shiwang Tang, "2002 ni yongshang kuandai le ma" (Did you use broadband service in 2002?), *BJKP*, accessed November 3, 2014, http://www.bjkp.gov.cn/zhuanti/old_bjkp/dnsj/wjwx/k30134-04.htm.

4. Dagang Feng, "Zhongguo Dianxin Hulian Xingkong quanmian shangyong; liyi gongxiang shoudao SP huanying" (China Telecom's VNET is ready for commercial use; SP welcomes revenue sharing), *Sohu IT*, last modified September 16, 2003, http://it.sohu.com/58/01/article213250158.shtml.

5. Xian Jia, "Zaixian shipin dianbo wangzhan de banian kangzhan" (Eight-year war of VOD websites), *ChinaByte*, last modified April 29, 2008, http://net.chinabyte.com/285/8097285.shtml.

6. D. Feng, "Zhongguo Dianxin Hulian Xingkong quanmian shangyong."

7. Hong Liu, "Xieshou 'SP', Hulian Xingkong dazao da pingtai" (VNET builds large platform with SP), *Telecommunications Weekly*, December 5, 2005, 056.

8. Jia, "Zaixian shipin dianbo wangzhan de banian kangzhan."

9. This conclusion about the role of online service/content providers in copyright infringement in China was drawn from users' online comments, commercial market research, and the subsequent state-led antipiracy campaigns and corporate-initiated copyright lawsuits around 2008.

10. Qianshan Muxue, "Xiaozhang de daoban dianying shoufei wangzhan—'Hulian Xingkong'" (Daring paid pirate film site—"VNET"), *JYSQ.Net* (forum), April 6, 2007 (6:49 p.m.), http://bbs.jysq.net/thread-865133-1-1.html.

11. Mingsi Li, "Hulian Xingkong 'shehuang'; yunyingshang buneng jidang yundongyuan youdang caipanyuan" (VNET gets involved in providing pornography), *Legal Daily*, July 15, 2007.

12. In the beginning, these download-managing softwares only supported protocols, such as Hypertext Transfer Protocol (HTTP) and File Transfer Protocol (FTP), that were used to transfer files between a server and clients on a computer network. They began to support protocols such as BitTorrent (BT) after P2P technology took over the client-server model. GB, telephone interview with author, July 19, 2014.

13. Guobin Yang, *The Power of the Internet in China: Citizen Activism Online* (New York: Columbia University Press, 2009).

14. A. Wu, "Broadening the Scope of Cultural Preferences."

15. See Michel Hockx, *Internet Literature in China* (New York: Columbia University Press, 2015).

16. Jessie Jiang and Simon Elegant, "Avoiding Censors, Chinese Authors Go Online." *Time*, March 16, 2009, http://content.time.com/time/world/article/0,8599,1885399,00 .html.

17. For an extended discussion of Flash culture in China, see, Weihua Wu, *Chinese Animation, Creative Industries, and Digital Culture* (London: Routledge, 2017).

18. Wu, *Chinese Animation, Creative Industries, and Digital Culture*, 115.

19. GB, telephone interview with author, July 19, 2014. GB's reminiscences were checked against accounts in contemporaneous niche magazines and trade newspapers.

20. Tian Fu, "BT xiazai: yong falv jiayu shouzhong de shuangrenjian" (BT downloading: Double-edged sword harnessed by law), *China Intellectual Property News*, May 31, 2006.

21. Chao Liu, "P2p shi yao bangsha haishi zhao'an" (Should P2P be forbidden or incorporated?), *China Intellectual Property News*, March 3, 2006, 012.

22. GB, telephone interview with author, July 19, 2014.

23. Chuantao Li, "Hulian Xingkong wunian zhibian: cong pingtai dao menhu" (Five-year transformation of VNET: From platform to portal), *Telecommunications Weekly*, May 28, 2007, 008.

24. GB, telephone interview with author, July 19, 2014.

25. Na Yang, "Bubble or Future? The Challenge of Web 2.0 in China," *Intercultural Communication Studies* 17, no. 3 (2008): 93–103.

26. Wen Man, interview with author, Beijing, April 23, 2014; See also Xinyuan Li, "Zaixian shipin fenxiang ni de jingcai" (Online video emerging for self-expression), *Computer World*, August 14, 2006.

27. Gary Wang, "Toodou.com zenme lai de?" (How was Toodou.com born?), *Visible Mind* (blog), March 9, 2005, http://visiblemind.org/?p=811.

28. Wang, "Toodou.com zenme lai de?" (How was Toodou.com born?).

29. Zhen Zhang and Angela Zito, eds. *DV-Made China: Digital Subjects and Social Transformations after Independent Film* (Honolulu: University of Hawai'i Press, 2015).

30. Paola Voci, *China on Video: Smaller-Screen Realities* (Abingdon, UK: Routledge, 2010).

31. Hu, interview with author, Shanghai, July 25, 2014. In this book, I use aliases instead of the real names of my informants except for Hu and two professionally generated content (PGC) producers, Siwen and Tong, cited in chapter 7. Hu's productions, especially his spoof "A Murder Caused by a Steamed Bun," are widely known, which makes him easily identifiable, as the details I mention do for Siwen and Tong.

32. Urban-management police, commonly called "Chengguan" in China, are responsible for maintaining urban order. In past years, reports of intensified confrontations between Chengguan and marginalized urban social groups filled the Chinese internet.

33. Haomin Gong and Xin Yang, "Digitized Parody: The Politics of Egao in Contemporary China," *China Information* 24, no. 1 (March 1, 2010): 3–26.

34. Bingchun Meng, "From Steamed Bun to Grass Mud Horse: E Gao as Alternative Political Discourse on the Chinese Internet," *Global Media and Communication* 7, no. 1 (April 1, 2011): 33–51.

35. Meng, "From Steamed Bun to Grass Mud Horse"; Hongmei Li, "Parody and Resistance on the Chinese Internet," in David Kurt Herold and Peter Marolt, eds., *Online Society in China: Creating, Celebrating, and Instrumentalising the Online Carnival*, (Abingdon, UK: Routledge, 2011): 71–88; Voci, *China on Video*.

36. Hongmei Li, "Parody and Resistance on the Chinese Internet."

37. Paul Clark, *Youth Culture in China: From Red Guards to Netizens* (Cambridge: Cambridge University Press, 2012).

38. Gang Zhong, "Yi kaobei chudao, kaiqi Zhongguo yaogunyue lieche" (Chinese rock started with copycat), *Southern Metropolis Daily*, October 12, 2008.

39. Living in the work-unit compound of the Ministry of the Foreign Affairs, Ma presumably possessed privileged cultural capital, and Wang's connection to him shows that they shared the same or adjacent social space. In fact, Wang's parents taught at the Central Academy of Fine Arts, the most renowned art academy in China. Perhaps his family background enabled him to connect to the outside world, even during the Cultural Revolution. In this way, unevenly distributed cultural capital across classes and social spaces structured the patterns of cultural consumption, especially at the very beginning of the reform. In this sense, early rock music in China was a product of elite cultural practices rather than a form of subculture. See Jinyue Cui and Min Yuan, "Cuijian men de 30 nian fengyu" (Thirty years of China's rock stars), *Sohu News*, last modified September 9, 2010, http://news.sohu.com/20100909/n274819952.shtml.

40. G. Zhong, "Yi copy chudao, kaiqi zhongguo yaogunyue lieche."

41. Baranovitch, *China's New Voices.*

42. Wai, interview with author, Shanghai, June 8, 2016.

43. Hu, interview with author, Shanghai, July 25, 2014.

44. Tudou used to ask its users to tag the content they uploaded as "original" or "nonoriginal" so it could estimate the percentage of content originally created by them, as opposed to content they imported (pirated) from elsewhere. But when they often failed to use either tag, Tudou's choice of "original" as the default tag made an accurate estimate of original spoofing impossible. Wai, interview with author, Shanghai, June 8, 2016.

45. Jean Burgess and Joshua Green, *YouTube: Online Video and Participatory Culture* (Cambridge: Polity Press, 2009); Limor Shifman, "An Anatomy of a YouTube Meme," *New Media & Society* 14, no. 2 (2011): 187–203.

46. GB, telephone interview with author, July 19, 2014.

47. Yi Chen, as quoted in Wenjie Jin, "Meiju hefa rujing hou de zimuzu: bei shoubian, buzai qiang shoufa" (Fansubbing groups after official import of U.S. television series), *Sina Tech*, last modified June 16, 2014, http://tech.sina.com.cn/i/2014-06-16/08499438956.shtml.

48. GB, telephone interview with author, July 19, 2014.

49. Linhua Yang, "Rongzi guanjun Tudou Wang: shizhong jianchi 'caogen da juchang'" (Fundraising champion Tudou keeps its grassroots orientation), *21st Century Business Herald*, October 12, 2007.

50. Bingchun Meng, "Underdetermined Globalization: Media Consumption via P2P Networks." *International Journal of Communication* 6, (2012): 467–483.

51. Gary Hall, "Introduction: Pirate Philosophy," *Culture Machine: Pirate Philosophy* 10, no. 0 (2009): 1–5; quotation on p. 2.

52. L. Yang "Rongzi guanjun Tudou Wang."

53. Feng Wu, "Shipin fenxiang wangzhan mianlin chengzhang fannao" (Growing pains of video-sharing websites), *China InfoWorld*, August 21, 2006.

54. L. Yang, "Rongzi guanjun Tudou Wang."

55. Jiyong Hou, "San'ge Web 2.0 de rongzi meng" (Fundraising dreams of three Web 2.0s), *21st Century Business Herald*, March 13, 2006.

56. Xiaoyan Li, "Fengxian touzi buqi shipin wangzhan; Xuxin biaotai 'yang ta san-nian'" (Venture capitalists promise to stay with video sites for another three years). *21st Century Business Herald*, October 12, 2007, 024.

57. Xudong Zhang, "Heyi Wangluo tuichu Youku Wang" (1Verge Inc. launches Youku), *China InfoWorld*, July 19, 2006.

58. Hui Gu, "Shipin wangzhan rongzi cheng bifu youxi?" (Fundraising of video sites turning into game for rich?), *China Business Journal*, December 3, 2007.

59. Wen Man, interview with author, Beijing, April 23, 2014.

60. Peng, interview with author, Shanghai, June 1, 2016.

61. Wai, interview with author, Shanghai, June 8, 2016.

62. Zhao and Keane, "Between Formal and Informal."

63. Yuhong Lin, "Wangshang 'egao' zhi feng dang sha" (Online "spoofing" should be stopped), *Guangming Daily*, August 10, 2006, accessed November 15, 2014, http://tech.sina.com.cn/i/2006-08-11/15321082387.shtml.

64. Guangming Daily, "Wangshang 'egao' youbei hexie linian" (Online "spoofing" counters harmonious ideals), *GMW*, November 29, 2006, accessed November 15, 2014, http://www.gmw.cn/01gmrb/2006-11/29/content_514452.htm.

65. G. Yang, *Power of the Internet in China.*

66. All kinds of capital production involve risk to some extent, cultural production in particular, whose high risk stems from the inherent uncertainty of popular tastes. As Richard Caves points out, uncertain demand means that neither producers nor consumers know in advance what audiences want in the cultural productions. Con-sidered from this perspective, early video culture was a bellwether of popular tastes and informed video companies' various initiatives, including their commercial in-house projects. See Richard Caves, *Creative Industries: Contracts between Art and Commerce* (Cambridge, MA: Harvard University Press, 2000).

Chapter 6: Bidding on the Rights to Stream

1. Sohu Corporation, "Tudou Wang Wangwei: 2009 jiangshi shipin wangzhan jian-nan de yinian" (Gary Wang: 2009 will be a tough year for video sites), Sohu IT, September 19, 2008, http://it.sohu.com/20080919/n259649951.shtml.

2. See Liang Chen and Qiuju Shi, "Di'erbo hulianwang rechao jisu tuishao" (Second wave of internet fever is cooling down), *Nanfang Daily*, October 31, 2006; A Ding, "Web 2.0 jinyu hanliu erfei yandong" (Web 2.0 encounters cold spell), *Computer World*, September 18, 2006.

3. Sina Corporation, "Tudou Wang xuanbu huode disanlun rongzi" (Tudou.com announces third round of financing), Sina Tech, April 16, 2007, http://tech.sina .com.cn/i/2007-04-16/17531467661.shtml.

4. Guoqiang Yang, "Youku Wang wancheng disanlun rongzi 2500 wan meiyuan" (Youku completed a third-round financing of $25 million), *Yicai*, November 22, 2007.

5. Na Zhao, "56 Wang 8000 wan meiyuan jiaru Renren" (Renren acquired 56.com for $80 million), *PE Daily*, September 27, 2011.

6. Wei Liao, "Wangwei naixin zhong 'Tudou'" (Gary Wang plants "Tudou" with patience), *China Securities News*, September 16, 2006.

7. Yilan Li, "Shipin wangzhan: neirong, zhengce he guanggao gege doushi 'kan'" (Video websites: Content, policy, and advertising are all obstacles), *China Culture Daily*, December 8, 2006.

8. Guoxun Li and Yufeng Rao, "Shipin wangzhan de yingli tuwei" (Video sites attempt to break through in profit making), *China Business Post*, November 30, 2007.

9. iResearch, *China Online Advertising Research Report* 2006 (Shanghai: iResearch Consulting Group, 2007); Shengmin Huang et al., *Zhongguo guanggaozhu yingxiao qushi baogao 2007–2008 (Report on the marketing trends of advertisers in China, 2007–2008)* (Beijing: Social Science Literature Press, 2008), 39.

10. Sh. Huang et al., *Zhongguo guanggaozhu yingxiao qushi baogao 2007–2008*, 524.

11. Xiaoyan Li, "Fengxian touzi buqi shipin wangzhan."

12. Vice president of ku6.com, as quoted in Guoxun Li and Rao, "Shipin wangzhan de yingli tuwei."

13. Li and Rao, "Shipin wangzhan de yingli tuwei."

14. Dan Schiller and Christian Sandvig, "Is YouTube the Successor to Television—Or to Life Magazine?" *Huffington Post*, May 12, 2010, http://www.huffingtonpost.com/ dan-schiller/is-youtube-the-successor_b_497198.html.

15. Zhijun Zhou, "Pinpin qianshou dianshiye; shipin wangzhan qiangzhan neirong 'lanhai'" (Video sites cooperated with television industry), *China Culture Daily*, September 14, 2007.

16. Joseph Turow, *The Daily You: How the New Advertising Industry Is Defining Your Identity and Your Worth* (New Haven: Yale University Press, 2011).

17. Yan Liu, as quoted in Zhou, "Pinpin qianshou dianshiye."

18. Zhiping Zheng, "Chousi bolv; liangchu wangzhan qinquan zhenxiong" (Real criminal of online copyright infringement), *China Intellectual Property News*, September 7, 2007.

19. Qiushi Shi, "P2p-VC de xia yitong jin?" (P2p-VC's next pot of gold?), *China High-Tech Industry Herald*, April 3, 2006.

20. See Guoxun Li, "Banquan chezhou shipin wangzhan" (Copyright becomes obstacle for video websites), *China Business Post*, November 20, 2006.

21. Chinese copyright owners were willing to transfer exclusive digital rights to single intermediaries instead of selling nonexclusive rights to many for two principal reasons. First, because of the underdeveloped nature of the new media market, they could expect to get only meager revenues from the content of their projects, and single-package transfers of exclusive rights saved them the bother of trying to find many buyers for nonexclusive ones. Hao, interview with author, Beijing, April 16, 2014. And, second, given the high level of informality in television drama and film production in China, most producers/investors would withdraw from projects soon after distribution and monetization, and, of those who did remain, few would be interested in selling nonexclusive rights one by one.

22. Xiangbao Hu, "Shipin luanxiang diaocha: banquan fenxiaoshang beizhi 'diaoyu qizha'" (Survey of chaos in video sector), *Tencent Tech*, November 15, 2010, http://tech.qq.com/a/20101115/000146.htm.

23. "Leshi chaoji dianshi: meilaoban baozhuang chu de disanjia shangshi gongsi gainian" (LeTV super television: Third concept coined by Yueting Jia), May 9, 2013, http://biz.zjol.com.cn/system/2013/05/08/019326291.shtml.

24. See Xiaoping Xie, "Linglei jingshang Jia Yueting: mouhua sijia gongsi shangshi" (Yueting Jia's alternative business style), May 29, 2013, http://tech.163.com/13/0529/04/90105BFD000915BF.html.

25. "Leshi chaoji dianshi."

26. Hao, interview with author, Beijing, April 16, 2014.

27. "Leshi chaoji dianshi."

28. Hao, telephone interview with author, December 2, 2017.

29. Jia, "Zaixian shipin dianbo wangzhan de banian kangzhan."

30. Hao, interview with author, Beijing, April 16, 2014.

31. Siyue Fang, "Shipin wangzhan zhuzuoquan qinquan jianjie zeren tanjiu" (Exploration of indirect responsibility of video websites in rights infringement), *China Intellectual Property News*, February 25, 2011.

32. Ming Zhao, "Banquan susong: shipinye tanglang yu huangque youxi" (Copyright lawsuits in video industry), *China Economic Times*, April 1, 2010.

33. Na Li, "Shipin wangzhan baisulv yu jiucheng reng qinquan buzhi" (Video websites' copyright infringement continues despite more than 90 percent denial rate in lawsuits), *Legal Daily*, November 20, 2006.

34. Long, interview with author, Shanghai, June 3, 2016.

35. Hao, interview with author, Beijing, April 16, 2014.

36. *Xinxi wangluo chuanboquan baohu tiaoli*, 2006.

37. Fangyuan Liu, "Jidong jiemeng su Tudou; shipin fenxiang moshi yukao" (Joy.cn sued Tudou; Video sharing encountered challenges), *21st Century Business Herald*, January 8, 2009.

38. Peng Xie, "'Meiyou le shengcun yali, jiu buhui xiang zuo'e le'" ("No evils if there is no survival pressure"), *Nanfang Daily*, October 15, 2009.

39. Hui Bo, "Kunrao wangluo shipin hangye de banquan miju" (Copyright labyrinth in online video industry), *China Intellectual Property News*, March 13, 2009.

40. Xi Wu, "Wangluo banquan 'wanji' nanzhi; 'bifenggang yuanze' dai tiaozheng" (Online infringement is difficult to eradicate; "Safe harbor rule" needs adjustment), *China High-Tech Industry Herald*, July 25, 2011.

41. Hao, interview with author, Beijing, April 16, 2014.

42. X. Hu, "Shipin luanxiang diaocha"; P. Xie, "'Meiyou le shengcun yali, jiu buhui xiang zuo'e le'."

43. Zhang Li, "Daguansi kefou zhongjie wangluo qinquan?" (Can lawsuits end online infringement?), *Procuratorial Daily*, August 7, 2009.

44. Hao, interview with author, Beijing, April 16, 2014.

45. Tian Luo, "Shipin wangzhan mianlin 'bu qinquan jiu si'?" (Video websites could only survive by infringement?), *Beijing Business Today*, January 6, 2009.

46. X. Hu, "Shipin luanxiang diaocha."

47. Luo, "Shipin wangzhan mianlin 'bu qinquan jiu si'?"

48. N. Li, "Shipin wangzhan baisulv yu jiucheng reng qinquan buzhi."

49. Rong Wang, "Leshi Wang banquan fenxiao tuidong yeji dazeng" (Rights business makes big contribution to LeTV), *China Securities Journal*, March 16, 2012.

50. Jin Sun, "Shipin wangzhan dongri zhongguoshi jiushu: gaibian dianshiju chanye" (Video sites change television drama industry), *Yicai*, November 26, 2008.

51. Sina Corporation, "Leshi Wang guapai shangshi; A Gu shoujia wangluo shipin gongsi dansheng" (LeTV launched IPO), *Sina Tech*, August 12, 2010, http://tech.sina .com.cn/i/2010-08-12/09454536935.shtml.

52. Wen Man, interview with author, Beijing, April 23, 2014.

53. Kazunori Takada, "Youku to Buy Tudou, Creating China Online Video Giant," *Reuters*, March 12, 2012, https://www.reuters.com/article/us-youku-tudou/youku-to -buy-tudou-creating-china-online-video-giant-idUSBRE82B0HD20120312.

54. Qingping Ge, "Baituo qinquan kunjing; shipin wangzhan mou chulu" (Video sites seeking ways out of infringement dilemma), *China High-Tech Industry Herald*, December 7, 2009; NetEase, "6.cn zhuanxing shipin shequ; huo xukezheng jingying zaixian yanchu" (6.cn received permit to run online performance business), *NetEase Tech*, accessed January 21, 2015, http://tech.163.com/10/1209/03/ 6NED5SHS000915BF.html; "Why Does Renren Acquire 56.com?" *Business Insider*, September 28, 2011, http://www.businessinsider.com/why-renren-acquired-video -site-56com-2011-9.

55. Sohu Corporation, "Sohu.com to Deliver Exclusive Online Video Content for FIFA World Cup 2006," March 23, 2006, http://corp.sohu.com/20060323/ n242442471.shtml.

56. Xinying Dou, "Shenxian banquan jiufen nitan; shipin hangye youdian luan" (Chaotic video industry deeply implicated in rights disputes), *China Intellectual Property News*, December 4, 2009.

57. Yaqing Hu, "Shipin fengyun" (Ebb and flow of video), *China Business Journal*, September 21, 2009; and Hao, interview with author, Beijing, April 16, 2014.

58. Jieyun Xu, "Lei Tengxun moshi de youhuo yu bianjie" (Lures and boundaries of the semi-Tencent model), *Yicai*, July 14, 2011.

59. P. Xie, "'Meiyou le shengcun yali, jiu buhui xiang zuo'e le'."

60. Chunyan Gao, "Qianwan yuan qianggou reboju; wei qiang dipan shipin wangzhan sha hongyan" (Video sites dogfight over hot television series), *China InfoWorld*, August 1, 2011.

61. "Internet TV Battle," *Global Times*, May 10, 2012, http://www.globaltimes.cn/ content/708849.shtml.

62. Hao, interview with author, Beijing, April 22, 2014.

63. Yina Gou, "Remen dianshiju wangluo banquan jiage baodie wucheng" (Price of hot television series drops by half), May 2, 2012, http://tech.163.com/12/0502/03/80FGR93V000915BF.html.

64. Mengwei Jiang, "Yingyuan shipin wangzhan boyi dianying 'chuangkouqi'" (Cinema chains and video sites fight over "release window"), *Beijing Business Today*, March 23, 2012.

65. Shanghai Media Group (SMG) Research and Development Office, "Zhongguo fufei dianshi huanman tuijin; ruhe dapo fazhan jiangju" (Slow development of paid TV in China requires solutions), *Satellite TV and Broadband Multimedia*, 2008.

66. Campbell Cowie and Sandeep Kapur, "The Management of Digital Rights in Pay TV," in Martin Cave and Kiyoshi Nakamura, eds., *Digital Broadcasting: Policy and Practice in the Americas, Europe and Japan* (Cheltenham, UK: Edward Elgar, 2006): 162–186.

67. Hao, interview with author, Beijing, April 22, 2014.

68. M. Jiang, "Yingyuan shipin wangzhan boyi dianying 'chuangkouqi'."

69. Hao, interview with author, Beijing, April 22, 2014.

70. Jeff Ulin, *The Business of Media Distribution: Monetizing Film, TV, and Video Content* (Abingdon, UK: Taylor & Francis, 2010).

71. Hao, interview with author, Beijing, April 22, 2014.

72. Hao, interview with author, Beijing, April 22, 2014.

73. Michael Curtin, "The Future of Chinese Cinema: Some Lessons from Hong Kong and Taiwan," in Chin-Chuan Lee, ed., *Chinese Media, Global Contexts* (London: Routledge, 2003), 237–256.

74. Hao, interview with author, Beijing, April 22, 2014. The "Big Six" refers, of course, to the current six "Hollywood majors" or leading Hollywood studios: Columbia, Disney, Paramount, 20th Century Fox, Universal, and Warner (Warner Bros.).

75. Toby Miller et al., *Global Hollywood 2* (London: British Film Institute, 2004).

76. Hao, interview with author, Beijing, April 22, 2014.

77. Hongjun Liu, "Meiju zhengduozhan" (Business war on American televisions series), *Global Entrepreneur*, April 1–15, 2013.

78. Sohu Corporation, "Meiju zhengban geming: rang mengxiang zhaojin xianshi" (Legalizing American television series), *Sohu Television Monthly*, accessed February 2, 2015, http://yule.sohu.com/s2012/3608/s353540936/.

79. Hao, interview with author, Beijing, April 22, 2014.

80. Herbert Schiller, *Mass Communications and American Empire* (New York: A. M. Kelley, 1969).

81. Alan Lau, "Succeeding in China's Online Video Market," July 2011, https://www.mckinsey.com/industries/media-and-entertainment/our-insights/succeeding-in-chinas-online-video-market; Hao, interview with author, Beijing, April 22, 2014.

82. Hao, interview with author, Beijing, April 22, 2014.

83. Hongjun Liu, "Meiju zhengduozhan"; Yeksy, "Souhu yinjin Suoni yingshi 600 dapian; jianli Haolaiwu pianyuanku" (Sohu imported 600 titles from Sony), *Yesky*, April 6, 2012, http://news.yesky.com/204/31060704.shtml; TechWeb, "Souhu Shipin yinjin duobu dapian fali haiwai banquan shichang" (Sohu Video imported numerous blockbusters), November 28, 2012, http://www.techweb.com.cn/internet/2012-11-28/1258881.shtml.

84. Sohu Corporation, "Meiju zhengban geming."

85. Hongjun Liu, "Meiju zhengduozhan."

86. Xiazhi Li, "Meiju dubo beihou de banquan jiaoliang" (Copyright wrestling behind exclusive streaming of American television series), *Beijing Daily*, February 15, 2014.

87. Yingying Dou, "Souhu Shipin: caigou meiju you jiqiao" (Sohu Video: Acquiring American television series requires skills), *China Economic Times*, March 19, 2013.

88. In earlier years, the companies had relied on online piracy communities to find out about popular American television series. At one point, for example, Sohu Video's acquisitions director had used pirated videos to watch the first three seasons of *Gossip Girl* before the company decided to buy the series in 2010. Hongjun Liu, "Meiju zhengduozhan."

89. "Shipin wangzhan goumai meiju shengyi jing" (Video websites' business of acquiring American television series), *Yicai*, November 5, 2013, http://www.yicai.com/news/3087973.html.

90. Chao Han, "'Bing yu huo' 35 nian: meiju zai Zhongguo" (35 years of "ice and fire": American television series in China), *Yicai*, April 30, 2014.

91. Hao, interview with author, Beijing, April 22, 2014.

92. Juan Xue, "Shipin qiye anzhan meiju" (Video companies fought over American television series), *China Economic Times*, October 29, 2013.

93. Y. Dou, "Souhu Shipin."

94. Xiaowei Cai, "Shipin wangzhan shi ruhe tiaoxuan meiju de?" (How do video sites select U.S. television series?), *Dongfang Daily*, October 10, 2013.

95. Jing Li, "Shipin wangzhan xin jueli: yinjin yu zizhi" (Video sites' new war: Import and in-house production), *Economic Observer*, May 11, 2013.

96. This subheading quotes my informant Nan, a fansubber I will turn to in this section. Nan, interview with author, Shanghai, July 20, 2014.

97. Hao, interview with author, Beijing, April 22, 2014.

98. Patrick Brzeski, "Chinese Internet Giant Tencent Licenses Disney Films for Streaming Video Service," *Hollywood Reporter*, September 9, 2013, https://www.hollywoodreporter.com/news/chinese-internet-giant-tencent-licenses-624403.

99. Hao, interview with author, Beijing, April 22, 2014.

100. Nelson Granados, "Changes to Hollywood Release Windows Are Coming Fast and Furious," *Forbes*, April 8, 2015, https://www.forbes.com/sites/nelsongranados/2015/04/08/changes-to-hollywood-release-windows-are-coming-fast-and-furious/#2420d6076dc7.

101. Hao, interview with author, Beijing, April 22, 2014.

102. Bruce M. Owen and Steven S. Wildman, *Video Economics* (Cambridge, MA: Harvard University Press, 1992).

103. Hongjun Liu, "Meiju zhengduozhan"; "Shipin wangzhan goumai meiju shengyi jing."

104. "Shipin wangzhan goumai meiju shengyi jing."

105. Hao, interview with author, Beijing, April 22, 2014.

106. Meng Cai, "Duojia shipin wangzhan shishui zhengban yingshiju tongbu bochu; mianfei dacan keyi chi duojiu?" (Video sites test water on copyright; How long can free meal last?), *China Culture Daily*, March 10, 2011.

107. Nan, interview with author, Shanghai, July 20, 2014.

108. Nan, interview with author, Shanghai, July 20, 2014.

109. Jin, "Meiju hefa rujing hou de zimuzu.

110. Hao, interview with author, Beijing, April 11, 2014. Since the video companies had been granted streaming rights for mainland China only, they were required to block access by overseas viewers and to disable video downloads for offline viewing in order to protect the copyright owners' properties from piracy.

111. Nan, interview with author, Shanghai, July 20, 2014.

112. Xiaolong Cao, "Zimuzu banquan kunjing" (Copyright dilemma of fansubbing groups), *New Finance Observer*, December 1, 2014, http://tech.hexun.com/2014-12-01/170956506.html.

113. Nan, interview with author, Shanghai, July 20, 2014.

114. Michael Wayne, "Post-Fordism, Monopoly Capitalism, and Hollywood's Media Industrial Complex." *International Journal of Cultural Studies* 6, no. 1 (March 1, 2003): 82–103.

115. Mark Andrejevic, "Watching Television without Pity: The Productivity of Online Fans," *Television & New Media* 9, no. 1 (January 1, 2008): 24–46.

116. Hao, interview with author, Beijing, April 28, 2014.

117. Zhongxiaolu Chen, "Viki: zimu ban de Weiji Baike" (Viki: Wikipedia in fansubbing), *Nanfang Daily*, November 17, 2011.

118. Bo Yuan, "Zimuzu bei jiaoting tuxian banquan yishi tishen" (Halt in fansubbing shows improvement of copyright awareness), *China Intellectual Property News*, December 3, 2014; Chenguang Wu, "BT lei wangluo xiazai gongju yinglai shengsijie" (Impending death of BT downloading tools), *Beijing Business Today*, December 16, 2009.

119. Wenhui Ya, "Mianfei zimu wangzhan guanbi; zhenggui shipin wangzhan shouyi" (Closure of fansubbing groups benefits video websites), *China High-Tech Industry Herald*, December 8, 2014.

120. Jin, "Meiju hefa rujing hou de zimuzu."

121. Hao, interview with author, Beijing, April 28, 2014.

122. Jun Feng, "'Zimuzu' guanbi zhihou" (Afterward of closure of fansubbing groups), *China Culture Daily*, December 12, 2014.

123. Yuan Fang, "Zimuzu wangzhan yuanhe bei guanting" (Why were fansubbing websites closed?), *China Press and Publishing Journal*, December 24, 2014.

124. This subheading quotes my informant Hao, LeTV's copyright director. Hao, interview with author, Beijing, April 11, 2014.

125. Sui Yu, "Yinian qianbu guize fuza; Zhongguo dianying jinkou xianzhuang jiemi" (Demystifying film import in China: 1,000 titles each year with complicated rules), *MTIME*, accessed February 4, 2015. http://news.mtime.com/2012/10/11/1499044.html.

126. Jonathan Papish, "Foreign Films in China: How Does It Work?" *China Film Insider*, March 2, 2017, http://chinafilminsider.com/foreign-films-in-china-how-does-it-work/.

127. S. Yu, "Yinian qianbu guize fuza."

128. Sohu Corporation, "Jiejiu 'Jiangge' shibai shimo: shencha zhidu de gongkai NG" (A failed censorship of *Django Unchained*), *Sohu Television Monthly*, April 15, 2013, http://yule.sohu.com/20130415/n372648812_1.shtml.

129. SARFT, "Jingwai dianshi jiemu yinjin, bochu guanli guiding" (Rules on Importing and Scheduling Overseas Television Programs), 2004.

130. SARFT, "Guanyu jiaqiang hulianwang chuanbo yingshiju guanli de tongzhi" (Notice Concerning Strengthening Regulations of Films and Television Dramas Transmitted via Internet), 2007.

131. SARFT, "Guanyu jiaqiang hulianwang shiting jiemu neirong guanli de tongzhi" (Notice to Strengthen the Content Regulation of Online Audiovisual Programs), 2009.

132. See, Yan Li, "Zhishi chanquan baohu jinru 'xingdong nian'" (Intellectual property protection entered "Year of Action"), *Beijing Business Today*, April 13, 2009; Zhai Qun and Jian Biao, "Zhengsu BT, yingshi jiemu zai wu mianfei wucan" (No free lunch anymore after BT crackdown), *China Culture Daily*, December 18, 2009.

133. Jiulong Cheng, "Guangdian 'jingu zhou' tuxi shipin wangzhan" (SARFT raided video websites), *21st Century Business Herald*, April 9, 2009.

134. Hao, interview with author, Beijing, April 11, 2014.

135. Hao, interview with author, Beijing, April 22, 2014.

136. Hao, interview with author, Beijing, April 22, 2014.

137. "The SARFT Decides to Introduce *Ted*, Reducing 105 Minutes to One Minute," Douban.com, January 25, 2013, http://www.douban.com/group/topic/36272980/.

138. Hao, interview with author, Beijing, April 22, 2014.

139. "Yangshi, Shangshi: jinqi bu dasuan yinjin meiju" (CCTV and STV have no plan to import U.S. television series), *Shanghai Morning Post*, September 18, 2007.

140. Hao, interview with author, Beijing, April 11, 2014.

141. Steven Jiang, "*House of Cards* in China: Surprisingly Available and Popular," *CNN*, February 19, 2014, http://www.cnn.com/2014/02/19/world/asia/china-house -of-cards-jiang/index.html.

142. "Souhu Shipin de Zhipaiwu you shanjian ma?" (Is Sohu Video's *House of Cards* deleted?), Zhihu.com, accessed February 13, 2015, http://www.zhihu.com/question/22856972.

143. Hao, interview with author, Beijing, April 11, 2014.

144. Brett Christophers, "Television's Power Relations in the Transition to Digital: The Case of the United Kingdom," *Television & New Media* 9, no. 3 (2008): 239–257; Michael Curtin, "Media Capital: Towards the Study of Spatial Flows," *International Journal of Cultural Studies* 6, no. 2 (2003): 202–228.

Chapter 7: Online Video as an Emerging Network of Cultural Production

1. Fan Yang, "Wangju, shipin wangzhan de xinchong?" (Web soaps: video sites' new favorite?), *Workers' Daily*, May 21, 2010.

2. Yang, "Wangju, shipin wangzhan de xinchong?"

3. Stuart Cunningham and Jon Silver, *Screen Distribution and the New King Kongs of the Online World* (Houndmills, UK: Palgrave Macmillan, 2013).

4. Youku.com, "Youku Original Announces New Seasons of In-House Produced Evergreen Web Series," Youku.com—Investor Relations—Press Release, accessed February 16, 2015. http://ir.youku.com/phoenix.zhtml?c=241246&p=irol-newsArticle &ID=1660354.

5. Hao, interview with author, Beijing, April 22, 2014.

6. Hao, interview with author, Beijing, April 22, 2014.

7. Qifan Deng, "Wangzhan zizhiju: damu yiqi haomeng nanyuan" (Tough journey of web soaps), *Workers' Daily*, June 4, 2012.

8. Jie Chen, "Xinmeiti dianying tansuo huali xijin xin tujing" (New media films explore new ways to profit), *Beijing Business Today*, June 13, 2011.

9. Yongyi Wu, "'Shuangxian ling' huo dailai liangbai yi guanggao, wangluo shipin youwang yinglai 'di'er chun'" (Two restraining orders expected to bring the second spring to video sites), *Communication Information News*, December 7, 2011.

10. Jing Lu, "Zizhi dangdao: shipin wangzhan pingtai zhan shengji" (Upgraded war among video sites on content production), *China Business Journal*, May 2, 2011.

11. SARFT, "Guanyu jinyibu jiaqiang dianshi shangxing zonghe pindao jiemu guanli de yijian" (Opinions on Further Strengthening the Regulation of Television Programs on General Interest Satellite Channels), 2011.

12. SARFT, "'Guangbo dianshi guanggao bochu guanli banfa' de buchong guiding" (Supplementary Rules on "The Measures for the Administration of Radio and Television Commercials"), 2011.

13. Mengjie Jiang, "Shipin wangzhan jiancheng jinbo jiemu jiebangzhe" (Video websites becoming next runner for forbidden content), *Beijing Business Today*, December 5, 2011; Yongyi Wu, "'Shuangxian ling' huo dailai 2baiyi guanggao."

14. Yongyi Wu, "'Shuangxian ling' huo dailai 2baiyi guanggao."

15. Hua, interview with author, Beijing, April 24, 2014.

16. Hua, interview with author, Beijing, April 24, 2014.

17. Hua, interview with author, Beijing, April 24, 2014.

18. "Cooperative marriages" are between gays and lesbians, who face intense heteronormative pressures.

19. Qingsheng Liao, "Shipin wangzhan zoushang neirong chanyehua dadao, baituo banquan zhigu jiasu yingli bufa" (Video sites' content strategies help relieve pressure from copyright), *Communication Information News*, April 21, 2010.

20. Hua, interview with author, Beijing, April 24, 2014.

21. CNNIC, *Report on Internet Development in China 2013*, 28.

22. Jiang and Elegant, "Avoiding Censors, Chinese Authors Go Online."

23. Jiang and Elegant, "Avoiding Censors, Chinese Authors Go Online"; Edward Wong, "Pushing China's Limits on Web, If Not on Paper," *New York Times*, November 6, 2011, http://www.nytimes.com/2011/11/07/world/asia/murong-xuecun-pushes -censorship-limits-in-china.html.

24. See Hockx, *Internet Literature in China*.

25. Fan, interview with author, Beijing, April 18, 2014.

26. See, for example, Jean Burgess, "YouTube and the Formalization of Amateur Media," in Dan Hunter, Ramon Lobato, Megan Richardson and Julian Thomas, eds., *Amateur Media: Social, Cultural and Legal Perspectives* (London: Routledge, 2012), 53–58; Jin Kim, "The Institutionalization of YouTube: From User-generated Content to Professionally Generated Content," *Media, Culture & Society* 34, no. 1 (2012): 53–67; and Elaine Zhao, "Professionalization of Amateur Production in Online Screen Entertainment in China: Hopes, Frustrations and Uncertainties," *International Journal of Communication* 10 (2016): 5444–5462; Zhao and Keane, "Between Formal and Informal."

27. Hu, interview with author, Shanghai, July 25, 2014.

28. Siwen, telephone interview with author, July 19, 2014.

29. Oiwan Lam, "China: My Father Is Li Gang!" *Global Voices*, October 22, 2010, https://globalvoicesonline.org/2010/10/22/china-my-father-is-li-gang/.

30. See Yiannis Mylonas, "Amateur Creation and Entrepreneurialism: A Critical Study of Artistic Production in Post-Fordist Structures," *tripleC: Communication, Capitalism & Critique* 10, no. 1 (2012): 1–11.

31. Tong, interview with author, Shanghai, July 27, 2014.

32. Tarleton Gillespie, "The Politics of 'Platforms'," *New Media & Society* 12, no. 3 (2010): 347–364.

33. Tong, interview with author, Shanghai, July 27, 2014.

34. Tong, interview with author, Shanghai, July 27, 2014.

35. Jing Li, "Shipin wangzhan chonggui UGC" (Video sites return to UGC), *Economic Observer*, July 12, 2013.

36. Gillespie, "The Politics of 'Platforms'."

37. Siwen, telephone interview with author, July 19, 2014; Tong, interview with author, Shanghai, July 27, 2014.

38. Miao Yang, "iQiyi kaifang shipin bofang pingtai; zhizuozhe ke huode guanggao fencheng" (iQiyi opens its platform for video producers), *Beijing News*, March 27, 2012.

39. Xuan Mo, "Tengxun Shipin jujiao yuanchuang jingpin zhanlue" (Tencent Video focuses on quality original productions), *International Financial News*, June 20, 2013.

40. Meng Ning, "Shipin boke guanggao fencheng qubian, zhuli UGC yewu huo lunwei zitai" (Effectiveness of ad revenue divide in video sharing remains unclear), *TechWeb*, accessed February 28, 2015. http://www.techweb.com.cn/internet/2013 -06-16/1303248.shtml.

41. Ning, "Shipin boke guanggao fencheng qubian, zhuli UGC yewu huo lunwei zitai"; Siwen, telephone interview with author, July 19, 2014; Tong, interview with author, Shanghai, July 27, 2014.

42. Siwen, telephone interview with author, July 19, 2014; Tong, interview with author, Shanghai, July 27, 2014.

43. Siwen, telephone interview with author, July 19, 2014; Tong, interview with author, Shanghai, July 27, 2014.

44. Gillespie, "The Politics of 'Platforms.'"

45. Siwen, telephone interview with author, July 19, 2014; Tong, interview with author, Shanghai, July 27, 2014.

46. This subheading is a quote from my informant Fan, whom I briefly mentioned in the first section "Video Companies' In-House Initiatives" and whom I will quote again in this section. Fan, interview with author, Beijing, April 17, 2014.

47. *Guanyu jinyibu jiaqiang wangluoju, weidianying deng wangluo shiting jiemu guanli de tongzhi*, 2012.

48. Mengwei Jiang, "Neirong chidu guokuan; shipin wangzhan tiaozhan jianguan dixian" (Video sites challenged regulatory bottom line), *Beijing Business Today*, May 30, 2012.

49. Jiang, "Neirong chidu guokuan."

50. Fan, interview with author, Beijing, April 17, 2014.

51. Fan, interview with author, Beijing, April 17, 2014.

52. Qingping Ge, "Zizhi ju shencha lidu jiada; shipin wangzhan ying kaoyan" (Censorship of web soaps strengthened; Video companies facing challenges), *China High-Tech Industry Herald*, July 30, 2012; Yanping Chen, "Wangluo ju wei dianying jianguan shoujin; chidu bakong cheng guifan guanjian" (Regulations of web soaps and micro movies strengthened; Grasping yardstick becomes key), *Communication Information News*, July 18, 2012.

53. Yonghai He, "Wangluo ju 'xianshen houbo' buying zhiyu zishen" (Regulation of web soaps should not be limited to self-censorship), *Workers' Daily*, July 23, 2012.

54. Fan, interview with author, Beijing, April 17, 2014.

55. Tao, interview with author, Beijing, April 24, 2014.

56. Lin, interview with author, Shanghai, June 7, 2016.

57. Fan, interview with author, Beijing, April 17, 2014.

58. Lin, interview with author, Shanghai, June 7, 2016.

59. SARFT, *China Radio & TV Yearbook 2013*, 195.

60. Hua, interview with author, Beijing, April 24, 2014.

61. Fan, interview with author, Beijing, April 18, 2014.

62. Fan, interview with author, Beijing, April 18, 2014.

63. Hao, interview with author, Beijing, April 11, 2014.

64. Siwen, telephone interview with author, July 19, 2014; Tong, interview with author, Shanghai, July 27, 2014.

65. Tong, interview with author, Shanghai, July 27, 2014.

66. Youku, "What Does the China Earthquake Administration Do?" *UFO Talk*, April 25, 2013.

67. Garnham, *Capitalism and Communication*.

68. Youku, *Absolutely Unexpected*, season 2, episode 3, 2014.

Chapter 8: Epilogue

1. In telling contrast, however, an episode of Youku's web soap *Absolutely Unexpected* (*Wanwan meixiangdao*) the year before had aptly satirized the moral hypocrisy of the *Voice of China* in showing off the success of Zhejiang TV's commercial pursuits even while going through the motions of fulfilling the channel's political obligations. Youku, *Absolutely Unexpected*, season 1, episode 10, 2013.

2. Doyle Greene, "2 Broke Girls (Or, One American Dream with a Side of Alienation)," *Flow*, November 13, 2011, http://flowtv.org/2011/11/2-broke-girls/.

3. Lin, interview with author, Shanghai, June 7, 2016.

4. Ronen Palan, "Trying to Have Your Cake and Eating It: How and Why the State System Has Created Offshore," *International Studies Quarterly* 42 (1998): 626.

5. Sarah Nuttall and Achille Mbembe, "Secrecy's Softwares," *Current Anthropology* 56 (December 2015): 317–324.

6. Lee C. Bollinger, *Images of a Free Press* (Chicago: University of Chicago Press, 1991).

7. See, for example, David Mitchell, "Internet Content Regulation in Southeast Asia: Directions," *Media International Australia* 101, no. 1 (November 2001): 43–55; and Terence Lee, "Forging an 'Asian' Media Fusion: Singapore as a 21st Century Media Hub," *Media International Australia* 158, no. 1 (February 2016): 80–89.

8. Xi Jinping, as quoted in "Bawo chuanmei biange qushi; jiji zhanling xinxing yulun zhendi" (Mastering trends of media changes; Actively occupying new battles of public opinion), *XinhuaNet*, June 14, 2016, http://www.xinhuanet.com/politics/2016-06/14/c_1119039250.htm.

9. Xie Yu, "Why China's Plan to Launch the Highly Touted CDR Scheme Is Still on Hold," *South China Morning Post*, July 14, 2018, https://www.scmp.com/business/china-business/article/2155107/why-chinas-plan-launch-highly-touted-cdr-scheme-still-hold; Ming, telephone interview with author, November 1, 2018.

10. SAPPRFT, "Guanyu jinyibu luoshi wangshang jingwai yingshiju guanli youguan guiding de tongzhi" (Notice to Further Implement Related Regulations on Online Foreign Films and Television Dramas), 2014.

11. Hao, telephone interview with author, February 11, 2018.

12. Hao, telephone interview with author, February 11, 2018.

13. Sina Corporation, "Zongju jiaqiang wangju jianguan; dianshi wangluo shencha biaozhun tongyi" (SARFT strengthens regulations of web soaps; Censorship standards for television and internet to be unified), *Sina Entertainment*, February 27, 2016, http://ent.sina.com.cn/v/m/2016-02-27/doc-ifxpvysv4949295.shtml.

14. SAPPRFT, "Guanyu jinyibu jiaqiang wangluo yuanchuang shiting jiemu guihua jianshe he guanli de tongzhi" (Notice to Further Strengthen the Planning, Construction, and Management of Online Original Audiovisual Programs), 2016.

Bibliography

Interviews with Chinese Industry Professionals in Television and Online Video

Fan. April 17 and 18, 2014, Beijing; February 10, 2018, WeChat.

Gan. April 13, 2014, Beijing; June 2, 2016, Shanghai.

GB. July 19, 2014, telephone; October 17 and 29, 2016, WeChat.

Han. March 31, 2014, Beijing; June 10 and 11, 2014, Shanghai.

Hao. April 11, 16, 22, and 28, 2014, Beijing; December 2, 2017, telephone; February 11, 2018, telephone.

Hu. July 25, 2014, Shanghai.

Hua. April 24, 2014, Beijing.

Lin. June 7, 2016, Shanghai.

Long. June 3, 2016, Shanghai.

Ming. November 1, 2018, telephone.

Nan. July 20, 2014, Shanghai.

Peng. June 1, 2016, Shanghai.

Qin. June 27, 2014, Shanghai.

Shao. April 21, 2014, Beijing.

Siwen. July 19, 2014, telephone.

Tao. April 24, 2014, Beijing.

Tong. June 6, 2016, Shanghai; July 27, 2014, Shanghai.

Wai. June 8, 2016, Shanghai.

Wei. April 20, 2014, Beijing; October 17, 2014, telephone.

Wen Man. April 23, 2014, Beijing.

Xin. April 21, 2014, Beijing; October 19, 2014, telephone; June 8, 2016, Shanghai.

Chinese-Language Trade Publications and Mass-Circulation Newspapers/Magazines

Beijing Business Today (Beijing shangbao)

Beijing Daily (Beijing ribao)

Beijing News (Xin jing bao)

Caixin

CBN Weekly (Diyi caijing zhoukan)

China Business Journal (Zhongguo jingying bao)

China Business Post (Caijing shibao)

China Computer Education (Zhongguo diannao jiaoyu bao)

China Culture Daily (Zhongguo wenhua bao)

China Economic Times (Zhongguo jingji shibao)

China Enterprise News (Zhongguo qiye bao)

China Entrepreneur (Zhongguo qiyejia)

China High-Tech Industry Herald (Zhongguo gaoxin jishu chanye daobao)

China InfoWorld (Zhongguo jisuanji bao)

China Intellectual Property News (Zhongguo zhishi chanquan bao)

China News (Zhonghua xinwen bao)

China News Weekly (Zhongguo xinwen zhoukan)

China Press and Publishing Journal (Zhongguo xinwen chubanbao)

China Press Journal (Zhongguo xinwen bao)

China Securities News (Zhongguo zhengquan bao)

Communication Information News (Tongxin xinxi bao)

Computer Weekly (Diannao bao)

Computer World (Jisuanji shijie)

Dongfang Daily (Dongfang zaobao)

Economic Observer (Jingji guancha bao)

Global Entrepreneur (Huanqiu qiyejia)

Guangming Daily (Guangming ribao)

International Business Daily (Guoji shangbao)

International Financial News (Guoji jinrong bao)

Legal Daily (Fazhi ribao)

Money Weekly (Licai zhoubao)

Nanfang Daily (Nanfang ribao)

Network World (Wangluo shijie)

New Finance Observer (Xin jinrong guancha)

People's Posts and Telecommunications (Renmin youdian)

Procuratorial Daily (Jiancha ribao)

Satellite TV and Broadband Multimedia (Weixing dianshi yu kuandai duomeiti)

Securities Daily (Zhengquan ribao)

Shanghai Morning Post (Xinwen chenbao)

Shanghai Securities News (Shanghai zhengquan bao)

Southern Weekly (Nanfang zhoumo)

Telecommunications Weekly (Tongxin chanye bao)

Telecommunications World (Tongxin shijie)

Time Weekly (Shidai zhoubao)

21st Century Business Herald (21 shiji jingji baodao)

Worker's Daily (Gongren ribao)

Policy Database and Government Reports Consulted

China InfoBank (All laws and regulations cited in this book were retrieved from this database.)

CNNIC. *Report on Internet Development in China (Zhongguo hulianwang fazhan baogao)*. 2002–2012.

SARFT. *China Radio & TV Yearbook (Zhongguo guangbo dianshi nianjian)*. 1986–2015.

Report on the Development of Chinese Media Industry (Zhongguo chuanmei chanye fazhan baogao). 2004–2008, 2011–2013.

Report on the Development of China's Radio, Film, and Television (*Zhongguo guangbo dianying dianshi fanzhan baogao*). 2006, 2008, 2011–2013.

Report on the Development of Chinese Cultural Industry (*Zhongguo wenhua chanye fazhan baogao*). 2001–2013.

Report on the Marketing Trends of Advertisers in China (*Zhongguo guanggaozhu yingxiao chuanbo qushi baogao*). Nos. 3, 5, 6, and 7.

Other Sources Consulted

Reports from the following law firms:
Cadwalader Wickersham & Taft LLP
Hogan Lovells
O'Melveny & Myers LLP

Sina's registration statement: http://ir.sina.com/financial-information/sec-filings

Bibliography

Agamben, Giorgio. *State of Exception*. Chicago: University of Chicago Press, 2003.

Alford, William P. *To Steal a Book Is an Elegant Offense: Intellectual Property Law in Chinese Civilization*. Stanford: Stanford University Press, 1995.

Andrejevic, Mark. "Watching Television without Pity: The Productivity of Online Fans." *Television & New Media* 9, no. 1 (January 1, 2008): 24–46.

Andrews, Julia Frances. *Painters and Politics in the People's Republic of China, 1949–1979*. Berkeley: University of California Press, 1994.

Athique, Adrian. "The Global Dynamics of India Media Piracy: Export Markets, Playback Media and the Informal Economy." *Media, Culture & Society* 30, no. 5 (2008): 699–717.

Athique, Adrian. "Piracy at the Frontier: Uneven Development and the Public Sphere." *Media International Australia* 152 (2014): 87–97.

Bai, Ruoyun. *Staging Corruption: Chinese Television and Politics*. Vancouver: University of British Columbia Press, 2014.

Baranovitch, Nimrod. *China's New Voices: Popular Music, Ethnicity, Gender, and Politics, 1978–1997*. Berkeley: University of California Press, 2003.

Barmé, Geremie. "The Greying of Chinese Culture." *China Review* (1992): 13.1–13.52.

"Bawo chuanmei biange qushi; jiji zhanling xinxing yulun zhendi" (Mastering trends of media changes; Actively occupying new battles of public opinion).

XinhuaNet, June 14, 2016. http://www.xinhuanet.com/politics/2016-06/14/c _1119039250.htm.

"Beifang Wang kaiban wangshang chuanbo guangbo dianying dianshi lei jiemu yi huode Guojia Guangdian Zongju pizhun" (Enorth's quasi–radio, film, and television programs services approved by SARFT). enorth, February 20, 2003. http://news .enorth.com.cn/system/2003/02/19/000510568.shtml.

Bennett, James, and Niki Strange, eds. *Television as Digital Media*. Durham, NC: Duke University Press, 2011.

Bilton, Chris. "Risky Business: The Independent Production Sector in Britain's Creative Industries." *International Journal of Cultural Policy* 6, no. 1 (December 1, 1999): 17–39.

Bo, Hui. "Kunrao wangluo shipin hangye de banquan miju" (Copyright labyrinth in online video industry). *China Intellectual Property News*, March 13, 2009.

Bollinger, Lee C. *Images of a Free Press*. Chicago: University of Chicago Press, 1991.

Boyd, Douglas A., Joseph D. Straubhaar, and John A. Lent. *Video Cassette Recorders in the Third World*. White Plains, NY: Longman, 1989.

Braman, Sandra. *Change of State: Information, Policy, and Power*. Cambridge, MA: MIT Press, 2006.

Breznitz, Dan, and Michael Murphree. *Run of the Red Queen: Government, Innovation, Globalization, and Economic Growth in China*. New Haven: Yale University Press, 2011.

Brzeski, Patrick. "Chinese Internet Giant Tencent Licenses Disney Films for Streaming Video Service." *Hollywood Reporter*, September 9, 2013. https://www .hollywoodreporter.com/news/chinese-internet-giant-tencent-licenses-624403.

Bunn, Matthew. "Reimagining Repression: New Censorship Theory and After." *History and Theory* 54 (2015): 25–44.

Burgess, Jean. "YouTube and the Formalization of Amateur Media." In *Amateur Media: Social, Cultural and Legal Perspectives*, edited by Dan Hunter, Ramon Lobato, Megan Richardson, and Julian Thomas, 53–58. London: Routledge, 2012.

Burgess, Jean, and Joshua Green. *YouTube: Online Video and Participatory Culture*. Cambridge: Polity Press, 2009.

Cai, Meng. "Duojia shipin wangzhan shishui zhengban yingshiju tongbu bochu; mianfei dacan keyi chi duojiu?" (Video sites test water on copyright; How long can free meal last?). *China Culture Daily*, March 10, 2011.

Cai, Xiaowei. "Shipin wangzhan shi ruhe tiaoxuan meiju de?" (How do video sites select U.S. television series?). *Dongfang Daily*, October 10, 2013.

"Cai Fuchao: xianshang xianxia tongyi biaozhun xianshen houbo" (Cai Fuchao: To unify online and offline standards). *Caixin*. Last modified December 16, 2014. http://companies.caixin.com/2014-12-16/100763622.html.

Calabrese, Andrew, and Colleen Mihal. "Liberal Fictions: The Public-Private Dichotomy in Media Policy." In *The Handbook of Political Economy of Communications*, edited by Janet Wasko, Graham Murdock, and Helena Sousa, 226–263. Chichester, UK: Wiley-Blackwell, 2011.

Caldwell, John. *Production Culture: Industrial Reflexivity and Critical Practice in Film and Television*. Durham: Duke University Press, 2008.

Cammett, John. *Antonio Gramsci and the Origins of Italian Communism*. Stanford: Stanford University Press, 1967.

Cao, Xiaolong. "Zimuzu banquan kunjing" (Copyright dilemma of fansubbing groups). *New Finance Observer*, December 1, 2014. http://tech.hexun.com/2014-12-01/170956506.html.

Caves, Richard. *Creative Industries: Contracts between Art and Commerce*. Cambridge, MA: Harvard University Press, 2000.

Cendrowski, Scott. "Local Investors Miss Out on Sizzling Chinese Tech Stocks." *Fortune*, July 11, 2014. http://fortune.com/2014/07/11/local-investors-miss-out-on-sizzling-chinese-tech-stocks/.

Chan, Joseph Man. "Administrative Boundaries and Media Marketization: A Comparative Analysis of the Newspaper, TV and Internet Markets in China." In *Chinese Media, Global Contexts*, edited by Chin-Chuan Lee, 156–172. London: Routledge, 2009.

Chan, Joseph Man. "Television in Greater China." In *Contemporary World Television*, edited by John Sinclair and Graeme Turner, 104–107. London: British Film Institute, 2004.

Chan, Joseph Man. "When Capitalist and Socialists Television Meet: The Impact of Hong Kong TV on Guangzhou Residents." In *Media, Money, and Power: Communication Patterns in Chinese Societies*, edited by Chin-Chuan Lee, 245–270. Evanston, IL: Northwestern University Press, 2000.

Chen, Jie. "Xinmeiti dianying tansuo huali xijin xin tujing" (New media films explore new ways to profit). *Beijing Business Today*, June 13, 2011.

Chen, Liang, and Qiuju Shi. "Di'erbo hulianwang rechao jisu tuishao" (Second wave of internet fever is cooling down). *Nanfang Daily*, October 31, 2006.

Chen, Xiaomei. *Acting the Right Part: Political Theater and Popular Drama in Contemporary China*. Honolulu: University of Hawai'i Press, 2002.

Chen, Yanping. "Wangluo ju wei dianying jianguan shoujin; chidu bakong cheng guifan guanjian" (Regulations of web soaps and micro movies strengthened; Grasping yardstick becomes key). *Communication Information News*, July 18, 2012.

Chen, Yanyan. "Yu bacheng wenhua chuanmei qiye zhongbao baoxi; binggou reqing bujian yijia gaoshao butui" (Cultural enterprises performing well on market; Enthusiasms in mergers continue). *Securities Daily*, August 29, 2013.

Chen, Zhongxiaolu. "Viki: zimu ban de Weiji Baike" (Viki: Wikipedia in fansubbing). *Nanfang Daily*, November 17, 2011.

Cheng, Jiulong. "Guangdian 'jingu zhou' tuxi shipin wangzhan" (SARFT raided video websites). *21st Century Business Herald*, April 9, 2009.

Chin, Yik Chan. "Policy Process, Policy Learning, and the Role of the Provincial Media in China." *Media, Culture & Society* 33, no. 2 (March 1, 2011): 193–210.

"China Bans Internet Investment." *BBC News*, September 15, 1999. http://news.bbc .co.uk/2/hi/business/448305.stm.

Christophers, Brett. "Television's Power Relations in the Transition to Digital: The Case of the United Kingdom." *Television & New Media* 9, no. 3 (2008): 239–257.

Chu, Godwin C., and Francis Hsu, eds. *Moving a Mountain: Cultural Change in China*. Honolulu: University of Hawai'i Press for East–West Center, 1979.

Clark, Donald. "Who Owns the Chinese Internet?" *Chinese Law Prof Blog*, July 7, 2011. http://lawprofessors.typepad.com/china_law_prof_blog/2011/07/who-owns-the -chinese-internet.html.

Clark, Paul. *Youth Culture in China: From Red Guards to Netizens*. Cambridge: Cambridge University Press, 2012.

Cowie, Campbell, and Sandeep Kapur. "The Management of Digital Rights in Pay TV." In *Digital Broadcasting: Policy and Practice in the Americas, Europe and Japan*, edited by Martin Cave and Kiyoshi Nakamura, 162–186. Cheltenham, UK: Edward Elgar, 2006.

Cui, Baoguo, ed. *2011 Zhongguo chuanmei chanye fazhan baogao* (2011 Report on the development of Chinese media industry). Beijing: Social Science Literature Press, 2011.

Cui, Jinyue, and Min Yuan. "Cuijian men de 30 nian fengyu" (Thirty years of China's rock stars). *Sohu News*. Last modified September 9, 2010. http://news.sohu .com/20100909/n274819952.shtml.

Cunningham, Stuart. "Emergent Innovation through the Co-Evolution of Informal and Formal Media Economies." *Television and New Media* 13, no. 5 (2012): 415–430.

Cunningham, Stuart, and Jon Silver. "Online Film Distribution: Its History and Global Complexion." In *Digital Disruption: Cinema Moves Online*, edited by Dina Iordanova and Stuart Cunningham, 53–95. St. Andrews, UK: St. Andrews Film Studies, 2012.

Cunningham, Stuart, and Jon Silver. *Screen Distribution and the New King Kongs of the Online World*. Houndmills, UK: Palgrave Macmillan, 2013.

Curtin, Michael. "Matrix Media." In *Television Studies after TV: Understanding Television in the Post-Broadcast Era*, edited by Graeme Turner and Jinna Tay, 19–29. Abingdon, UK: Routledge, 2009.

Curtin, Michael. "Media Capital: Towards the Study of Spatial Flows." *International Journal of Cultural Studies* 6, no. 2 (2003): 202–228.

Curtin, Michael. "The Future of Chinese Cinema: Some Lessons from Hong Kong and Taiwan." In *Chinese Media, Global Contexts*, edited by Chin-Chuan Lee, 237–256. London: Routledge, 2003.

Curtin, Michael, Jennifer Holt, and Kevin Sanson, eds. *Distribution Revolution: Conversations about the Digital Future of Film and Television*. Berkeley: University of California Press, 2014.

Dai, Jinhua. *Wuzhong fengjing: Zhongguo dianying wenhua 1978–1998* (Scenery in mist: Chinese cinema culture, 1978–1998). Beijing: Peking University Press, 2000.

Dai, Xiudian. "Digital Inclusion: A Case for Micro Perspectives." In *Digital World: Connectivity, Creativity and Rights*, edited by Gillian Youngs, 34–51. Abingdon, UK: Routledge, 2013.

Deibert, Ronald J. "Dark Guests and Great Firewalls: The Internet and Chinese Security Policy." *Journal of Social Issues* 58, no. 1 (2002): 143–159.

DeMare, Brian. *Mao's Cultural Army: Drama Troupes in China's Rural Revolution*. Cambridge: Cambridge University Press, 2015.

Deng, Qifan, "Wangzhan zizhiju: damu yiqi haomeng nanyuan" (Tough journey of web soaps), *Workers' Daily*, June 4, 2012.

Dimitrov, Martin. *Piracy and the State: The Politics of Intellectual Property Rights in China*. Cambridge: Cambridge University Press, 2009.

Dimitrov, Martin, ed. *Why Communism Did Not Collapse: Understanding Authoritarian Regime Resilience in Asia and Europe*. New York: Cambridge University Press, 2013.

Ding, A. "Web 2.0 jinyu hanliu erfei yandong" (Web 2.0 encounters cold spell). *Computer World*, September 18, 2006.

Dou, Xinying. "Shenxian banquan jiufen nitan; shipin hangye youdian luan" (Chaotic video industry deeply implicated in rights disputes). *China Intellectual Property News*, December 4, 2009.

Dou, Yingying. "Souhu Shipin: caigou meiju you jiqiao" (Sohu Video: Acquiring American television series requires skills). *China Economic Times*, March 19, 2013.

Egorov, Georgy, Sergei Guriev, and Konstantin Sonin. "Why Resource-Poor Dictators Allow Freer Media: A Theory and Evidence from Panel Data." *American Political Science Review* 103, no. 4 (2009): 645–668.

Evens, Tom. "The Political Economy of Retransmission Payments and Cable Rights: Implications for Private Television Companies." In *Private Television in Western Europe: Content, Markets, Policies*, edited by Karen Donders, Caroline Pauwels, and Jan Loisen, 182–196. Houndmills, UK: Palgrave Macmillan, 2013.

Fang, Siyue. "Shipin wangzhan zhuzuoquan qinquan jianjie zeren tanjiu" (Exploration of indirect responsibility of video websites in rights infringement). *China Intellectual Property News*, February 25, 2011.

Fang, Yuan. "Zimuzu wangzhan yuanhe bei guanting" (Why were fansubbing websites closed?). *China Press and Publishing Journal*, December 24, 2014.

Feng, Dagang. "Zhongguo Dianxin Hulian Xingkong quanmian shangyong; liyi gongxiang shoudao SP huanying" (China Telecom's VNET is ready for commercial use; SP welcomes revenue sharing). *Sohu IT*. Last modified September 16, 2003. http://it.sohu.com/58/01/article213250158.shtml.

Feng, Jun. "'Zimuzu' guanbi zhihou" (Afterward of closure of fansubbing groups). *China Culture Daily*, December 12, 2014.

Foster, William. "The Diffusion of the Internet in China." Ph.D. diss., University of Arizona, 2001.

Fu, Tian. "BT xiazai: yong falv jiayu shouzhong de shuangrenjian" (BT downloading: Double-edged sword harnessed by law). *China Intellectual Property News*, May 31, 2006.

Fung, Anthony. "Globalizing Televised Culture: The Case of China." In *Television Studies after TV: Understanding Television in the Post-Broadcast Era*, edited by Graeme Turner and Jinna Tay, 178–188. Abingdon, UK: Routledge, 2009.

Fung, Anthony, and Luzhou Li. "TV Box on the Internet: The Interplay between Politics and Market in China." In *Global Media Convergence and Cultural Transformation: Emerging Social Patterns and Characteristics*, edited by Dal Yong Jin, 327–339. Hershey, Pa.: IGI Global, 2010.

Fung, Anthony, and Xiaoxiao Zhang. "The Chinese *Ugly Betty*: TV Cloning and Local Modernity." *International Journal of Cultural Studies* 14 (2011): 265–276.

Ganley, Gladys D., and Oswald H. Ganley. *Global Political Fallout: The First Decade of the VCR, 1976–1985*. Cambridge, MA: Center for Information Policy Research, Harvard University, 1987.

Gao, Chunyan. "Qianwan yuan qianggou reboju; wei qiang dipan shipin wangzhan sha hongyan" (Video sites dogfight over hot television series). *China InfoWorld*, August 1, 2011.

Gao, Hongbin. "The Present and Prospect of China Internet Data Center." Accessed October 23, 2014. http://unpan1.un.org/intradoc/groups/public/documents/apcity/unpan001519.pdf.

Garnham, Nicholas. *Capitalism and Communication: Global Culture and the Economics of Information*. London: Sage, 1990.

Garnham, Nicholas. "From Cultural to Creative Industries." *International Journal of Cultural Policy* 11, no. 1 (March 1, 2005): 15–29.

Ge, Qingping. "Baituo qinquan kunjing; shipin wangzhan mou chulu" (Video sites seeking ways out of infringement dilemma). *China High-Tech Industry Herald*, December 7, 2009.

Ge, Qingping. "Zizhi ju shencha lidu jiada; shipin wangzhan ying kaoyan" (Censorship of web soaps strengthened; Video companies facing challenges). *China High-Tech Industry Herald*, July 30, 2012.

Genesis Capital. "Dui Zhongguo IDC shichang de yuce" (Predicting China's IDC market). Accessed October 23, 2014. http://tech.sina.com.cn/r/m/53883.shtml.

Genesis Capital. "Gaiyao: Zhongguo IDC shichang de guimo yu zengzhang" (Scale and growth of IDC market in China). Accessed October 25, 2014. http://tech.sina.com.cn/r/m/53860.shtml.

Geng, Yanbing. "Shangwubu: waizi binggou jin zhan liyong waizi 3.1%" (Ministry of Commerce: Foreign mergers only account for 3.1% of foreign investments). *21st Century Business Herald*, September 21, 2011.

Gillespie, Tarleton. "The Politics of 'Platforms.'" *New Media & Society* 12, no. 3 (2010): 347–364.

Gitelman, Lisa. *Always Already New: Media, History, and the Data of Culture*. Cambridge, MA: MIT Press, 2006.

Godwin C. Chu, ed. *Moving a Mountain: Cultural Change in China*. Honolulu: University of Hawai'i Press, 1979.

Gold, Thomas. "Go with Your Feelings: Hong Kong and Taiwan Popular Culture in Greater China." *China Quarterly* 136 (1993): 907–925.

Gong, Haomin, and Xin Yang. "Digitized Parody: The Politics of Egao in Contemporary China." *China Information* 24, no. 1 (March 1, 2010): 3–26.

Gou, Yina. "Remen dianshiju wangluo banquan jiage baodie wucheng" (Price of hot television series drops by half). May 2, 2012. http://tech.163.com/12/0502/03/80FGR93V000915BF.html.

Granados, Nelson. "Changes to Hollywood Release Windows Are Coming Fast And Furious." *Forbes*, April 8, 2015. https://www.forbes.com/sites/nelsongranados/2015/04/08/changes-to-hollywood-release-windows-are-coming-fast-and-furious/#2420d6076dc7.

Greene, Doyle. "2 Broke Girls (Or, One American Dream with a Side of Alienation)." *Flow*, November 13, 2011. http://flowtv.org/2011/11/2-broke-girls/.

Grossberg, Lawrence. *Bringing It All Back Home: Essays on Cultural Studies.* Durham: Duke University Press, 1997.

Gu, Hui. "Shipin wangzhan rongzi cheng bifu youxi?" (Fundraising of video sites turning into game for rich?] *China Business Journal*, December 3, 2007.

Guangming Daily. "Wangshang 'egao' youbei hexie linian" (Online "spoofing" counters harmonious ideals). *GMW*, November 29, 2006. Accessed November 15, 2014. http://www.gmw.cn/01gmrb/2006-11/29/content_514452.htm.

Hai, Da. "Wangluo dianshi taidong" (Emerging online television). *Computer World*, June 7, 2004.

Hall, Gary. "Introduction: Pirate Philosophy." *Culture Machine: Pirate Philosophy* 10 (2009): 1–5.

Han, Chao. "'Bing yu huo' 35 nian: meiju zai Zhongguo" (35 years of "ice and fire"': American television series in China). *Yicai*, April 30, 2014.

Han, Rongbin. "Defending the Authoritarian Regime Online: China's 'Voluntary Fifty-Cent Army'." *China Quarterly* 224 (2015): 1006–1025.

Hanson, Lisa. "The Chinese Internet Gets a Stronger Backbone." *Forbes*, February 24, 2015. https://www.forbes.com/sites/lisachanson/2015/02/24/the-chinese-internet-gets-a-stronger-backbone/#77b7bd411ff4.

Harvey, David. *A Brief History of Neoliberalism.* Oxford: Oxford University Press, 2005.

Harwit, Eric. *China's Telecommunications Revolution.* Oxford: Oxford University Press, 2008.

Harwit, Eric, and Duncan Clark. "Government Policy and Political Control over China's Internet." In *Chinese Cyberspaces: Technological Changes and Political Effects*, edited by Jens Damm and Simona Thomas, 12–41. Abingdon, UK: Routledge, 2006.

He, Qiliang. "Between Accommodation and Resistance: Pingtan Storytelling in 1960s Shanghai." *Modern Asian Studies* 48, no. 3 (2014): 524–549.

He, Qiliang. "Between Business and Bureaucrats: Pingtan Storytelling in Maoist and Post-Maoist China." *Modern China* 36, no. 3 (2010): 243–268.

He, Yonghai. "Wangluo ju 'xianshen houbo' buying zhiyu zishen" (Regulation of web soaps should not be limited to self-censorship). *Workers' Daily*, July 23, 2012.

Heilmann, Sebastian. *Red Swan: How Unorthodox Policy-Making Facilitated China's Rise*. Columbia University Press, 2018.

Heilmann, Sebastian, and Elizabeth Perry. "Embracing Uncertainty: Guerrilla Policy Style and Adaptive Governance in China." In *Mao's Invisible Hand: The Political Foundations of Adaptive Governance in China*, edited by Sebastian Heilmann and Elizabeth Perry, 1–29. Cambridge, MA: Harvard University Press, 2011.

Hille, Kathrin, and Joseph Menn. "Alibaba Settles Alipay Dispute with Yahoo." *Financial Times*, July 30, 2011. https://www.ft.com/content/40a66dd2-b9ec-11e0-8171 -00144feabdc0.

Hockx, Michel. *Internet Literature in China*. New York: Columbia University Press, 2015.

Holm, David. *Art and Ideology in Revolutionary China*. Oxford: Clarendon Press, 1991.

Holt, Jennifer, and Kevin Sanson, eds. *Connected Viewing: Selling, Streaming, and Sharing Media in the Digital Era*. London: Routledge, 2013.

Hong, Junhao. *The Internationalization of Television in China: The Evolution of Ideology, Society, and Media Since the Reform*. Westport, Conn.: Praeger, 1994.

Hong, Yu. *Networking China: The Digital Transformation of the Chinese Economy*. Champaign: University of Illinois Press, 2017.

Hong, Yu. "Pivot to Internet Plus: Molding China's Digital Economy for Economic Restructuring?" *International Journal of Communication* 11 (2017): 1486–1506.

Hou, Jiyong. "San'ge Web 2.0 de rongzi meng" (Fundraising dreams of three Web 2.0s). *21st Century Business Herald*, March 13, 2006.

Howell, Jude. "Striking a New Balance: New Social Organisations in Post-Mao China." *Capital & Class* 18, no. 3 (1999): 89–111.

Hsueh, Roselyn. "Nations or Sectors in the Age of Globalization: China's Policy toward Foreign Direct Investment in Telecommunications." *Review of Policy Research* 32, no. 6 (2015): 627–648.

Hu, Xiangbao. "Shipin luanxiang diaocha: banquan fenxiaoshang beizhi 'diaoyu qizha'" (Survey of chaos in video sector). *Tencent Tech*, November 15, 2010. http://tech.qq.com/a/20101115/000146.htm.

Hu, Yaqing. "Shipin fengyun" (Ebb and flow of video). *China Business Journal*, September 21, 2009.

Hu, Zhengrong, and Hong Li. "China's Television in Transition." In *Television and Public Policy: Change and Continuity in an Era of Global Liberalization*, edited by David Ward, 89–113. London: Routledge, 2008.

Hu, Zhongbin. "Waizi PE 'lao yi'" (Foreign PE is outdated). *Economic Observer Online*, July 22, 2011. http://www.eeo.com.cn/2011/0722/206907.shtml.

Huang, Guo. "18 wei gaoren bamai Zhongguo IDC" (18 Experts diagnose problems for Chinese IDC). *Computer World*, 2001.

Huang, Guo. "IDC bubi cong jian jifang kaishi" (IDC does not need to start with self-built space). *Computer World*, 2001.

Huang, Shengmin, et al. *Zhongguo guanggaozhu yingxiao qushi baogao 2007–2008* (Report on the marketing trends of advertisers in China, 2007–2008). Beijing: Social Science Literature Press, 2008.

Huang, Yu. "Peaceful Evolution: The Case of Television Reform in Post-Mao China." *Media, Culture & Society* 16, no. 2 (1994): 217–241.

Huang, Yu, and Andrew Green. "From Mao to the Millennium: 40 Years of Television in China." In *Television in Contemporary China*, edited by David French and Michael Richards, 267–291. London: Sage, 2000.

Hung, Chang-tai. *Mao's New World: Political Culture in the Early People's Republic.* Ithaca: Cornell University Press, 2011.

"Internet TV Battle." *Global Times*, May 10, 2012. http://www.globaltimes.cn/content/708849.shtml.

iResearch. *China Online Advertising Research Report: 2006.* Shanghai: iResearch Consulting Group, 2007.

Jenkins, Henry. *Convergence Culture: Where Old and New Media Collide.* New York: New York University Press, 2008.

Jia, Xian. "Zaixian shipin dianbo wangzhan de banian kangzhan" (Eight-year war of VOD websites). *ChinaByte.* Last modified April 29, 2008. http://net.chinabyte.com/285/8097285.shtml.

Jiang, Jessie, and Simon Elegant. "Avoiding Censors, Chinese Authors Go Online." *Time*, March 16, 2009. http://content.time.com/time/world/article/0,8599,1885399,00.html.

Jiang, Mengjie. "Shipin wangzhan jiancheng jinbo jiemu jiebangzhe" (Video websites becoming next runner for forbidden content). *Beijing Business Today*, December 5, 2011.

Jiang, Mengwei. "Neirong chidu guokuan; shipin wangzhan tiaozhan jianguan dixian" (Video sites challenged regulatory bottom line). *Beijing Business Today,* May 30, 2012.

Jiang, Mengwei. "Yingyuan shipin wangzhan boyi dianying 'chuangkouqi'" (Cinema chains and video sites fight over "release window"). *Beijing Business Today,* March 23, 2012.

Jiang, Steven. "*House of Cards* in China: Surprisingly Available and Popular." *CNN,* February 19, 2014. http://www.cnn.com/2014/02/19/world/asia/china-house-of-cards-jiang/index.html.

Jin, Wenjie. "Meiju hefa rujing hou de zimuzu: bei shoubian, buzai qiang shoufa" (Fansubbing groups after official import of U.S. television series). *Sina Tech.* Last modified June 16, 2014. http://tech.sina.com.cn/i/2014-06-16/08499438956.shtml.

Jones, Andrew. *Like a Knife: Ideology and Genre in Contemporary Chinese Popular Music.* Ithaca: Cornell University Press, 1992.

Kalathil, Shanthi. *Open Networks, Closed Regimes: The Impact of the Internet on Authoritarian Rule.* Washington, D.C.: Carnegie Endowment for International Peace, 2003.

Kataoka, Tetsuya. *Resistance and Revolution in China: The Communists and the Second United Front.* Berkeley: University of California Press, 1974.

Keane, Michael. *The Chinese Television Industry.* London: British Film Institute, 2015.

Keane, Michael. *Creative Industries in China: Art, Design and Media.* Cambridge: Polity Press, 2013.

Keane, Michael. "Disconnecting, Connecting, and Reconnecting: How Chinese Television Found Its Way Out of the Box." *International Journal of Communication* 10 (2016): 5426–5443.

Keane, Michael. "Television Drama in China: Engineering Souls for the Market." In *Global Goes Local: Popular Culture in Asia,* edited by Timothy J. Craig and Richard King, 120–137. Vancouver: University of British Columbia, 2001.

Keane, Michael. "Television Drama in China: Remaking the Market." *Media International Australia* 115 (2005): 82–93.

Kim, Jin. "The Institutionalization of YouTube: From User-Generated Content to Professionally Generated Content." *Media, Culture & Society* 34, no. 1 (2012): 53–67.

Kim, Samuel S. "China and Globalization: Confronting Myriad Challenges and Opportunities." *Asian Perspectives* 33, no. 3 (2009): 41–80.

King, Gary, Jennifer Pan, and Margaret E. Roberts. "How Censorship in China Allows Government Criticism but Silences Collective Expression." *American Political Science Review* 107, no. 2 (2013): 326–343.

Kristof, Nicholas. "Satellites Bring Information Revolution to China." *New York Times*, April 11, 1993. http://www.nytimes.com/1993/04/11/world/satellites-bring -information-revolution-to-china.html.

Kuhn, Anthony. "Company Town: Chinese Wiring the Countryside for Satellite TV; Television: Program Is the First Experimental Step in Building a Nationwide Direct-to-Home System." *Los Angeles Times*, September 23, 1999. http://articles.latimes .com/1999/sep/23/business/fi-13335.

Lagerkvist, Johan. "The Techno-Cadre's Dream: Administrative Reform by Electronic Governance in China Today?" *China Information* 19, 2 (2005): 189–216.

Lam, Oiwan. "China: My Father Is Li Gang!" *Global Voices*, October 22, 2010. https:// globalvoicesonline.org/2010/10/22/china-my-father-is-li-gang/.

Lampton, David M., ed. *Policy Implementation in Post-Mao China*. Berkeley: University of California Press, 1987.

Lansheng, Jiang, and Shengwu Xie, eds. *2001–2002 Zhongguo wenhua chanye fazhan baogao* (2001–2002 Report on the development of Chinese cultural industry). Beijing: Social Science Literature Press, 2002.

Laperrouza, Marc. "China's Telecommunication Policy-Making in the Context of Trade and Economic Reforms." Ph.D. diss., London School of Economics and Political Science, 2006.

Larkin, Brian. "Degraded Images, Distorted Sounds: Nigerian Video and the Infrastructure of Piracy." *Public Culture* 16, no. 2 (2004): 289–314.

Larkin, Brian. *Signal and Noise: Media, Infrastructure, and Urban Culture in Nigeria*. Durham: Duke University Press, 2008.

Lau, Alan. "Succeeding in China's Online Video Market." July 2011. https://www .mckinsey.com/industries/media-and-entertainment/our-insights/succeeding-in -chinas-online-video-market.

Lee, Chin-Chuan. "The Global and the National of Chinese Media: Discourses, Market, Technology and Identity." In *Chinese Media, Global Contexts*, edited by Chin-Chuan Lee, 1–31. London: Routledge, 2003.

Lee, Rocky. "Understanding the VIE Structure: Necessary Elements for Success and the Legal Risks Involved." *Cadwalader Wickersham & Taft LLP*, August 10, 2011. https:// www.lexology.com/library/detail.aspx?g=aa820b96-ff4a-4704-b457-243dce432a81.

Lee, Terence. "Forging an 'Asian' Media Fusion: Singapore as a 21st Century Media Hub." *Media International Australia* 158, no. 1 (February 2016): 80–89.

Lei, Hai. "Shipin fenxiang wangzhan; Matai Xiaoying tuxian" (Matthew effect among video-sharing sites). *China Computer Education*, July 23, 2007.

"Leshi chaoji dianshi: meilaoban baozhuang chu de disanjia shangshi gongsi gainian" (LeTV super television: Third concept coined by Yueting Jia). May 9, 2013. http://biz.zjol.com.cn/system/2013/05/08/019326291.shtml.

Li, Chuantao. "Hulian Xingkong wunian zhibian: cong pingtai dao menhu" (Five-year transformation of VNET: From platform to portal). *Telecommunications Weekly*, May 28, 2007, 008.

Li, Guohua. "Guangdian shenru 'jinqu'; wangluo jianguan xinhao jianqiang" (SARFT strengthens online regulation). *China Business Journal*, August 21, 2006.

Li, Guoxun. "Banquan chezhou shipin wangzhan" (Copyright becomes obstacle for video websites). *China Business Post*, November 20, 2006.

Li, Guoxun, and Yufeng Rao. "Shipin wangzhan de yingli tuwei" (Video sites attempt to break through in profit making). *China Business Post*, November 30, 2007.

Li, Hongmei. "Parody and Resistance on the Chinese Internet." In *Online Society in China: Creating, Celebrating, and Instrumentalising the Online Carnival*, edited by David Kurt Herold and Peter Marolt, 71–88. Abingdon, UK: Routledge, 2011.

Li, Hsiao-t'i. "Making a Name and a Culture for the Masses in Modern China." *Positions* 9, no. 1 (2001): 29–68.

Li, Jing. "Shipin wangzhan chonggui UGC" (Video sites return to UGC). *Economic Observer*, July 12, 2013.

Li, Jing. "Shipin wangzhan xin jueli: yinjin yu zizhi" (Video sites' new war: Import and in-house production). *Economic Observer*, May 11, 2013.

Li, Mingsi. "Hulian Xingkong 'shehuang'; yunyingshang buneng jidang yundongyuan youdang caipanyuan" (VNET gets involved in providing pornography). *Legal Daily*, July 15, 2007.

Li, Na. "Shipin wangzhan baisulv yu jiucheng reng qinquan buzhi" (Video websites' copyright infringement continues despite more than 90 percent denial rate in lawsuits). *Legal Daily*, November 20, 2006.

Li, Xiaoyan. "Fengxian touzi buqi shipin wangzhan; Xuxin biaotai 'yang ta sannian'" (Venture capitalists promise to stay with video sites for another three years). *21st Century Business Herald*, October 12, 2007, 024.

Li, Xiazhi. "Meiju dubo beihou de banquan jiaoliang" (Copyright wrestling behind exclusive streaming of American television series). *Beijing Daily*, February 15, 2014.

Li, Xinyuan. "Zaixian shipin fenxiang ni de jingcai" (Online video emerging for self-expression). *Computer World*, August 14, 2006.

Li, Yan. "Zhishi chanquan baohu jinru 'xingdong nian'" (Intellectual property protection entered "Year of Action"). *Beijing Business Today*, April 13, 2009.

Li, Yilan. "Shipin wangzhan: neirong, zhengce he guanggao gege doushi 'kan'." (Video websites: Content, policy, and advertising are all obstacles). *China Culture Daily*, December 8, 2006.

Li, Zhang. "Daguansi kefou zhongjie wangluo qinquan?" (Can lawsuits end online infringement?). *Procuratorial Daily*, August 7, 2009.

Li, Zixin, and Fan Hu. "Huanan IDC qidai shengju" (IDCs in southern China expect profits). *China InfoWorld*, 2001.

Liang, Bin, and Hong Lu. "Internet Development, Censorship, and Cyber Crimes in China." *Journal of Contemporary Criminal Justice* 26, no. 1 (2010): 103–120.

Liang, Zhang. "Hulianwang xin de paomo jiao IDC?" (New internet bubble called IDC?). *Yesky*. Last modified May 11, 2001. http://www.yesky.com/20010511/124520 .shtml.

Liao, Qingsheng. "Shipin wangzhan zoushang neirong chanyehua dadao, baituo banquan zhigu jiasu yingli bufa" (Video sites' content strategies help relieve pressure from copyright). *Communication Information News*, April 21, 2010.

Liao, Wei, "Wangwei naixin zhong 'Tudou'" (Gary Wang plants "Tudou" with patience). *China Securities News*, September 16, 2006.

Lieberthal, Kenneth. *Governing China: From Revolution Through Reform*. New York: W.W. Norton, 1995.

Lieberthal, Kenneth, and David M. Lampton, eds. *Bureaucracy, Politics and Decision Making in Post-Mao China*. Berkeley: University of California Press, 1992.

Lieberthal, Kenneth, and Michel Oksenberg. *Policy Making in China: Leaders, Structures, and Processes*. Princeton: Princeton University Press, 1988.

Lightman, Alex, and William Rojas. *Brave New Unwired World: The Digital Big Bang and the Infinite Internet*. New York: Wiley & Sons, 2002.

Lin, Yuhong. "Wangshang 'egao' zhi feng dang sha" (Online "spoofing" should be stopped). *Guangming Daily*, August 10, 2006. Accessed November 15, 2014. http://tech.sina.com.cn/i/2006-08-11/15321082387.shtml.

Link, Perry. "Hand-Copied Entertainment Fiction from the Cultural Revolution." In *Unofficial China: Popular Culture and Thought in the People's Republic*, edited by Perry Link, Richard Madsen, and Paul Pickowicz, 17–36. Boulder: Westview Press, 1989.

Link, Perry. "The Crocodile Bird: Xiangsheng in the Early 1950s." In *Dilemmas of Victory: The Early Years of the People's Republic of China*, edited by Jeremy Brown and Paul Pickowicz, 207–231. Cambridge, MA: Harvard University Press, 2007.

Link, Perry. "The Limits of Cultural Reform in Deng Xiaoping's China." *Modern China* 13, no. 2 (1987): 115–176.

Link, Perry, Richard Madsen, and Paul Pickowicz, eds. *Unofficial China: Popular Culture and Thought in the People's Republic*. Boulder, CO: Westview Press, 1990.

Liu, Chao. "P2P shi yao bangsha haishi zhao'an?" (Should P2P be forbidden or incorporated?). *China Intellectual Property News*, March 3, 2006, 012.

Liu, Chuan. "Zuo dianxin shichang de linglei wanjia" (To be alternative telecom market player). *Network World*, 2001.

Liu, Fangyuan. "Jidong jiemeng su Tudou; shipin fenxiang moshi yukao" (Joy.cn sued Tudou; Video sharing encountered challenges). *21st Century Business Herald*, January 8, 2009.

Liu, Hong. "Xieshou 'SP,' Hulian Xingkong dazao da pingtai" (VNET builds large platform with SP). *Telecommunications Weekly*, December 5, 2005, 056.

Liu, Hongjun. "Meiju zhengduozhan" (Business war on American televisions series). *Global Entrepreneur*, April 1–15, 2013.

Liu, Jia, and Jieyun Xu. "Ma Yun shiyi Zhifubao 'danfei'; xieyi kongzhi buke xing?" (Jack Ma internalized Alipay; VIE no longer works?). *Yicai*, June 15, 2011.

Lobato, Ramon, Julian Thomas, and Dan Hunter. "Histories of User-generated Content: Between Formal and Informal Media Economies." *International Journal of Communication* 5 (2011): 899–914.

Lorentzen, Peter. "China's Strategic Censorship." *American Journal of Political Science* 58, no. 2 (2014): 402–414.

Lorentzen, Peter L. "Regularizing Rioting: Permitting Public Protest in an Authoritarian Regime." *Quarterly Journal of Political Science*, 8, no. 2 (2013): 127–158.

Lotz, Amanda. *Portals: A Treatise on Internet-Distributed Television*. Ann Arbor: Michigan Publishing, 2017.

Lotz, Amanda. *The Television Will Be Revolutionized*. New York: New York University Press, 2007.

Lovell, Joseph. "Structures for International Private Equity Investment in the PRC." *International In-house Counsel Journal* 4, no. 13 (2010).

Lu, Jing. "Zizhi dangdao: shipin wangzhan pingtai zhan shengji" (Upgraded war among video sites on content production). *China Business Journal*, May 2, 2011.

Lu, Yue. "Shipin wangzhan tante miandui guangdian xingui; xiao wangzhan jiang-shou gengda chongji" (Video websites perturbed about new SARFT rules). *Yicai*, August 16, 2006.

Luo, Tian. "Shipin wangzhan mianlin 'bu qinquan jiu si'?" (Video websites could only survive by infringement?). *Beijing Business Today*, January 6, 2009.

"Luo Jianhui: chuantong meiti bu yunxu bochu de xin meiti yiyang buneng bo" (Luo Jianhui: What traditional media cannot show cannot be shown on new media either). *Sohu Media*. Last modified December 4, 2014. http://media.sohu.com/20141204/n406655434.shtml.

MacFarquhar, Roderick. "On 'Liberation'." *China Quarterly* 200 (2009): 891–894.

Mao, Zedong. "On New Democracy" (January 1940). In *Selected Works of Mao Tse-tung, Volume II*. Oxford: Pergamon Press, 1965.

Mao, Zedong. *"Talks at the Yan'an Conference on Literature and Art": A Translation of the 1943 Text with Commentary*. Ann Arbor: University of Michigan Center for Chinese Studies, 1980.

Mattelart, Armand, and Hector Schmucler. *Communication and Information Technologies: Freedom of Choice for Latin America?* Norwood, NJ: Ablex, 1985.

Mattelart, Tristan. "Audiovisual Piracy: Toward a Study of the Underground Networks of Cultural Globalization." *Global Media and Communication* 5, no. 3 (2009): 308–326.

Mayer, Vicki, Miranda Banks, and John Caldwell. *Production Studies: Cultural Studies of Media Industries*. London: Routledge, 2009.

McGinty, Andrew, Adrian Emch, Sherry Y. Gong, and James Zhang. "China VIE Structure for Foreign Investment under Attack from Multiple Directions: Will It Emerge (Relatively) Unscathed or Is Its Very Survival Threatened?" *Hogan Lovells*, January 20, 2012. https://www.lexology.com/library/detail.aspx?g=94767bad-0dc0-4f05-ab90-9bdffa49cbee.

McGrath, Jason. *Postsocialist Modernity: Chinese Cinema, Literature, and Criticism in the Market Age*. Stanford: Stanford University Press, 2008.

McGregor, James. *One Billion Customers: Lessons from the Front Lines of Doing Business in China*. New York: Free Press, 2005.

Meng, Bingchun. "From Steamed Bun to Grass Mud Horse: E Gao as Alternative Political Discourse on the Chinese Internet." *Global Media and Communication* 7, no. 1 (April 1, 2011): 33–51.

Meng, Bingchun. "Moving beyond Democratization: A Thought Piece on China Internet Research Agenda." *International Journal of Communication* 4 (2010): 501–508.

Meng, Bingchun. "Underdetermined Globalization: Media Consumption via P2P Networks." *International Journal of Communication* 6 (2012): 467–483.

Mertha, Andrew. *The Politics of Piracy: Intellectual Property in Contemporary China*. Ithaca: Cornell University Press, 2005.

Miller, Toby, Nitin Govil, John McMurria, Ting Wang, and Richard Maxwell. *Global Hollywood 2*. London: British Film Institute, 2004.

Min, Dahong, Binyan Yang, and Fei Jiang. "Yinshipin neirong zai hulianwang shang de chuanbo jiexi" (Analysis of online circulation of audiovisual content). *International Broadcasting, Film, and Television*, nos. 3–4, 2005.

Mitchell, David. "Internet Content Regulation in Southeast Asia: Directions." *Media International Australia* 101, no. 1 (November 2001): 43–55.

Mo, Xuan. "Tengxun Shipin jujiao yuanchuang jingpin zhanlue" (Tencent Video focuses on quality original productions). *International Financial News*, June 20, 2013.

Movius, Lisa. "Imitation Nation." Accessed July 8, 2002. https://www.salon.com/2002/07/08/imitation_nation/.

Murdock, Graham. "Political Economies as Moral Economies: Commodities, Gifts, and Public Goods." In *The Handbook of Political Economy of Communications*, edited by Janet Wasko, Graham Murdock, and Helena Sousa, 13–39. Chichester, UK: Wiley-Blackwell, 2011.

Muxue, Qianshan. "Xiaozhang de daoban dianying shoufei wangzhan—'Hulian Xingkong'" (Daring paid pirate film site—"VNET"). *JYSQ.Net* (forum), April 6, 2007 (6:49 p.m.). http://bbs.jysq.net/thread-865133-1-1.html.

Mylonas, Yiannis. "Amateur Creation and Entrepreneurialism: A Critical Study of Artistic Production in Post-Fordist Structures." *tripleC: Communication, Capitalism & Critique* 10, no. 1 (January 18, 2012): 1–11.

Nathan, Andrew. "Authoritarian Resilience." *Journal of Democracy* 14, no. 1 (2003): 6–17.

Naughton, Barry. "Hierarchy and the Bargaining Economy: Government and Enterprise in the Reform Process." In *Bureaucracy, Politics, and Decision Making in Post-Mao China*, edited by Kenneth Lieberthal and David Lampton, 245–281. Berkeley: University of California Press, 1992.

Naughton, Barry J., and Dali L. Yang, eds. *Holding China Together: Diversity and National Integration in the Post-Deng Era*. New York: Cambridge University Press, 2004.

NetEase. "6.cn zhuanxing shipin shequ; huo xukezheng jingying zaixian yanchu" (6.cn received permit to run online performance business). *NetEase Tech*. Accessed January 21, 2015. http://tech.163.com/10/1209/03/6NED5SHS000915BF.html.

Newman, Michael. *Video Revolutions: On the History of a Medium*. New York: Columbia University Press, 2014.

Ni, Hongzhang. "Shuzi dianshi 'xiaoao' IPTV" (Digital television outmaneuvered IPTV). *Sina Tech*, March 6, 2006. http://tech.sina.com.cn/t/2006-03-06/1126858615 .shtml?from=wap.

Ni, Hongzhang. "Wangluo dianshi weihe zaojin" (Why online television was banned). *Computer World*, March 26, 2007.

Ning, Meng. "Shipin boke guanggao fencheng qubian, zhuli UGC yewu huo lunwei zitai" (Effectiveness of ad revenue divide in video sharing remains unclear). *TechWeb*. Accessed February 28, 2015. http://www.techweb.com.cn/internet/2013 -06-16/1303248.shtml.

Nuttall, Sarah, and Achille Mbembe. "Secrecy's Softwares." *Current Anthropology* 56 (December 2015): 317–324.

Ong, Aihwa. *Neoliberalism as Exception: Mutations in Citizenship and Sovereignty*. Durham: Duke University Press, 2006.

O'Regan, Tom. "From Piracy to Sovereignty: International VCR Trends." *Continuum: Journal of Media and Cultural Studies* 4, no. 2 (1991): 112–135.

Owen, Bruce M., and Steven S. Wildman. *Video Economics*. Cambridge, MA: Harvard University Press, 1992.

Palan, Ronen. "Trying to Have Your Cake and Eating It: How and Why the State System Has Created Offshore." *International Studies Quarterly* 42 (1998): 625–644.

Pang, Laikwan. "Post-Socialism and Cultural Policy: China's Depoliticization of Culture in the Late 1970s and Early 1980s." In *Popular Culture and the State in East and Southeast Asia*, edited by Nissim Otmazgin and Eyal Ben-Ari, 147–161. London: Routledge, 2012.

Papish, Jonathan. "Foreign Films in China: How Does It Work?" *China Film Insider*, March 2, 2017. http://chinafilminsider.com/foreign-films-in-china-how-does -it-work/.

Parks, Lisa, and Nicole Starosielski. Introduction to *Signal Traffic: Critical Studies of Media Infrastructures*, edited by Lisa Parks and Nicole Starosielski, 1–27. Champaign: University of Illinois Press, 2015.

Pearl Research. "Chinese Authorities Punishes Tudou and 61 Other Online Video Sites for Violating Regulations." *Forbes*, March 20, 2008. http://www.forbes.com/2008/ 03/20/china-video-tudou-tech-cx_pco_0320paidcontent.html.

Perry, Elizabeth. "Cultural Governance in Contemporary China: 'Re-Orienting' Party Propaganda." Harvard-Yenching Institute Working Papers. Accessed November 20, 2014. http://dash.harvard.edu/handle/1/11386987.

Ping, Dongfang. "Hulianwang guanli, cong pojie 'jiulong zhishui' qibu" (Internet governance starts from breaking bureaucratic turf war). *East Day*, October 19, 2014. http://pinglun.eastday.com/p/20141019/u1ai8398239.html.

Ping, Yue. "Goujian youxiao cujin IPTV yewu fazhan de jianguan tixi" (Constructing regulatory system to effectively facilitate development of IPTV). *People's Posts and Telecommunications*, August 22, 2006.

Post, Robert. *Censorship and Silencing: Practices of Cultural Regulation*. Los Angeles: Getty Research Institute, 1998.

Pow, Choon-Piew. *Gated Communities in China: Class, Privilege and the Moral Politics of the Good Life*. London: Routledge, 2009.

Punathambekar, Aswin. *From Bombay to Bollywood: The Making of a Global Media Industry*. New York: New York University Press, 2013.

Qun, Zhai, and Jian Biao. "Zhengsu BT, yingshi jiemu zai wu mianfei wucan" (No free lunch anymore after BT crackdown). *China Culture Daily*, December 18, 2009.

Roberts, David, and Thomas Hall. "VIE Structures in China: What You Need to Know." *An O'Melveny & Myers LLP Research Report*, October 2011.

Rose, Ewan W. "Will China Allow Itself to Enter the New Economy?" *Duke Journal of Comparative & International Law* 11, no. 2 (2001): 451–466.

SARFT. "Guangdian Zongju guanyu 2008 nian 1 yue quanguo paishe zhizuo dianshiju beian gongshi de tongzhi" (SARFT notice on national television drama production in January 2008). Accessed October 22, 2014. http://dsj.sarft.gov.cn/tims/site/views/applications/note/view.shanty?appName=note&id=011fd9e3fc550454402881f71fd9e2a5

SARFT. "Guangdian Zongju xinwen fayanren jiu Zhejiang guangdian gaige fazhan jingyan dawen" (SARFT spokesman answered questions regarding broadcasting reform in Zhejiang Province). April 29, 2010. http://www.gov.cn/gzdt/2010-04/29/content_1595568.htm.

SARFT Development and Research Center. *2006 Zhongguo guangbo dianying dianshi fazhan baogao* (2006 Report on the development of China's radio, film, and television). Beijing: Xinhua Press, 2006.

"The SARFT Decides to Introduce *Ted*, Reducing 105 Minutes to One Minute." Douban.com, January 25, 2013. http://www.douban.com/group/topic/36272980/.

Schell, Orville. *Mandate of Heaven: The Legacy of Tiananmen Square and the Next Generation of China's Leaders*. New York: Simon & Schuster, 1995.

Schiller, Dan. *How to Think about Information*. Urbana: University of Illinois Press, 2007.

Schiller, Dan, and Christian Sandvig. "Is YouTube the Successor to Television—Or to *Life* Magazine?" *Huffington Post*, May 12, 2010. http://www.huffingtonpost.com/dan-schiller/is-youtube-the-successor_b_497198.html.

Schiller, Herbert. *Mass Communications and American Empire*. New York: A. M. Kelley, 1969.

Shambaugh, David. *China's Communist Party: Atrophy and Adaptation*. Washington, D.C.: Woodrow Wilson Center Press; Berkeley: University of California Press, 2008.

Shanghai Media Group (SMG) Research and Development Office. "Zhongguo fufei dianshi huanman tuijin; ruhe dapo fazhan jiangju" (Slow development of paid TV in China requires solutions). *Satellite TV and Broadband Multimedia*, 2008.

Shi, Baochun. "Shuju zhongxin de dianli baozhang" (Power supply to IDC). *China InfoWorld*, 2001.

Shi, Qiushi. "P2P-VC de xia yitong jin?" (P2P-VC's next pot of gold?). *China High-Tech Industry Herald*, April 3, 2006.

Shi, Yan. "Shanghai Wenguang shouhuo IPTV paizhao beihou" (Behind SMG's IPTV granted permit). Sina Tech, May 21, 2005. http://tech.sina.com.cn/t/2005-05-21/1454613793.shtml.

Shifman, Limor. "An Anatomy of a YouTube Meme." *New Media & Society* 14, no. 2 (2011): 187–203.

"Shipin wangzhan goumai meiju shengyi jing" (Video websites' business of acquiring American television series). *Yicai*, November 5, 2013. http://www.yicai.com/news/3087973.html.

Simon, Karla W. *Civil Society in China: The Legal Framework from Ancient Times to the New Reform Era*. Oxford: Oxford University Press, 2013.

Sina Corporation. "Largest Chinese Internet Portal, Sina.com, Completes $25-Million Round of Financing." May 10, 1999. http://phx.corporate-ir.net/phoenix.zhtml?c=121288&p=irol-newsArticle&ID=68766.

Sina Corporation. "Leshi Wang guapai shangshi; A Gu shoujia wangluo shipin gongsi dansheng" (LeTV launched IPO). *Sina Tech*, August 12, 2010. http://tech.sina.com.cn/i/2010-08-12/09454536935.shtml.

Sina Corporation. "Tudou Wang bashe jiuge yue zhong huo shipin paizhao" (Tudou finally received video permit after nine months). *Sina Tech*, September 10, 2008. http://tech.sina.com.cn/i/2008-09-10/15032448867.shtml.

Sina Corporation. "Walden International Investment Group Announces the Nasdaq Listing and Successful Initial Public Offering of Portfolio Company SINA.com." June 28, 2000. http://phx.corporate-ir.net/phoenix.zhtml?c=121288&p=irol-newsArticle&ID=101569

Sina Corporation. "Zongju jiaqiang wangju jianguan; dianshi wangluo shencha biaozhun tongyi" (SARFT strengthens regulations of web soaps; Censorship standards for television and internet to be unified). *Sina Entertainment*, February 27, 2016. http://ent.sina.com.cn/v/m/2016-02-27/doc-ifxpvysv4949295.shtml.

Smith, Philip, and Alexander Riley. *Cultural Theory: An Introduction*. Malden, MA: Blackwell, 2009.

Sohu Corporation. "Jiejiu 'Jiangge' shibai shimo: shencha zhidu de gongkai NG" (A failed censorship of *Django Unchained*). *Sohu Television Monthly*, April 15, 2013. http://yule.sohu.com/20130415/n372648812_1.shtml.

Sohu Corporation. "Meiju zhengban geming: rang mengxiang zhaojin xianshi" (Legalizing American television series). *Sohu Television Monthly*, accessed February 2, 2015. http://yule.sohu.com/s2012/3608/s353540936/.

Sohu Corporation. "Sohu.com to Deliver Exclusive Online Video Content for FIFA World Cup 2006." March 23, 2006. http://corp.sohu.com/20060323/n242442471.shtml.

Sohu Corporation. "Tudou Wang Wangwei: 2009 jiangshi shipin wangzhan jiannan de yinian" (Gary Wang: 2009 will be a tough year for video sites). *Sohu IT*, September 19, 2008. http://it.sohu.com/20080919/n259649951.shtml.

"Souhu Shipin de Zhipaiwu you shanjian ma?" (Is Sohu Video's *House of Cards* deleted?). Zhihu.com. Accessed February 13, 2015. http://www.zhihu.com/question/22856972.

Sun, Dingling. "Wangluo egao jiang taoshang 'jinguzhou'" (Regulation strengthened on online spoofing). *China Press Journal*, September 6, 2006.

Sun, Jin. "Shipin wangzhan dongri zhongguoshi jiushu: gaibian dianshiju chanye" (Video sites change television drama industry). *Yicai*, November 26, 2008.

Sun, Wanning. *Maid in China: Media, Morality, and the Cultural Politics of Boundaries*. Routledge, 2010.

Sun, Wanning. *Subaltern China: Rural Migrants, Media, and Cultural Practices*. Lanham, MD: Rowman & Littlefield, 2014.

Sun, Wanning, and Yuezhi Zhao. "Television Culture with 'Chinese Characteristics': The Politics of Compassion and Education." In *Television Studies after TV: Understanding Television in the Post-Broadcast Era*, edited by Graeme Turner and Jinna Tay, 96–104. Abingdon, UK: Routledge, 2009.

Sundaram, Ravi. *Pirate Modernity: Delhi's Media Urbanism*. London: Routledge, 2009.

Takada, Kazunori. "Youku to Buy Tudou, Creating China Online Video Giant." *Reuters*, March 12, 2012. https://www.reuters.com/article/us-youku-tudou/youku-to-buy-tudou-creating-china-online-video-giant-idUSBRE82B0HD20120312.

Tan, Zixiang, William Foster, and Seymour Goodman. "China's Unique Internet Infrastructure." *Communications of the ACM* 42, no. 6 (June, 1999): 44–52.

Tang, Shiwang. "2002 ni yongshang kuandai le ma?" (Did you use broadband service in 2002?). *BJKP*. Accessed November 3, 2014. http://www.bjkp.gov.cn/zhuanti/old_bjkp/dnsj/wjwx/k30134-04.htm.

Tao, Xinian. "Huace Yingshi shenmi ren 'bei gudong' zhi mi" (Mysterious shareholders of Huace). *Time Weekly*, no. 121 (March 2011).

Taubman, Geoffry. "A Not-So World Wide Web: The Internet, China, and the Challenges to Nondemocratic Rule." *Political Communication* 15, no. 2 (1998): 255–272.

TechWeb. "Souhu Shipin yinjin duobu dapian fali haiwai banquan shichang" (Sohu Video imported numerous blockbusters). *TechWeb*, November 28, 2012. http://www.techweb.com.cn/internet/2012-11-28/1258881.shtml.

Thomas, Julian, and Ramon Lobato. *The Informal Media Economy.* Cambridge: Polity Press, 2015.

Todd, Nigel. "Ideological Superstructure in Gramsci and Mao Tse-Tung." *Journal of the History of Ideas* 35, no. 1 (1974): 148–156.

Tong, Ming, et al. "IDC shichang jiujing you duoda?" (How large is the IDC market?). *China InfoWorld,* 2000.

Tong, Yanqi, and Shaohua Lei. *Social Protest in Contemporary China, 2003–2010: Transitional Pains and Regime Legitimacy.* New York: Routledge, 2014.

Tsai, Chung-min. "The Paradox of Regulatory Development in China: The Case of the Electricity Industry." Ph.D. diss., University of California, 2010.

Tsai, Kellee S. *Capitalism without Democracy: The Private Sector in Contemporary China.* Ithaca: Cornell University Press, 2007.

Tsai, Lily L. *Accountability without Democracy: Solidary Groups and Public Goods Provision in Rural China.* New York: Cambridge University Press, 2007.

Tsui, Lokman. "The Panopticon as the Antithesis of a Space of Freedom Control and Regulation of the Internet in China." *China Information* 17, no. 2 (2003): 65–82.

Turner, Graeme, and Jinna Tay, eds. *Television Studies after TV: Understanding Television in the Post-Broadcast Era.* Abingdon, UK: Routledge, 2009.

Turow, Joseph. *The Daily You: How the New Advertising Industry Is Defining Your Identity and Your Worth.* New Haven: Yale University Press, 2011.

Ulin, Jeff. *The Business of Media Distribution: Monetizing Film, TV, and Video Content.* Abingdon, UK: Taylor & Francis, 2010.

Uricchio, William. "The Future of a Medium Once Known as Television." In *The YouTube Reader*, edited by Pelle Snickars and Patrick Vonderau, 24–39. Stockholm: National Library of Sweden, 2009.

VNET. "Toushi IDC" (Deep analysis of IDC industry). *Computer World*, 2000.

Voci, Paola. *China on Video: Smaller-Screen Realities*. Abingdon, UK: Routledge, 2010.

Wang, Gary. "Toodou.com zenme lai de?" (How was Toodou.com born?). *Visible Mind* (blog), March 9, 2005. http://visiblemind.org/?p=811.

Wang, Ji. "YouTube men de zhongguoshi shengcun: 'tou' lai de daikuan" (Chinese YouTubes' survival: Living on "stolen" bandwidth). *Telecommunications Weekly*, June 11, 2007.

Wang, Jing. "Culture as Leisure and Culture as Capital." *Positions: East Asia Cultures Critique* 9, no. 1 (2001): 69–104.

Wang, Rong. "Leshi Wang banquan fenxiao tuidong yeji dazeng" (Rights business makes big contribution to LeTV). *China Securities Journal*, March 16, 2012.

Wang, Shujen. *Framing Piracy: Globalization and Film Distribution in Greater China*. Lanham, Md.: Rowman & Littlefield, 2003.

Wang, Xiaomei. "Huace mishi: Lou Zhongfu cuoshi de kongzhi quan" (Hidden history of Huace: Fortunes Zhongfu Lou missed). *Money Weekly*, May 7, 2012.

Wang, Zeyun. "Liumeiti zhandian tashang 'leiqu'" (Streaming sites stepped on minefield). *China InfoWorld*, March 26, 2007.

Wayne, Michael. "Post-Fordism, Monopoly Capitalism, and Hollywood's Media Industrial Complex." *International Journal of Cultural Studies* 6, no. 1 (March 1, 2003): 82–103.

"Why Does Renren Acquire 56.com." *Business Insider*, September 28, 2011. http://www.businessinsider.com/why-renren-acquired-video-site-56com-2011-9.

Williams, Raymond. *Television: Technology and Cultural Form*. Middletown, Conn.: Wesleyan University Press, 1992.

Wong, Edward. "Pushing China's Limits on Web, If Not on Paper." *New York Times*, November 6, 2011. http://www.nytimes.com/2011/11/07/world/asia/murong -xuecun-pushes-censorship-limits-in-china.html.

World Bank. "OKR: Deepening Public Service Unit Reform to Improve Service Delivery." Accessed October 20, 2014. https://openknowledge.worldbank.org/ handle/10986/8648.

Wu, Angela Xiao. "Broadening the Scope of Cultural Preferences: Movie Talk and Chinese Pirate Film Consumption from the Mid-1980s to 2005." *International Journal of Communication* 6, no. 1 (2012): 501–529.

Wu, Chenguang. "BT lei wangluo xiazai gongju yinglai shengsijie" (Impending death of BT downloading tools). *Beijing Business Today*, December 16, 2009.

Wu, Feng. "Shipin fenxiang wangzhan mianlin chengzhang fannao" (Growing pain of video-sharing websites). *China InfoWorld*, August 21, 2006.

Wu, Weihua. *Chinese Animation, Creative Industries, and Digital Culture*. London: Routledge, 2017.

Wu, Xi. "Wangluo banquan 'wanji' nanzhi; 'bifenggang yuanze' dai tiaozheng" (Online infringement is difficult to eradicate; "Safe harbor rule" needs adjustment). *China High-Tech Industry Herald*, July 25, 2011.

Wu, Xiaobo. *Jidang sanshinian: Zhongguo qiye 1978–2008* (Thirty years of Chinese business, 1978–2008), Vol. 2. Beijing: Zhongxin Press, 2008.

Wu, Ying. "Minying IDC zaoyu hanliu" (Private IDCs encountered cold spell). *China Enterprise News*, 2001.

Wu, Yongyi. "'Shuangxian ling' huo dailai liangbai yi guanggao; wangluo shipin youwang yinglai 'di'er chun'" (Two restraining orders expected to bring second spring to video sites). *Communication Information News*, December 7, 2011.

Xie, Liang. "'Zuoxiu' de Tudou; qianwei de 'boke'" (Tudou is staging show). *CPPCC Daily*, December 23, 2005.

Xie, Peng. "'Meiyou le shengcun yali, jiu buhui xiang zuo'e le'" ("No evils if there is no survival pressure"). *Nanfang Daily*, October 15, 2009.

Xie, Peng. "Shui zhizao le VIE konghuang?" (Who manufactured VIE panic?). *Southern Weekly*, October 13, 2011.

Xie, Xiaoping. "Linglei jingshang Jia Yueting: mouhua sijia gongsi shangshi" (Yueting Jia's alternative business style). May 29, 2013. http://tech.163.com/13/0529/04/90105BFD000915BF.html.

Wei, Xiong. "Hulianwang xin guiding yinchu wenhua huati" (Internet new rules bring about cultural topics). *Computer World*, 2003.

Xu, Jieyun. "Lei Tengxun moshi de youhuo yu bianjie" (Lures and boundaries of semi-Tencent model). *Yicai*, July 14, 2011.

Xue, Juan. "Shipin qiye anzhan meiju" (Video companies fought over American television series). *China Economic Times*, October 29, 2013.

Ya, Wenhui. "Mianfei zimu wangzhan guanbi; zhenggui shipin wangzhan shouyi" (Closure of fansubbing groups benefits video websites). *China High-Tech Industry Herald*, December 8, 2014.

Yang, Fan. "Rethinking China's Internet Censorship: The Practice of Recoding and the Politics of Visibility." *New Media & Society* 18, no. 7 (2016): 1364–1381.

Yang, Fan. "Wangju, shipin wangzhan de xinchong?" (Web soaps: video sites' new favorite?). *Workers' Daily*, May 21, 2010.

Yang, Guang. "Zhongguo IDC: wang mei zhi ke" (IDCs in China: Longing for success). *Computer World*, 2001.

Yang, Guobin. "Killing Emotions Softly: The Civilizing Process of Online Emotional Mobilization." (in Chinese) *Chinese Journal of Communication and Society* 40 (2017): 75–104.

Yang, Guobin. *The Power of the Internet in China: Citizen Activism Online*. New York: Columbia University Press, 2009.

Yang, Guobin. *The Red Guard Generation and Political Activism in China*. New York: Columbia University Press, 2016.

Yang, Guoqiang. "Youku Wang wancheng disanlun rongzi 2500 wan meiyuan" (Youku completed a third-round financing of $25 million). *Yicai*, November 22, 2007.

Yang, Linhua. "Rongzi guanjun Tudou Wang: shizhong jianchi 'caogen da juchang'" (Fundraising champion Tudou keeps its grassroots orientation). *21st Century Business Herald*, October 12, 2007.

Yang, Miao. "iQiyi kaifang shipin bofang pingtai; zhizuozhe ke huode guanggao fencheng" (iQiyi opens its platform for video producers). *Beijing News*, March 27, 2012.

Yang, Na. "Bubble or Future? The Challenge of Web 2.0 in China." *Intercultural Communication Studies* 17, no. 3 (2008): 93–103.

Yang, Qingfeng. "Shuju zhongxin anju zhinan" (Guide to IDC location). *Network World*, August 20, 2007.

Yang, Xiaqing. "Wangluo shipin jianguan nanti" (Thorny issue in online video regulation). *Computer World*, August 21, 2006.

"Yangshi, Shangshi: jinqi bu dasuan yinjin meiju" (CCTV and STV have no plan to import U.S. television series). *Shanghai Morning Post*, September 18, 2007.

Yao, Rui. "Gao Hongbing: 'guaiquan' zhong de IDC" (Hongbing Gao: IDC caught in loop). *Computer World*, 2001.

Ye, Yong. "Youku Wang zaihuo fengtou 2500 wan meiyuan zhuzi" (Youku received another $25 million). *Shanghai Securities News*, November 22, 2007.

Yesky. "Souhu yinjin Suoni yingshi 600 dapian; jianli haolaiwu pianyuanku" (Sohu imported 600 titles from Sony). *Yesky*, April 6, 2012. http://news.yesky.com/204/31060704.shtml.

Youku. *Absolutely Unexpected*. Season 1, episode 10. 2013.

Youku. *Absolutely Unexpected*. Season 2, episode 3. 2014.

Youku. "What Does the China Earthquake Administration Do?" *UFO Talk*, April 25, 2013.

Youku.com. "Youku Original Announces New Seasons of In-House Produced Evergreen Web Series," Youku.com—Investor Relations—Press Release. Accessed February 16, 2015. http://ir.youku.com/phoenix.zhtml?c=241246&p=irol-newsArticle&ID=1660354.

Yuan, Bo. "Zimuzu bei jiaoting tuxian banquan yishi tishen" (Halt in fansubbing shows improvement of copyright awareness). *China Intellectual Property News*, December 3, 2014.

Yu, Sui. "Yinian qianbu guize fuza; Zhongguo dianying jinkou xianzhuang jiemi" (Demystifying film import in China: 1,000 titles each year with complicated rules). *MTIME*. Accessed February 4, 2015. http://news.mtime.com/2012/10/11/1499044.html.

Yu, Xie. "Why China's Plan to Launch the Highly Touted CDR Scheme Is Still on Hold," *South China Morning Post*, July 14, 2018. https://www.scmp.com/business/china-business/article/2155107/why-chinas-plan-launch-highly-touted-cdr-scheme-still-hold.

Yurchak, Alexei. *Everything Was Forever, Until It Was No More: The Last Soviet Generation*. Princeton: Princeton University Press, 2005.

Zhai, Xuemei. "Zouzai jishu zhiqian de jianguan moshi tantao" (Exploration of regulatory model ahead of technologies). *Telecommunications Weekly*, September 5, 2005.

Zhang, Chengdong. "Daikuan taotie" (Gulosity of bandwidth), *Network World*, August 6, 2007.

Zhang, Gang. "Xiang 92 pai zhijing" (Salute to '92 school). *China Entrepreneur*, no. 6 (March 2012).

Zhang, Lena L. "Behind the 'Great Firewall': Decoding China's Internet Media Policies from the Inside." *Convergence: International Journal of Research into New Media Technologies* 12, no. 3 (2006): 271–291.

Zhang, Xiaoling. *The Transformation of Political Communication in China: From Propaganda to Hegemony*. Singapore: World Scientific, 2011.

Zhang, Xiaoxiao, and Anthony Fung. "TV Formatting of the Chinese *Ugly Betty*: An Ethnographic Observation of the Production Community." *Television & New Media* 15 (2014): 507–522.

Zhang, Xudong. "Heyi Wangluo tuichu Youku Wang" (1Verge Inc. launches Youku). *China InfoWorld*, July 19, 2006.

Zhang, Zhen, and Angela Zito, eds. *DV-Made China: Digital Subjects and Social Transformations after Independent Film*. Honolulu: University of Hawai'i Press, 2015.

Zhao, Elaine. "Professionalization of Amateur Production in Online Screen Entertainment in China: Hopes, Frustrations and Uncertainties." *International Journal of Communication* 10 (2016): 5444–5462.

Zhao, Elaine, and Michael Keane. "Between Formal and Informal: The Shakeout in China's Online Video Industry." *Media, Culture & Society* 35 (2013): 724–741.

Zhao, Ming. "Banquan susong: shipinye tanglang yu huangque youxi" (Copyright lawsuits in video industry). *China Economic Times*, April 1, 2010.

Zhao, Na. "56 Wang 8000 wan meiyuan jiaru Renren" (Renren acquired 56.com for $80 million). *PE Daily*, September 27, 2011.

Zhao, Xu. *Shao.com* (Burning.com). Beijing: Guangming Daily, 2001.

Zhao, Yining. "Zhuanfang yuan Xinxi Chanye Bu Fagui Si sizhang Liu Cai" (Interview with former head of Regulation Department of MII Cai Liu). *21st Century Business Herald*, November 21, 2011.

Zhao, Yuezhi. *Communication in China: Political Economy, Power, and Conflict*. Lanham, Md.: Rowman & Littlefield, 2008.

Zhao, Yuezhi. *Media, Market, and Democracy in China*. Urbana: University of Illinois Press, 1998.

Zhou, Jiansen. "Wangtong shouhuo wangshang chuanbo shiting jiemu xukezheng" (Netcom becomes first receiver of online audiovisual program transmission permit). *Sina News*, May 27, 2004. http://news.sina.com.cn/c/2004-05-27/12362643791s.shtml.

Zhe, Hu, et al. "Juezhan Web 2.0" (Decisive battle on Web 2.0). *Computer Weekly*, September 19, 2005.

Zheng, Jane. "'Creative Industry Clusters' and the 'Entrepreneurial City' of Shanghai." *Urban Studies* 48, no. 16 (December, 2011): 3561–3582.

Zheng, Zhiping. "Chousi bolv; liangchu wangzhan qinquan zhenxiong" (Real criminal of online copyright infringement). *China Intellectual Property News*, September 7, 2007.

Zhong, Gang. "Yi kaobei chudao, kaiqi Zhongguo yaogunyue lieche" (Chinese rock started with copycat). *Southern Metropolis Daily*, October 12, 2008.

Zhong, Yong. "Hunan Satellite Television over China." *Journal of International Communication* 16, no. 1 (January 1, 2010): 41–57.

"Zhongguo Liantong chengli" (Founding of China Unicom). *Telecommunications World*. Accessed April 10, 2017. http://tech.sina.com.cn/t/2007-07-06/20041603151 .shtml.

Zhou, Zhijun. "Pinpin qianshou dianshiye; shipin wangzhan qiangzhan neirong 'lanhai'" (Video sites cooperated with television industry). *China Culture Daily*, September 14, 2007.

Zhu, Jonathan, and Shujen Wang. "Mapping Film Piracy in China." *Theory, Culture and Society* 20, no. 4 (2003): 97–125.

Zhu, Ying. *Television in Post-Reform China: Serial Dramas, Confucian Leadership and the Global Television Market.* London: Routledge, 2008.

Zhu, Yuchao, and Dongyan Blachford. "'Old Bottle, New Wine'? Xinjiang Bingtuan and China's Ethnic Frontier Governance." *Journal of Contemporary China* 25, no. 97 (2016): 25–40.

Index